SEA OF DEATH

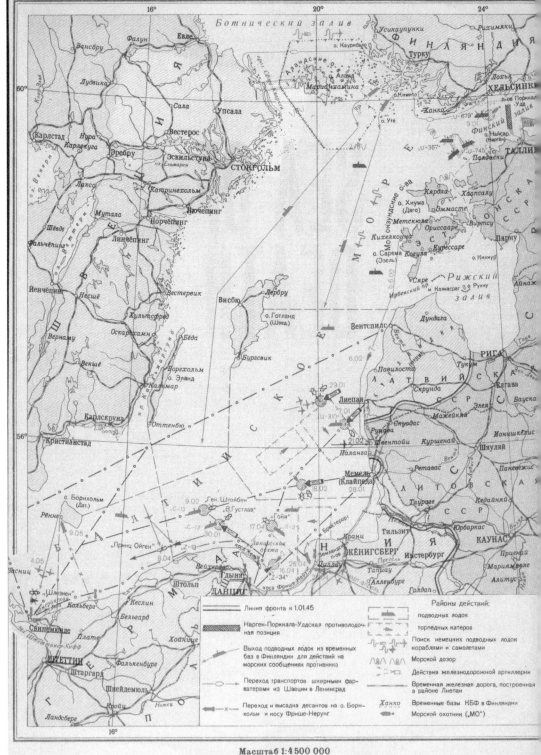

Масштаб 1:4 500 000

км 50   0   50   100   150 км

SEA OF DEATH

THE BALTIC, 1945

CLAES-GÖRAN WETTERHOLM

TRANSLATED BY ERIC KENTLEY

The
History
Press

Front cover: The *Cap Arcona* in the grip of an uncontrollable fire, 3 May 1945 (© Imperial War Museum)

Frontispiece: A Russian map of naval movements in the Baltic, January to May 1945. It also identifies (inaccurately) the wreck sites of the *Wilhelm Gustloff*, the *Steuben* and the *Goya*.

First published 2021

The History Press
97 St George's Place, Cheltenham,
Gloucestershire, GL50 3QB
www.thehistorypress.co.uk

British Library Cataloguing in Publication Data.
A catalogue record for this book is available from the British Library.

ISBN 978 0 7509 9507 8

Typesetting and origination by The History Press
Printed and bound in Great Britain by TJ International Ltd.

MIX
Paper from
responsible sources
FSC
www.fsc.org   FSC® C013056

CONTENTS

INTRODUCTION

It was the incongruity that I've never forgotten: the incongruity between where I was listening and what I was hearing. I sat in a spacious apartment in Hamburg's exclusive Uhlenhorst area, amid the conservative and expensive furnishings of a successful German businessman – dark wooden furniture, gilt furnishings, deep carpets and oil paintings of sailing ships on the wall. As he poured coffee, my host explained:

> What you must understand, Mr Wetterholm, is that if you take a jar of peas and press it under the water and the jar splits, then the peas come out and the jar is left down there.[1]

My host was searching for an analogy to describe events he had witnessed half a century earlier – part of the worst, and arguably the most tragic, of all disasters at sea. The 'jar' was a ship you have almost certainly never heard of: the *Thielbek*. The 'peas' were the people who drowned when she went down and then bobbed to the surface. In the comfort of his beautiful apartment he was describing a scene of almost unimaginable horror.

Not only almost unimaginable but also now mostly forgotten.

For many people, and Swedes like myself in particular, it is the sinking of the ferry *Estonia* that springs to mind as one of the greatest tragedies ever to occur in the Baltic Sea, when in the early hours of 28 September 1994, 852 people died. It was a disaster that continues to haunt Sweden to this day. But, without diminishing the tragedy of the *Estonia*, the number of the dead seems almost insignificant compared to the 10,000 lives that were lost on ships in the same sea in the final weeks of the Second World War.

Wilhelm Gustloff in Hamburg harbour around 1938.

Every year thousands of passengers make the seven-hour ferry crossing from Trelleborg, the southern-most town in Sweden, to Travemünde in Germany. I doubt that more than a handful realise that they are passing close to the site where Europe's worst maritime disasters took place. While everyone recognises the name *Titanic,* the names *Cap Arcona, Goya, General von Steuben* and *Thielbek* draw little more than blank stares. A few may have heard of *Wilhelm Gustloff,* but probably because of the Günter Grass novel *Crabwalk* (published in 2002), which takes her sinking as the central theme, not because what happened to her is etched onto our collective memory. Yet the number of lives lost on these ships in the Baltic far, far outnumber those that died when the *Titanic* slipped under the Atlantic waters.

It is perhaps not entirely a surprise that these enormous disasters in the Baltic are now largely forgotten: they occurred during the chaos that surrounded the end of the German Reich, and were lost in the mass of news as the war drew to a close. Eastern Europe was one enormous tragedy, played out in numberless heartbreaking events. And after the defeat of the Nazis, there was little interest in stories where Germans could not be portrayed as the villains but in which they were the victims; nor was there much sympathetic interest in the bigger story of the mass movement of Germans from the East, even though it still ranks as modern history's greatest exercise in ethnic expulsion.

If the loss of these ships is recalled at all, it seems easier to dismiss them with a lazy comparison. To take a single example: the magazine *Der Spiegel* described the *Wilhelm Gustloff* as 'the German *Titanic*', seemingly oblivious to the enormous difference in the casualty numbers and the very different causes of their sinking.

I have to confess that I too knew almost nothing of the *Wilhelm Gustloff* or the other ships that are the subject of this book until 1972, when in a bookshop in Hamburg I chanced upon Arnold Kludas's newly published *Die Deutschen Grossen Passagierschiffe*. When the enormity of what happened to these German ships in the Baltic began to dawn on me, I was amazed – and continue to be amazed – at how little attention their stories receive. Even among the hundreds of maritime experts and enthusiasts I have met over the years, very few of them knew about the *Wilhelm Gustloff*, which took more than 9,000 to the bottom of the Baltic, or the loss of the MV *Goya*, with perhaps as many as 7,000 dead, or of the similar catastrophe that befell the *General von Steuben*. Of course, none of these ships had encountered icebergs, or had orchestras on board or rich and famous passengers. These were tragedies caused by war, and amid all the abominations that took place during the Second World War, the stories of these ships have been lost from view.

My research began with the extensive archive material that survives in Germany. This led me to contact the historian and expert on (and survivor of) the *Wilhelm Gustloff*, Heinz Schön, who was also the author of several books on the expulsion of Germans from East Prussia. Heinz invited me to a memorial meeting that he had organised in Ostseebad Damp, not far from Kiel, in January 1995 to coincide with the fiftieth anniversary of the *Wilhelm Gustloff's* sinking. Held over a weekend, it was an extraordinary and very moving event.

I am perhaps best known as an author and curator of *Titanic* exhibitions. Over many years I have undertaken a considerable amount of research into the loss of that ship. I have been to many commemorative events over these years: they were mostly attended by young enthusiasts, but if I was lucky, I might get to meet one or two survivors (although in Boston in 1988 I met ten on a single day). Yet in Ostseebad Damp, the young were in a minority: the majority were either survivors – around 200 of them – or had participated in the rescue. I found myself walking amid living history: this was a reunion of people with crystal-clear memories of the night the *Wilhelm Gustloff* went down.

Over that weekend, I interviewed several of these survivors (the results of which formed the basis of a broadcast for Swedish radio). Many of them told me that this was the first time they had spoken about their experiences since 1945: the memories had been too painful and they had chosen to stay silent, burying what had happened to them deep inside. Perhaps it was liberating to be among those who shared the experience of the ship sinking; perhaps it was liberating to speak to a complete stranger.

This is not the only book that has been written about these wartime disasters in the Baltic, but I have been lucky enough to meet a great many survivors, both at that meeting and subsequently, and it is their accounts that form the core of this book. It is not about comparing disasters or establishing one as the 'greatest': as survivors from the *Wilhelm Gustloff* and another lost ship, the *Cap Arcona* often emphasised to me, it is about learning these disasters, to respect what happened, to understand how war generates terrible tragedies, and to try and ensure they are not repeated. I hope these are the lessons we can learn from the *Sea of Death*.

Heinz Schön in his archive in 1995. He was the pre-eminent *Wilhelm Gustloff* researcher.

The *Cap Arcona* (left) and *Wilhelm Gustloff* in Hamburg harbour around 1938. Together they represent the two largest shipping disasters in history.

A NOTE ON FATALITIES

One question my research has not been able to answer definitively is how many people were on the ships whose stories are told in this book at the time of their sinking, and how many died. This will never be known: I can give only broad-brush figures. In *SOS Wilhelm Gustloff*, Heinz Schön gives the number of those on board that ship as 10,582 and the number of fatalities as 9,343 but I am not confident of such exactness. The final day before her departure from Gotenhafen was chaotic in the extreme and we do not know exactly how many people were transferred later from the *Reval*. However, in terms of the lives lost, I am certain that Heinz is right when he says that the *Wilhelm Gustloff*'s sinking is the worst shipping disaster in history.

When I met the expert Wilhelm Lange in 2001 he suggested a figure of 7,000 on board the *Cap Arcona* on 3 May 1945, but he emphasised that it could have been many more. In the crumbling German Reich, records were lost or never made. We can only make approximate estimates and I now think that perhaps there were 8,000 people on board.

The track of a torpedo from an unknown submarine.

A NOTE ON PLACE NAMES

Most of the events described took place in East Prussia and for consistency I have used the German place names at the time. Their present-day appellations are listed below.

Angerapp river	Angrapa, Kaliningrad Oblast
Argemünde	[no longer exists, the site is in Kaliningrad Oblast]
Auschwitz	Oświęcim, Poland
Braunsberg	Braniewo, Poland
Danzig	Gdańsk, Poland
Elbing	Elbląg, Poland
Frisches Haff	Zalew Wiślany (Vistula Lagoon), Poland
Gotenhafen	Gdynia, Poland
Gotenhafen-Oxhöft	Oksywie, Poland
Gumbinnen	Gusev, Kaliningrad Oblast
Heilsberg	Lidzbark Warmińsk, Poland
Hela	Hel, Poland
Kahlberg	Krynica Morska, Poland
Kolberg	Kołobrzeg, Poland

Königsberg	Kaliningrad
Libau	Liepāja, Latvia
Memel	Klaipéda, Lithuania
Nemmersdorf	Mayakovskoye, Kaliningrad Oblast
Neufahrwasse	Nowy Port, Poland
Pillau	Baltiysk, Kaliningrad Oblast
Reval	Tallinn, Estonia
Schiewenhorst	Świbno, Poland
Stolpmünde	Ustka, Poland
Stutthof	Sztutowo, Poland
Swinemünde	Świnoujście, Poland
Windau	Ventspils, Latvia
Zoppot	Sopot, Poland

1

THE BEGINNING

It could have started anywhere but it began in the small village of Nemmersdorf.

This was a small settlement in the East Prussian countryside beside the River Angerapp, in the district of Gumbinnen. It was like many others in the area: quiet and peaceful, as it had been for generations.

The war was not being fought here.

Nemmersdorf lay in an administrative area that extended from the Baltic to the Black Sea, controlled by the infamous Gauleiter Erich Koch. Brutal and ruthless, he was an ardent devotee of Chancellor Adolf Hitler and wedded to the ideology of German supremacy. His attitude was typical of the Nazis: a belief that Slavs were and should always be a slave people:

> We have to lay the foundations for victory. We are a master race who must consider that the humblest German workers are racially and biologically a thousand times superior to the people who are here.[1]

The terror that Nazi Germany had launched and carried through with singular efficiency and brutality against the Russian people would be paid back as soon as Soviet forces trod on German soil.

Sooner or later, all the hate that had festered during the German occupation of western Russia had to erupt. There was barely a single Russian family that had not been affected in some way or another by the war. The Nazi leadership had publicly declared its desire to enslave or kill as many Russians as possible and now when the great counter-offensive began in September 1944 the Russian attitude was reciprocated. Few literate Russians would have been unaware of the exhortations of the Soviet writer Ilya Ehrenburg:

Kill, kill! There's nothing a German is not guilty of; not among the living, nor among the unborn! Follow the precepts of Comrade Stalin and trample the fascist animal in its burrow forever. Violently break the racist arrogance of the German women. Take them as legitimate prey. Kill, you brave advancing men of the Red Army![2]

Although the Soviet authorities eventually distanced themselves from Ehrenburg's views, he expressed the feelings of a great many Russians:

There is nothing more beautiful to us than German corpses. 'Kill the Germans!' your old mother asks you. 'Kill the Germans!' beseeches the child.[3]

The wave of refugees that began in the autumn of 1944 continued long after the war: it was the largest ethnic expulsion in history.

The German surrender to the Soviets after the Battle of Stalingrad on 2 February 1943 marked the beginning of the end of the Thousand Year Reich: now the war would turn against them. Whatever the Nazi leadership believed, in the autumn of 1944 the Red Army were on the move westwards, with the ultimate goal, via a crushed Germany, of Berlin. Yet even though it was now seventeen months after the Battle of Stalingrad, the inhabitants of Nemmersdorf probably had no idea that a massive Russian invasion of East Prussia was under way. However, on 16 October 1944, Russian aircraft attacked Gumbinnen, triggering an exodus of hundreds of civilians westwards.

It was half past eight in the morning of 21 October 1944 when the T34 tanks of the 2nd Battalion of General Burdejnys' 25th Guards Tank Brigade tore across the River Angerapp bridge, smashing into wagons, people, anything in their way as they raced towards Nemmersdorf. The attack was so sudden that the German soldiers stationed there had no time to destroy the bridge, nor had the villagers time to flee.

A few days later, the German army struck back with equal ferocity and retook the village. But what they found was a village of the dead. All the women had been raped before their murder, some had been crucified. One of the German officers recorded:

> When we moved through the village, we found no more Soviets. But we were greeted by grisly scenes of people who had been caught up there, which reminded me of the atrocities suffered by Soviet villagers from their own soldiers, something I had often seen during our retreats early in 1944. Here there were German women, whose clothing had been torn from their bodies, so that they could be violated and finally mutilated in horrific ways. In one barn, we found an old man, whose throat had been pierced by a pitch fork, pinning him to the door. All of the feather mattresses in one of the bedrooms had been sliced open, and were stained with blood. Two cut-up female corpses were lying amongst the feathers, with two murdered children. The sight was so gruesome that some of our recruits fled in panic.[4]

Captain Jaedtke, the commanding officer, recalled:

> Apparently the Russian attack on Nemmersdorf and Brauersdorf [8km east of Nemmersdorf] had overrun German refugee columns; the scene that

Any vessel that floated could be used for the evacuation – and for some it meant salvation.

greeted us was grim. Amongst approximately 50 shot-up wagons and along the edge of a wood, about 200 meters away, the bodies of shot women and children were strewn everywhere. In Brauersdorf itself, there were many women next to the village road who had their breasts cut off. I saw this with my own eyes. I received many reports of many other atrocities from units in other areas, but particularity from Nemmersdorf.[5]

For the survivors and relatives of the victims, this atrocity was traumatising. But for the Nazi propaganda minister, Joseph Goebbels, it was a gift from the gods. He immediately ordered documentary photography and the detailed recording of eyewitness accounts of the results of the Russian soldiers' rampage. International observers were summoned. The German people would understand of just what Soviet soldiers were capable.

However, using Nemmersdorf as a propaganda weapon turned out to be a double-edged sword. Although it may have stiffened the resolve of some to resist the Russian advance, it was also a clear warning to those in East Prussia that such a fate might await them, too. Confidence in the Nazis' assurances was weakened. Could they really keep the Red Army back? Or, even though it was forbidden at the time, should civilians flee westwards?

Yet there was some hope for these civilians – the Americans and British were known to be pushing up from the south and the west and the prospect of life under Anglo-American rule seemed far preferable to living under Soviet control.

A QUIET SEA

Germans had lived for generations in villages like Nemmersdorf, yet less than five years earlier this area had been part of Poland. When on 1 September 1939 the German armies attacked, the lives of millions in this part of Europe were changed forever.

A week before this invasion, on 23 August 1939, a secret so-called non-aggression pact between Germany and Russia had been signed by foreign ministers Ribbentrop and Molotov, effectively redrawing the map of Europe. Poland was to be divided between them: the Soviets would occupy the Baltic States and attack Finland unopposed; Germany had a free hand to invade France and was promised Lithuania. Most importantly for the Nazis, it meant that if the British decided to defend Poland there would not be a war on two fronts.

A by-product of this pact was that the Baltic became a 'quiet' sea. Importantly, iron from the Swedish ore fields, essential to the German war effort, could be transported without fear of attack. Grand Admiral Erich Raeder later commented:

> The Baltic coast and ore shipments from Sweden were thus secured during the summer, so combat forces did not have to be brought from the North Sea. Submarine Command believed that, thanks to the Hitler-Stalin Pact, we had the freedom from being attacked in the back and that in a crisis we could withstand a commercial war against England.[6]

The calm in the Baltic was also aided by the entrance to Öresund (which separates Denmark and Sweden) being heavily mined and only possible to navigate with the aid of a pilot. Thus, with the Soviet Union as an ally, an illusory peace was created.

On 30 November 1939 a Russian force of about 200,000 men, 900 artillery pieces, 1,500 tanks and 300 aircraft pushed north along the Karelian Isthmus, north of Leningrad, and attacked Finland. Opposing them was a Finnish defence of 129,000 men, poorly equipped and with no armoured weapons. Finns stationed further north, all along the Russian–Finnish border that stretched almost to the Arctic Sea, were similarly outmanned and outgunned.

However, the Soviet leadership had not taken account of the fanatical, desperate resistance they would face. Russian soldiers were trained to obey orders blindly, not to take the initiative; Finnish soldiers, in contrast, often acted very independently. They did not simply wait for orders but instead hit as fast as they could whenever the opportunity arose. The result was a series of extremely worrying Russian defeats, which Stalin found unacceptable. While the Soviet Union did its best to hide its huge losses, the rest of the world followed this courageous struggle of David against Goliath in astonishment.

But the Finnish defence forces could not hold back the Russian onslaught forever. After 105 days, hostilities were suspended and on 12 March 1940 the Moscow Peace Treaty formally ended the so-called Winter War. The peace agreed upon resulted in huge land losses for Finland but the independence of the remainder of the country was secured.

Meanwhile, German military successes had, by the spring of 1940, brought a large part of Europe under Nazi control. This included Denmark and Norway, as well as the Netherlands, Belgium and France. Germany had thus built an 'Atlantic Wall', which would prove vital in the fight against Britain.

OPERATION BARBAROSSA

For the Nazis, the non-aggression pact with the Soviet Union was simply a pragmatic, temporary peace. Russians were considered sub-human and Hitler's real intention was to occupy Russia, turning it into a colony that would supply slave labour. But Soviet successes in the occupation of the Baltic States and eastern Poland, as well as the Winter War, threatened to create a strong communist bloc. So on 18 December 1940, Hitler signed Directive No. 21 – his crusade against the East, which was to become known as Operation Barbarossa: the invasion of Russia. Originally scheduled for mid-May 1941, it began on Sunday, 22 June that year.

At first, Stalin refused to believe that his ally Hitler was really attacking him and this naivety allowed the German army to quickly gain considerable ground. The Germans now also sought new allies and turned to Finland: co-operation between the two countries would make it possible to sever Soviet access to the Baltic Sea completely. Not only that, Russian troop and fleet movements could be monitored from Finnish territory and the Finnish navy promised to secretly lay mines along parts of the Estonian coast.

The Russians put up an ineffective resistance and were driven back on all fronts. The city of Leningrad, with a million inhabitants, was almost completely strangled in a siege that lasted for 900 days.

When German forces reached the Estonian town of Kunda, on the southern coast of the Gulf of Finland, the Soviet 10th Rifle Corps found itself cut off and had to be rescued by sea. On 28–29 August the men were evacuated on more than 160 ships with the intention to take them to Leningrad. But what the rescuers did not realise was 1,700 German and Finnish mines and 700 explosives had been laid in the sea to the north. And German bombers were ready and waiting. What has been called 'the Tragedy at Juminda' began.

Among the vessels were twenty-nine large freighters. Of these, twenty-five were sunk, three grounded themselves at Hogland and only one reached Leningrad. Ship after ship ran into mines; the beautiful August night was rocked by incessant explosions. The exact number of people on the ships has never been released by the Russian authorities, if it was ever known, but it is estimated that between 5,000 and 6,000 men were killed. What might have been remembered as Russia's Dunkirk turned out to be probably history's biggest shipping loss caused by mines.

As if this were not enough, the Russians lost more men and ships during the evacuation of the Hanko peninsula on the Finnish coast, which had been leased to the Soviet Navy as part of the Moscow Peace Treaty. On 2 December 1941, the steamer *Josif Stalin* left Hanko in a convoy of twenty warships. On board were more than 6,000 men, with several thousand more on the other vessels. At Porkkalanniemi, close to

Helsinki, the steamer came under attack from Finnish batteries and was severely damaged. *Hufvudstadsbladet*, a Swedish language Finnish newspaper, published an article a few days later that made it all seem like a boy's adventure story:

> The [Finnish] heavy guns open fire. The mighty muzzles fire flames. The boys shoot to their hearts' content … The big cannon fire a few shots at the large transport ship. She must now choose: to try to get past MacElliot [Mäkiluoto, a fort guarding the entrance to the Gulf of Finland] or go into the minefield. It seems a hard decision. Or is she damaged, unable to navigate? In any case, she will disappear with the wind out into the minefield, where twelve minutes later a mighty explosion is heard, perhaps the grandest ever seen in the Gulf of Finland. A clear, white pillar of fire, approximately 150 metres wide, rises up to 600 metres.[7]

Josif Stalin did not sink, but her officers decided to run her aground. Those on board not killed by the explosions were drowned as the water poured into her damaged hull, or in the panic that broke out. Although the Soviet propaganda machine again did its best to supress the news, 3,849 men died.

With Russian combat units trapped in Leningrad, a relative – but deceptive – calm returned to the Baltic. It is a shallow Mediterranean (in the oceanographic sense) sea, nicknamed '*der Ententeich*', 'the Duck Pond', by the German navy but '*die Badewanne*', 'the bathtub', by German submarine officers. It offers few deep places to elude depth changes. For a submarine it is one of the most difficult seas in the world in which to operate.

Despite the challenges, submarines still carried out some spectacular sinkings. One of them occurred on 22 June 1942 when the Russian Shchuka-class submarine *SC-317*, under the command of Captain Moschow, attacked the Swedish merchant ship *Ada Gorthon* south of the island of Öland. She was loaded with 3,700 tons of iron ore bound for German factories. The lookout on the cargo steamer spotted a periscope on the port side, and soon afterwards a torpedo track:

> He immediately ran aft to alert the duty officer, shouting 'Torpedo!'. He managed to shout once more as he passed the companion hatchway, before the torpedo hit the ship at about the hatch cover of the second hold.[8]

The *Ada Gorthon* broke in two and disappeared in less than a minute. Amazingly, eight of her fourteen-man crew survived.

After the loss of the *Ada Gorthon*, convoys were introduced but Russian submarines still managed to sink a number of Swedish iron-ore vessels, among them the *Margareta* on 9 July 1942, *Luleå* on 11 July and *C.F. Liljevalch* on 18 August.

THE FISHING EXPEDITION

The challenge for Germany's naval leaders was to close the Gulf of Finland to Russian submarines. Plans had been first considered as early as spring 1942 and at the time had been dismissed as almost impossible to achieve, but now one idea was revived: a steel net stretching right across the Gulf, between the Estonian island of Naissaar and the Finnish island of Kallbådan, which was the Gulf's narrowest point. Combined with a minefield and constant patrolling, it would be impenetrable to submarines.

Running for 55½km, with depths ranging from 60 to 90m, the installation of the net – Operation Walrus – was a huge technical achievement. It was a double mesh, each side of the square mesh measuring 4m and supported by a dense rows of buoys that the Finnish and German patrol boats did their best to disguise.

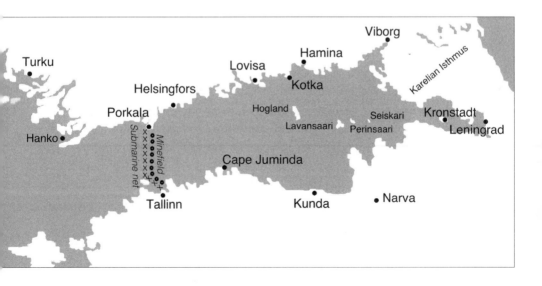

The net was installed without serious interference from the Russians. Reconnaissance aircraft, and later attack planes, that approached were effectively driven off. Then, on 15 May 1943, Submarine *SC-303*, under the command of Ivan Travkin, was ordered to penetrate the net. At the time neither he nor his superiors knew its length, depth or strength. Travkin was instructed to get through it at night, so the submarine waited on the sea bottom, right next to the net, until darkness fell:

> The first attempt to penetrate the net was on course 230°, or straight on, at the minimum speed along the bottom at 90 m depth. After ten minutes *SC-303* drove its blunt nose into a mesh and the horizontal rudder was blocked. With slow backing, it came loose. A second attempt was made in the same place with course 280° angle to the net. The submarine was tangled up even worse and full engine power was required to get loose. Travkin then groped southward along the fence to a place where the water depth was 100m, but this attempt to crawl under the net also failed. Again the boat was caught and came loose only with the greatest difficulty. Then the electricity began to fail, the boss gave up the attempt and let the crew rest on the bottom.[9]

The net worked and the 'fish' remained inside their cage. German and Finnish sea traffic began to sail normally, insofar as it could during a war, and Swedish iron-ore shipments once more travelled in safety.

The calm could continue only as long as the German armed forces controlled the Baltic. But the balance of the war had begun to turn – partly because Finland now defected from Germany's side. The Winter War of 1939–40 between Finland and Russia had resumed in the autumn of 1941 as 'the Continuation War'. Although the Finns initially succeeded in recouping their earlier land losses, Russia launched a huge offensive on 9 June 1944 (timed to coincide with the Normandy landings) which retook all their gains. The attacking troops destroyed everything in their path and on 20 June they reached Vyborg and the fierce Battle of Tali-Ihantala was fought from 25 June to 9 July.

Although the Finns managed to halt the Russian advance, it was clear that they were again the underdogs. After negotiations, an armistice was signed at four in the morning of 4 September 1944, and confirmed on 19 September. The price of peace was the permanent surrender of all the lands the Finns had retaken and lost, $300,000,000 in war reparations and the requirement that all German troops would leave Finnish territory by midnight on 14/15 September. This meant the hurried arrangement of large troop movements that, among other things, led to massive destruction in Finnish Lapland by German troops as they retreated.

THE WOLVES ARE ON THE PROWL

At the same time as there were Germans in Finland, there were Finnish soldiers and officers in German-occupied Estonia, collaborating with the German military. Per-Olof Ekman belonged to a group working in the Tallinn suburb of Nörme whose task was to collect information broadcast on the radio. On the evening of 3 September, the news came through of the Finnish ceasefire with Russia. They understood the implications immediately. Two days later, the group was back in Helsinki, and stationed at Suomenlinna, a sea fortress to the south of the city. Ekman and his colleagues were ordered to co-operate with the Russians, which turned out to mean helping their submarines clear the Gulf of Finland. They were to go on board a Russian warship to maintain radio contact with the Finnish coastal stations:

> Not a word on our previous collaboration with the Germans was mentioned. Although this mission was secret, it was indeed a sudden jump across to the opposite side.[10]

At its Finnish terminus, the great net began to be torn up: there was already a wide gap at Porkkalanniemi. And on 24 September, Marshal Zhukov obtained maps of the minefields. Ekman and his men were transferred to Hamina, to the east, where the headquarters of Eastern Finland Coastal Brigade was stationed:

> We would pilot the first couple of submarines from coastal fairway to open water, perhaps even to Åland and give the Russians all the help they wanted. The responsibility lay with us and the pilots … The same dangerous sea wolves the Germans had so effectively kept trapped in the eastern part of the Gulf would now be discharged into the Baltic Sea [where they had not been since 1942] … Targets for their torpedoes were in abundance.[11]

A small group of men was conducted at night in the motorboat *SM-3* to Lavansaari. Here, a patrol boat was waiting to escort them into the harbour, where a Russian minesweeper was moored.

There was a confusion of tongues: the Russian radio telegraphers could speak neither Finnish, German, nor English but fortunately there was an interpreter. After breakfast they joined a convoy behind the minesweeper, and were in turn followed by three submarines and four patrol boats. Eventually they passed Hanko and anchored overnight at Högsåra. The next morning the convoy continued and in the evening the submarines entered the Baltic Sea to begin their hunt.

After refuelling, the convoy returned to escort the next group of submarines. Off Pellinki they met four submarines, *D-2*, *L-3*, *S-13*, and the former Estonian submarine *Lembit*. Ekman got to know the captains of these submarines, including Vladimir Konovalov on *L-3*. Meetings were formal but never threatening. They all knew what the Russian submarines would be doing in the Baltic, but no one could know that *L-3* would cause one of the greatest ever shipping tragedies:

> The quartet [of submarines] was guided round the archipelago by the same route as the first group but to Sottunga [in the Åland Islands]. As well as submarines, other Russian vessels travelled along the protected route westwards: destroyers, gunboats, and freighters, most on their way to the newly acquired naval base at Porkala.[12]

One by one, the submarines slipped away into clear water. The sea wolves began as a pack, but then moved away to hunt on their own. Among the crews, there was not only hatred for Germans and hunger for revenge but also a desire for prestige and honour. They wanted to be part of the Russian history of the war, and they had been trapped in their bases for too long. Now finally there was a chance to demonstrate of what they were capable. There may have also been a gung-ho quality in the submarine commanders.

On the afternoon of 29 October 1944 the steamer *Bremerhaven* left Windau for Gotenhafen. On board were refugees, soldiers, injured troops and medics – in all 3,171 people including the crew. The 9th Security Division in Gotenhafen had provided minesweepers *M-155* and *M-435* as escorts. Nothing occurred during the night, but about half past nine the next morning Soviet aircraft attacked.

Bremerhaven was hit repeatedly and caught fire. Anti-aircraft ammunition on deck ignited and exploded. The fire was soon out of control and distress signals were broadcast. When the rescue ships arrived, a large portion of the aft part of the *Bremerhaven* was on fire. Those on board had moved as far forward as they could and now hastily started to evacuate the ship. More than 80 per cent of those on board were saved; around 400 died, which, in the context of the times, was not seen as a major disaster.

Nevertheless, the security arrangements regarding escorts came under scrutiny after the loss of *Bremerhaven*. Just days after the tragedy, 'Standing Force Escort Regulation No. 1' was enacted. Ships now stayed closer to the coast whenever possible, and escorts were tightened significantly. A special radio wavelength was set up for them, and in November 1944 an additional security division for evacuations and escorts was created. All this was to be of great importance for what was to come.

When there was no other route to the West, the Baltic was the only option.

RUSSIAN HONOUR AND A SMALL GOTLAND BOAT

More than once, a Russian submarine commander exaggerated his successes to convince his home base that he had done a decent job and not been out in vain. It was very difficult to check commanders' claims, but the tonnage they reported as sunk did not always reflect reality. For example, during a summer offensive in 1942, in their home base of Kronstadt submarine captains posted twenty ships sunk totalling 160,000 gross tons. According to the Germans, Russian submarines sank eight ships, totalling 15,745 gross tons. There may be several explanations for this discrepancy, but sometimes it was simply believed that vessels were larger than they actually were. However, the longing for honour and fame is hard to discount as a contributory factor in exaggerating the truth.

On their return, submarine crews would be given a magnificent reception. The quay was adorned with a triumphal arch, with red banners and slogan-inscribed placards, and in this festive manner the crews were welcomed back to their barracks:

> The Submarine Brigade's political branch edited the magazine Podvodnik Baltiki, which, in enthusiastic terms, related the Soviet submariners' noble war effort against the fascists in the seas. The Political Department distributed richly illustrated leaflets portraying heroes and glorifying their deeds. Medals rained over them: Lenin, Red Banner, Red Star, The Bravery …[13]

The desire to succeed and achieve honours combined with a sense of freedom after a long period of confinement, a desire for revenge and a gung-ho attitude may have all been factors when the submarine *L-21*, under the command of Captain Third Rank S.S. Mogilevskij, sighted the Gotland Company's *Hansa* early in the morning of 24 November 1944.

Hansa was the Gotland Company's workhorse, a ship that was almost a sea-going bus. She flew the Swedish flag: she could not be mistaken for anything other than a neutral vessel. Although Russian submarines had previously disrupted Swedish ore shipments to the German munition foundries, passenger ships were not thought to be likely targets.

L-21's war record up to this point had been unremarkable. She had had a fairly unsuccessful time laying mines, and her torpedoes had missed the German cruiser *Nürnberg*. Now the submarine had problems with her steering gear and Captain Mogilevskij decided to return to base. Like many other Russian submarine commanders, Mogilevskij chose to go west of Gotland, perhaps in case something more interesting than an ore vessel might appear.

At four o'clock in the morning on 24 November 1944 the call was made that a large vessel was fast approaching. *Hansa* was, however, only 563 gross tons and could only do 8 knots into the wind. But perhaps to Mogilevskij she may have seemed like a larger transport vessel, possibly laden with munitions. The Swedes sold iron ore to Germany: it was not difficult to imagine that this could be some kind of shipment to the enemy. *L-21* took up a firing position at about 1,500m. Although she was effectively cloaked in the pre-dawn darkness, there was a risk of detection if she went closer.

Three torpedoes were fired. One hit *Hansa* just aft of the forward mast, 1½m below the waterline. It literally tore the bow off and the ship immediately began to sink. Most of those on board were asleep: no distress signal was ever sent and the little ship's agony lasted only a few minutes.

Those in their cabins were drowned when the sea rushed in. A few made it up to the main deck, but of the eighty-six on board only two survived: Third Officer Arne Thuresson and a passenger, Army Staff Captain Arne Mohlin.

The sinking of *Hansa* attracted enormous attention in Sweden: the loss of a merchant ship in this way made it one of the most talked about events of the war.

It cannot be proven, but there may be another explanation for *Hansa's* sinking, other than it simply being mistaken for a larger vessel. She may have been misidentified as a large passenger ship: there was already a steady stream of refugees across the Baltic to Sweden. Russian radio was already criticising the Swedish position: fleeing from the Soviet forces, even by civilians, was seen with much disfavour in Moscow.

The Soviet authorities categorically denied any involvement in this incident, as well as the torpedoing of the *Ada Gorthon* in 1942. However, the Swedish government eventually undertook an extensive investigation – the *Hansa* Commission – in December 1944. Gathering all the wreckage that could be found, *Hansa* was reconstructed in a cavern under the Engelbrekt church in Stockholm. Detective Stellan Cleveland was able to prove that it was not a mine, sabotage or an on–board explosion that sank the ship: it was a torpedo. He could even show where the torpedo hit. But the torpedo's origin was unknown. It would take another forty-eight years before Russia officially admitted that *Hansa* was sunk by one of its submarines.

In the autumn and early winter of 1944, Russian submarines in the Baltic increased in number and they became more aggressive. On 7 October, before *Hansa* was sunk, *SC-404* attacked the *Nordstern*, a ship bound from Saaremaa, the largest island in Estonia, with more than 600 people on board, most of them refugees. First Mate Reinhard Prahm was off duty but lay on his bunk fully dressed with a life jacket on. A huge explosion threw him out of the bunk: he understood immediately that the ship had been struck by a torpedo and he rushed up to the boat deck:

> As there was no time to release and launch the undamaged lifeboats, a few men and I jumped from the stern into the water. It was literally at the last second. The next moment MS *Nord Stern* sank below the Baltic waves. The suction from the sinking ship took me under water for a few brief moments, but then threw me to the surface. When I could see again, there was no ship left. All around me lay just shipwrecked people and flotsam.[14]

Ninety-four were rescued: 535 died.

It was around this time that a huge wave of refugees was moving towards the West, towards the parts of Germany not under threat from the Russians. Those who could took the trains or, if sufficiently privileged, travelled by car. Others took horses and carts. Enormous numbers simply walked. However, the Russian onslaught, with its tanks, its foot soldiers and its aeroplanes, began to pour over them, sweeping away all hope of reaching the West.

A HERO COMES HOME

The cruiser *Emden* left Königsberg on 24 January 1945, a city to which she never returned, with the help of tugboats. She was towed to Pillau, where her own crew repaired her engines. But before she left Königsberg, she loaded a strange cargo. On the evening of 23 January, *Emden*'s crew had set up a triumphal arch consisting of lifebuoys and floats, surrounded

The sinking of the *Hansa* attracted enormous attention in Sweden and was the subject of one of the largest wreck investigations in the country's history.

The *Hansa* was a faithful old servant in the trade with Gotland. At the outbreak of the war, she was repainted white to mark her neutral status.

by flags and standards from the Tannenberg Monument, which had been erected to commemorate the German soldiers lost at the Second Battle of Tannenberg in 1914. The ship's cranes later lifted two lead coffins on board. They contained the remains of Chancellor Paul von Hindenburg, who had been the victorious German commander at the battle, and his wife. The Tannenberg Monument had been completed in 1927 and when Hindenburg died in 1934 he and his wife (who had died in 1921) were interred there. The remains of this national hero could not be allowed to fall into Russian hands. Once the coffins were removed, the Germans destroyed the mausoleum with dynamite.

In every harbour on the East Prussian coastline, those who wanted to get away before it was too late became desperate. A soldier later described what he saw in Pillau:

> In the harbour everyone was pushed against the ships. Terrible scenes were enacted. People were transformed into animals. Women threw their children into the water, just to get on board or not let them be killed in congestion. At the same time, the general confusion was further increased by the fact that totally disorganised troops had streamed into the city, plundered houses, joined the refugees, and also pushed towards the ships. To get through the gates of the harbour, soldiers robbed mothers of their children, claiming they wanted to board with their families. Others had dressed in women's clothes and so tried to get to the ships.[15]

Shortly afterwards, Königsberg was besieged and isolated from the other coastal towns. The struggle for the city then began, which led to most of Königsberg's heritage being erased forever. Rumours began to circulate about the so-called Amber Room, rumours that persist to this day. The Amber Room was a gift from the Prussian King Frederick William I to Tsar Peter I (Peter the Great). There were panels made of amber so beautiful and so costly that the fame of the Amber Room spread around Europe. When the German troops besieged Leningrad, they removed the panels from the Tsar's summer palace and transported them in wooden chests to Königsberg, presumably with the intention of transporting them further west. However, here the trail ends. But there is a persistent rumour that the panels did move on – to Gotenhafen, where they were loaded on to the *Wilhelm Gustloff*.

The Russian submarine fleet in the Baltic Sea consisted of three submarine brigades organised in three to five divisions, each division having between three and five submarines. The submarine fleet had been insignificant when the Communists had taken over the country in 1917, but it had been steadily built up. During the Siege of Leningrad, they were trapped, but once this was over, and the submarines were relocated to Turku after the settlement with Finland, the situation changed radically. From then on, submarines were a threat to all Baltic shipping.

Under the command of Captain Third Grade Alexander Marinesco, Submarine *S-13* had – according to Marinesco – sunk a large ship in Danzig Bay on 14 October 1944. It was a steamer of at least 5,000 tonnes but Marinesco's report to the home base in Turku was greeted with enormous scepticism. When it later turned out that it was the freighter *Siegfried* of 563 tonnes, they became even more suspicious of the captain. A note was added to Marinesco's file with the Narodnyy Komissariat Vnutrennikh Del: the NKVD – the Soviet interior ministry and security police. This was not the only entry in the file. Marinesco had great fondness for vodka equalled by that for women, sometimes of doubtful character. This in itself may not be so remarkable but what concerned the security police and his superiors was his independent, almost anarchic way of waging war. It was as if Marinesco was fighting his own private war against Germany and he was deliberately not following the orders he received. On the other hand, he was highly regarded by his crew, and they had a high level of confidence in him, both of which were prerequisites for success.

Marinesco was born in 1913, in Odessa. The family was poor and he left school at 15 with poor academic grades. His sea career began as a deck hand on a coastal voyager, and the shipping company later enrolled him in Odessa's navigation school. He advanced to Mate and achieved some fame by rescuing the crew of a stricken torpedo boat, and as a result of this he was given the opportunity to undertake naval training, which in turn led him to a career in submarines.

On 2 January 1945, *S-13* was ready to go. On board were twelve torpedoes, 120 100mm grenades, air-defence ammunition and provisions for two months' hunting in the southern Baltic. But the most valuable element was missing: the Master. Where was Marinesco? He had been missing for three days and when the departure date arrived, the military police began to search for him. When they finally found him and returned him to the base, he was found to be 'in a less than presentable condition'. Completely inebriated, he had no memory of where he had been. It was discovered that he had spent some of the time in a brothel. The question was: had someone spied on him there?

Police Department Chief Zjankotjian interrogated Marinesco thoroughly and made it clear that despite his popularity he could easily face prosecution. As a result of his behaviour the authorities dared not let him return to command *S-13*. However, this enraged the crew, who filed a petition in defence of Marinesco. While this dispute raged, it was decided to send *S-13* to Hanko anyway, where it could more easily slip out to sea once Marinesco's fate had been decided.

The Soviet navy, however, needed to sink all the enemy tonnage it could and to do so needed all its skilled submariners. So Marinesco was released and allowed to return to his vessel. He was now under double pressure: first he had to show to his superiors that he was a competent submarine captain by sinking ships of some significance; and secondly he must do what his superiors and the party demanded – be a good and obedient officer.

Alexander Marinesco, 42 at the time of the sinking of the *Wilhelm Gustloff,* was an experienced sailor whose crew had great confidence in him. (Heinz Schön)

In many cases, a depth-charge explosion was the end for a submarine and her crew, who often left no trace.

Marinesco was, of course, aware of the Russian army's great counter-offensive, which in turn meant an increase in the enemy's activity at sea. He reasoned that, after crossing the Baltic near Memel, the area around Danzig Bay would be a good place for his hunt. But the bay was shallow, and for a submarine it could be fatal if there was an aeroplane attack or, worse, depth charges. Every crew on a submarine knew what depth charges meant:

> The pressure waves made all loose goods on board tumble willy-nilly or caused the seawater to pour through the consequent leaks. During long-term attacks, the air was almost at an end in there … The highly risky back-and-forth evasion was only mastered by a skilled master and well-trained, resolute crews. The master had a heavy responsibility for his men and his boat.[16]

Marinesco set off in the company of *SC-307* and *SC-310* until they neared Memel. Having spotted nothing of interest and knowing that the Russians now occupied Memel, Marinesco decided to leave the other two submarines and head south:

We went back and forth in front of the nose of the fascists, but the dogs did not want to come out to fight. I decided to take the war to their own territory, I was going to take the position from Hela's lighthouse and then slam into Danzig Bay.[17]

Late in the afternoon of 30 January, *S-13* was off Hela, the peninsula that lies on the north-western side of Danzig Bay. Marinesco gave orders for silence, listening for any propeller noise that would indicate a ship nearby. The submarine was combat-ready: four torpedoes were loaded and sailor Andrej Pichut had even inscribed the torpedoes. Torpedo 1 he called 'For the Motherland'; Torpedo 2 'For Stalin'; Torpedo 3 'For the Soviet people' and Torpedo 4 'For Leningrad'. The latter inscription was particularly apt for *S-13*'s crew: everyone on board had lost one or more relatives during the siege of the city.

Through the periscope, Marinesco strained to detect something, but the Baltic seemed completely deserted. So he decided to surface. It was dreadfully cold and he was wearing a thick sheepskin coat as he climbed the submarine tower. Following him was Boatswain Lew Jefremenkow, who had served under Marinesco for three years. Then Boatswain Winogradow joined them but none of the three men could see anything.

Marinesco went down, leaving the two boatswains. The two men stared into the darkness. Suddenly, Winogradow saw a light. He pointed it out to Jefremenkow. Neither could he understand it. Could it be the lighthouse at Hela? More crewmen came up to look at the lights. When Marinesco was finally called he immediately realised that what Winogradow had spotted were the sidelights of a ship, a big ship. He ordered all men to their places and to get the submarine ready to attack. But the big ship was still too far away for Marinesco to have the chance to intercept it. But what he could not understand was why such a big ship was sailing with all her lights ablaze:

The lights we had spotted suddenly disappeared; a snowstorm had swept over us and our vision was lost. When the snow suddenly stopped falling, I saw the silhouette of an ocean steamer. She was large. She even had lanterns out. I was immediately convinced that it was certainly 20,000 tons, definitely not less. I was also sure that she was packed with men who had trampled Mother Russia's land and were now on the run. The steamer

has to be sunk immediately, I decided, and that would be *S-13*'s task …
And then the idea came to attack the big ship and its small escort from the
coast-ward side. From that point of view, they could not have anticipated an
attack. The lookouts concentrated on looking out to the sea.[18]

Marinesco now ordered *S-13* to go at full speed on a course parallel
to the ship but between her and the coast. The preparations had taken
about two hours. The atmosphere in *S-13* was very tense but controlled.
Marinesco had to be sure he reached the right angle of attack, but he
trusted his crew.

S-13 drew closer and when she was 700m from the ship Marinesco
judged the moment was right. Through the binoculars of First Officer
Jefremenko, the ship looked huge. When Marinesco finally had the ship
in the middle of the periscope's crosshairs, he gave the order '*Fire!*'

2

KRAFT DURCH FREUDE

When Hitler seized power in 1933, trade unions were effectively eradicated and replaced by the *Deutsche Arbeitsfront* (DAF), the German Labour Front. In a speech delivered on 2 May 1933, the leader of DAF, Dr Robert Ley, explained that society was now transformed into a co-operative organisation where leadership and unions were one and the same:

> We go now into the second part of the National Socialist revolution. You say then: what do you want? You already have all the power. Yes, we have the power but we do not have power over the people. You workers, we still do not have one hundred per cent of your thoughts and therefore we will not release you until you honestly admit that you belong to us. You will also be relieved of the last Marxist shackles, so you can find your own people's way. For this we know: without the German worker there is no German people![1]

The abolition of the trade unions naturally caused discontent, and one way in which this was mollified was through the establishment, within DAF's control, of the leisure organisation.

Kraft durch Freude (KdF) – 'Strength through Joy'– was an offshoot of DAF. It arranged a variety of activities from plays to sports, built swimming baths and other recreational facilities (and was responsible for commissioning the People's Car, the Volkswagen 'Beetle'), but they also organised incredibly popular and affordable sea cruises. Ley stated that it was the Führer's wish that every worker and the employee should be able to participate in a KdF trip:

> There should not just be trips to the most beautiful German vacation spots, but also sea voyages to foreign countries.[2]

Above: The leisure organisation *Kraft durch Freude* quickly became popular by, among other things, offering holiday trips at bargain prices. Their large cruise ships were built with money confiscated from the banned trade unions.

Left: To the left of the sack race competitor with his arm outstretched is the leader of KfD Robert Ley on board one of his ships.

Initially the KdF chartered vessels, ranging from excursion boats to ocean liners. In May 1934, for its first overseas voyage, Hamburg America Line's *Monte Olivia* and the North German Lloyd steamship *Dresden* undertook a five-day cruise to the Isle of Wight. Disembarking at the destination was, however, forbidden, even though the passengers for this first voyage had been carefully selected, as were the journalists reporting it. Inevitably, it was deemed a huge success both in print and on radio. Cruises along the Norwegian coast and into the fjords soon followed.

A book about KdF, published in 1936, praised the organisation and Robert Ley:

Freut euch des Lebens!
Als wir fuhr'n in diesen Tagen
In die weite Welt hinein,
Tat der Doktor Ley uns sagen:
'kommt mir nicht mit Leid und klagen!
Ihr sollt euch des Lebens freun!'

Ja, wir waren tapfre Streiter
Dieses Worts, und mit Genuß
Hat des Schiffes Reiseleiter
Melden könne: froh und heiter
War die Bande bis zum Schluß!

[Approximate translation]
Enjoy life!
When we travelled in these days
Out on the wide earth
Teach us Dr Ley to consider:
'Take not your woe and lamentation!
You shall rejoice these days'

Yes, we have fought bravely,
Oh for these words and
With joy, our chief
Here on the trip told us
That we delightfully enjoyed every moment![3]

Even though reporting of the wreck of the *Dresden* was restricted, the bringing ashore of the two dead passengers was turned into a Nazi propaganda opportunity.

In June 1934, on the seventh KdF cruise to Norway, *Dresden* sailed with *Monte Rosa*, but the latter, the faster ship, was far ahead when, in the vicinity of Haugesund (halfway between Bergen and Stavanger) *Dresden* found herself in rapidly deteriorating weather. A storm had torn away a marker buoy and even though there was a pilot on board, the ship scraped along the underground rocks, cutting a 30m-long, 4m-wide hole on the port side. The officers managed to run the ship aground, and although two women died of heart attacks, all the other passengers were successfully evacuated in the ship's lifeboats.

In an article in *Volkischer Beobachter*, Robert Ley lamented the deaths of the two women but stressed the German crew's successful rescue of the passengers. Other reporting was more strictly regulated: the sinking was only briefly mentioned, with no detailed descriptions of what had happened.

Despite the accident, the KdF continued to increase the number of cruises it offered. A small fleet of passenger ships – *Monte Olivia, St. Louis, Sierra Cordoba* and *Berlin* – was hired for voyages to the Mediterranean, Tenerife, Madeira and other places in southern Europe. Then the KdF purchased its first ship, the *Sierra Morena* from the North German Lloyd Line, and renamed her *Der Deutsche*. All these ships would later participate in the enormous East Prussian evacuation.

The cruises became very popular very quickly because the quality was high and the ticket prices were low. A Swedish propaganda leaflet described the bargain:

A voyage to Norway, which takes a week, on one of the most luxurious, modern passenger ships of 10,000 to 27,000 tonnes in the KdF fleet with seaward-facing cabins, good food, railway ticket to the departure harbour and back, guided tour of the port and dock installations, etc. costs 50 Rm. [Reichsmark]. This is around the figure a skilled worker makes per week, and this sum he still receives during the holiday week.[4]

Ordinary German workers and their families were taken in luxury to places they had only read about: they were making the same voyages as the affluent bourgeoisie and the upper classes.

The KdF's next step was to begin building its own ships. Ironically, it was the banning of the trade unions that made these ships for the workers possible: on 24 October 1934 Hitler decreed that the funds of the dissolved trade unions would be transferred to DAF and the KdF. Planning began immediately for a fleet of white KdF ships, and the world's first one-class cruise ships.

3

THE WORKERS' DREAM SHIP

THE EPONYMOUS WILHELM GUSTLOFF

On the evening of 4 February 1936, David Frankfurter, a young medical student, left the Hotel Metropol in Davos, Switzerland, where he had been staying for a few days. He walked towards a large house in the town and knocked on the door. It was opened by Hedwig Gustloff, who told him that her husband, Wilhelm, was on the telephone. The young man was shown into the study to wait.

Frankfurter was a Jew, the son of a Croatian rabbi. He had begun his medical studies in Vienna and continued in other cities, including Frankfurt, where he had witnessed the Nazi seizure of power. Grasping the consequences for the Jewish population, he had fled to Switzerland in October 1933. From the day he arrived he began collecting everything he could about Wilhelm Gustloff, leader of the Swiss Nazis, a man known as the 'Davos dictator' and one of Hitler's most loyal and dedicated devotees. He did so for one reason only: to assassinate him.

Wilhelm Gustloff ended his call and stepped into the study. At 190cm (almost 6ft 3in), he was much taller than Frankfurter, but fearlessly and without a word Frankfurter pulled out his gun, pointed it at Gustloff and quickly fired five shots into his chest and head. Frankfurter then walked out of the house and shortly afterwards rang the police to identify himself and admit to what he had done. He was eventually sentenced to eighteen years in prison followed by lifetime expulsion from Switzerland for the murder of Wilhelm Gustloff.

Adolf Hitler was not slow to exploit Gustloff's assassination, turning it into a propaganda extravaganza. Three days of national morning were ordered and around 35,000 people attended the funeral on 12 February, in

Left: Wilhelm Gustloff was one of the first martyrs to the Nazi cause, and his death was gratefully received for its propaganda value. He was given a funeral in Schwerin similar to that of a high-ranking statesman, and after seeing the emotion it raised, it was decided that the ship should be named after Hitler's friend and party member.

Below: The *Wilhelm Gustloff* was a very stable and seaworthy ship. Her bulkheads allowed the forward part of the ship to be sealed completely, giving her a much better chance of staying afloat after an accident.

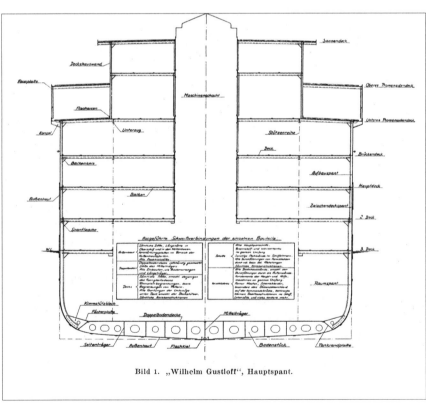

Bild 1. „Wilhelm Gustloff", Hauptspant.

Gustloff's hometown of Schwerin in northern Germany. Hitler declared they had 'lost a living person but gained an immortal'.

THE NEW SHIP

Around the time of Gustloff's assassination, Robert Ley had submitted an order to the Hamburg shipyard of Blohm & Voss for the first new KdF ship. It had been planned that she would bear the name *Adolf Hitler*, but to perpetuate the memory of his assassinated follower, the Führer decided that her name would be *Wilhelm Gustloff*.

She would be 25,000 gross registered tons and cost an estimated 25 million Reichsmarks. Very specific requirements were laid down: all cabins would have a sea view; they would be similarly decorated; there must be enough deck space for everyone; all passengers must be able to enjoy the sun and daylight on the deck without ventilators or equipment to interrupt the view; and there must be lounges and dining rooms to accommodate all the passengers. In addition, the crew cabins had to resemble those of the passengers, and the crew accommodation must be similarly generous. And none of these requirements should compromise the ship's stability or fire protection. This was to be a revolution in passenger ship design, and a very demanding brief for the naval architects. But on 1 May 1936 Robert Ley hammered home the first rivet in the ship's keel, witnessed by a large contingent of the press.

LAUNCH IN HAMBURG

A year after the keel was laid, it was announced that the ship would be launched on 5 May 1937. As the first KdF ship, it would be a spectacular event:

The Führer and National Chancellor Adolf Hitler is coming to this event to Hamburg. The launching ceremony will be performed by Mrs Hedwig Gustloff, widow of the NSDAP [National Socialist German Workers' Party] leader murdered in Switzerland and Dr Robert Ley is giving the launch speech. All Hamburg is in a fever because of it.[1]

Somewhere between 50,000 and a 100,000 people gathered along the piers, on the beaches and in the shipyard itself to watch the launch. Hitler arrived in Hamburg by train in the early morning and his motorcade to the Elbe was a public relations triumph.

Following the obligatory speeches, the widow Gustloff smashed the customary champagne bottle against the bow of the ship, the drapes fell away and a temporary nameboard with the words 'Wilhelm Gustloff' flapped down. Hitler did not go on board, preferring to inspect her from a harbour launch.

Fitting out took a further nine months, and the *Wilhelm Gustloff*'s sea trials took place on 23 and 24 March 1938. Usually, sea trials are a private affair between the builder and owner just before handover, but not in this case. On board were 1,300 guests and 165 journalists from every part of Germany. As the first of KdF's own ships, it was deemed vital to secure as much publicity as possible. Among the invited guests were Austrians: these trials were taking place shortly after the Anschluss that had integrated Austria into the Reich.

Adolf Hitler visited the *Wilhelm Gustloff* on 29 March 1938, but he hardly ever travelled on this or any other ship. He suffered from seasickness and did not want to show this 'weakness'.

Adolf Hitler on a rare trip on the *Robert Ley* from Hamburg to the German island Helgoland. The KdF director, Robert Ley, walks behind him (to the left).

The reporters were ecstatic, one of them writing:

> If [this] is an omen for the future, then the first KdF-ship is to be a happy ship. No vessel which went to sea from Hamburg, Bremen or any other port on the earth has ever seen so many happy people as on board Wilhelm Gustloff on her first trip.[2]

On 29 March, just five days after the trials, the ship was handed over to the KdF. There was also a ceremony for the launch of a sister ship – *Robert Ley* – at which Hitler himself delivered a speech in which he described the class-less *Wilhelm Gustloff* as 'the Europe to come for the German worker'.

Once the *Robert Ley* was in the water, Hitler was taken to inspect the *Wilhelm Gustloff*. Captain Carl Lübbe gave the Chancellor a full tour of her from the bridge to the engine room. He would have seen the two particular cabins: a special 'Führer-cabin' reserved for him (although he was never to use it), which consisted of a bedroom with bath and toilet and a living room, and the similar 'Robert Ley cabin', for the exclusive use of the KdF boss. These were the exceptions to the 'one-class principle'.

The *Wilhelm Gustloff* was described as a very handsome ship by the international press. In particular, the large public spaces and long promenades and sun decks that could be enjoyed by all passengers were noted.

Although the launch invitation described the *Wilhelm Gustloff* as a steamer, she was in fact a motor vessel, with a top speed of 16 knots. MV *Wilhelm Gustloff* was 25,484 gross tons, 208.5m (684ft) long, 23.6m (77ft) wide and 37m (121ft) high from the keel to top of the funnel, which itself was 13m (42ft) high. The ship's draft was 6.8m (22ft). She was partly riveted and partly welded, and came to be regarded as a very seaworthy vessel. The world's twenty-fifth largest passenger vessel, she was the fifth largest German passenger vessel ever built.

The ship was divided into twelve watertight compartments described as 'absolutely safe' (since the *Titanic* disaster in 1912, the concept of 'unsinkable' had fallen out of favour). The bulkheads sealed compartments completely – water could not flow from compartment to compartment as it had on the *Titanic* and which was the cause of her going down. There were a few exits from the forward compartments, but these were known only to the crew.

As well as the abundant strolling and recreational areas on the sun deck, there was a glazed area on the lower promenade deck for ambling. To protect passengers from the weather, it was fitted with armoured glass, which was nearly impossible to smash.

All cabins, as had been specified, had sea views and the drawing rooms, dining rooms and public areas were fitted out with great care. She lacked the distinctive luxury that was common in first-class accommodation on the great liners, but she was conceived according to different criteria: she reflected the National Socialist spirit.

Unlike most other passenger ships of the period, the *Wilhelm Gustloff* was not intended to sail between two ports or continents but was built as a cruise ship, a holiday vessel. The cabins were of a modest design because social life was to take place in the dining saloons, public areas, on decks and particularly on the promenade deck. This greatly pleased the journalists from the state-controlled press, who wrote enthusiastically about the new vessel. It was a time when a large passenger vessel was synonymous with the nation: the greatest ships often became a kind of unspoken symbol of the country and therefore the *Wilhelm Gustloff* was an important statement for the Nazi propaganda, who nicknamed her 'the Peace Ship'.

Cabins for passengers and crew were similar, and all faced the sea.

Above: Wilhelm Gustloff, probably photographed around the end of April 1938 as she prepared for her maiden voyage.

Left: In the ship's specification it was stated that every passenger should have access to the sun deck.

It was a requirement that all members of the crew on a KdF ship, from the captain to the pantry steward, must be members of the National Socialist Party. There were other party officials on board, who reported directly to the party, not the captain. This made the crew composition on KdF ships very different to those on other ships.

TROOP TRANSPORT

There is no evidence to suggest that when the *Wilhelm Gustloff* and her sister ship the *Robert Ley* were designed there was any thought that they could be excellent troop carriers. Nevertheless, a year after the *Wilhelm Gustloff* entered service, both ships, along with ships the KdF had hired, became exactly that.

On 16 May 1939, the captains of this KdF armada were ordered to disembark all female staff and many of the service personnel. They were then ordered to sea, where they opened their secret orders. Their destination was the port of Vigo on Spain's west coast. Here they embarked thousands of troops – volunteers of the Condor Legion who had fought for General Franco in the Spanish Civil War. Now that war was won, the ships were to bring the troops back to Hamburg.

The *Wilhelm Gustloff* on the Stockholm roads in July 1939 for the *Lingiaden*. To the left of her is the Canadian Pacific *Montcalm and* to the right is the training ship *Chapman,* which today is a youth hostel in Stockholm.

Part of the German *Lingiaden* troupe on board the *Wilhelm Gustloff*. Not only was it practical to accommodate the athletes on board, they were also easier to control. In the background are the masts of the *Chapman*, then a training ship.

Shortly afterwards, the *Wilhelm Gustloff* and another KdF ship, the *Stuttgart*, played another propaganda role. In the summer of 1939 the Swedish government, under the patronage of King Gustav V, had invited the German national sports leader to send athletes to participate in the first *Lingiaden* – the Swedish Olympic games – in Stockholm. This international event gave propaganda minister Joseph Goebbels the opportunity to showcase the best German gymnasts, who had been so successful at the Berlin Olympics in 1936. The *Lingiaden* ran between 20 July and 4 August, and the German sports management saw its importance in demonstrating the nature of the new progressive Germany and in strengthening ties with a 'Germanic brother people'. This was also reflected in the number of participants: the German team totalled 1,400 men and women, the third-largest contingent after Sweden and Denmark.

The athletes lived on board the ships. There were several advantages: the Swedish hosts were not required to provide accommodation and the gymnasts were all together and therefore easier to control. However, a large flotilla of small boats was needed to transport the athletes morning, noon and evening, when meals was taken. Nevertheless, they were not cut off from the Stockholm society – dances were organised on the *Wilhelm Gustloff* to which the locals were invited and the atmosphere was described as excellent.

A SECRET TELEGRAM

In summer 1939, as the atmosphere in Europe grew darker, the *Wilhelm Gustloff* made a number of cruises to the Norwegian fjords. Her fiftieth cruise would be her last.

The ship's quartermaster, Wilhelm Smelius, recalled the final trip. She was fully booked and no one was concerned that there was no opportunity to land, even though it was a five-day, and uneventful, cruise. Smelius was on watch between midnight and four on the night of 24/25 August when at about 1.00 a.m. Captain Heinrich Bertram came on to the bridge just as a coded telegram arrived:

> With the telegram in his hand, which was probably just a specific password, he left the bridge but soon came back with a sealed envelope. We looked intently at him as he broke the seal and opened the envelope. For a moment, dead silence reigned on the bridge. We did not know the meaning of the designation 'QWA 7' and five others with designation 'QWA 8-12' held by the captain and that the letter contained 'Special Instructions for German merchant ships in time of war'. What the order's content meant to us, we understood by the Captain's next decision: we need to cancel the trip immediately and return to Hamburg![3]

On the afternoon of 26 August *Wilhelm Gustloff* was back in Hamburg. Early in the morning of 1 September the crew understood Germany was at war and that they had just completed the ship's last peacetime journey.

4

THE BEGINNING OF THE END

A tidal wave of Russian troops swept into East Prussia, pouring over the plains into the villages and towns. The German defenders stubbornly held on, briefly holding back some of the deluge. But it was soon clear to them, and millions of others, that the Russians were unstoppable and they fled. Among those they abandoned were hundreds of thousands of women and children who had been evacuated from Berlin and the other major cities that were being obliterated by the Allied bombers to what had been seen as the safest parts of the country. The National Socialist party tried to reassure the population that everything was under control, but these were very soon proven to be hollow words. More and more Germans began to doubt that the Reich would emerge victorious from this war and as the Russian troops penetrated deeper and deeper into the country and stormed towards Berlin it eventually became clear to everyone.

Pincer movements cut off the German armies from each other and one by one the Russians encircled the coastal towns. Tallinn and Riga were evacuated but other towns became magnets for millions of refugees desperately trying to escape.

By 27 January 1945 (by coincidence, the birthday of the last German Kaiser) the whole of East Prussia was encircled. Russian forces severed land connections to the West, so there was only one place to go: the sea. For the hundreds of thousands, even millions of people who now left their homes, there was no turning back – the images from Nemmersdorf had shown what would happen if they stayed. Saving their lives was their only thought: possessions were gradually discarded as they made their way towards the coast. The small sleepy town of Pillau in Danzig Bay, for example, saw its population of 5,000 explode into a boiling cauldron of 40,000 refugees in just a few days.

At first Hitler and his close commanders ignored the refugee crisis. The Führer, after all, had displayed the same attitude to the bombed cities – he seemed unmoved by the tragedies that took place daily and with increasing intensity. It was Admiral Karl Dönitz, his highest-ranking naval officer, who first assessed the situation soberly and in January 1945 he ordered a rescue to begin. Its aim, according to Dönitz, was to evacuate troops and supplies, but wherever possible refugees could also be boarded. However, the evacuation was not to interfere in any way with the German navy's strategic operations.

But as the flow of refugees assumed gigantic proportions the distinction between troops and refugees vanished, and as spring 1945 came, the evacuation focused on saving any German lives possible, whether military or civilian.

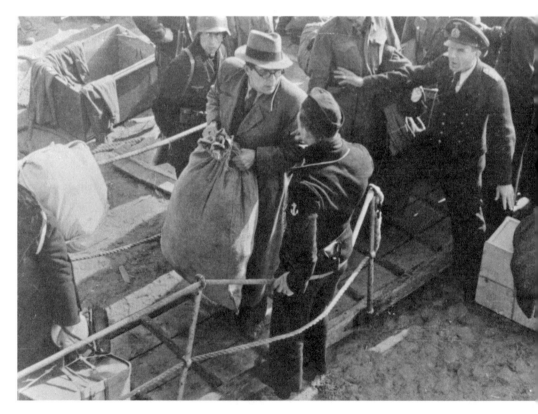

Many believed in Hitler's promise that Germany would not be invaded. It became clear that this promise could not be kept too late for far too many. Panic spread like wildfire through Eastern Germany. The majority would flee overland but when this became impossible, the sea became the only route for escape.

A tiny piece of National Socialist history: the Hamburg America line's *Albert Ballin* was named after Germany's greatest shipping tycoon, the man who built the company into an empire and one of the largest shipping lines in the world. But Ballin was a Jew and as such he became a non-person in Germany. His name was expunged from history, including in pictures like this, where the ship's name has been retouched to read *Hansa*.

Operation Hannibal, or 'Unternehmen Rettung' (Operation Rescue) as it was also known, was the greatest evacuation by sea of all time. Yet even if every German ship afloat had sufficient fuel and was able to participate, the scale of the rescue needed made it impossible to achieve more than a partial success.

REAR ADMIRAL KONRAD ENGELHARDT

Organising the rescue was delegated to someone in whom Dönitz had the utmost confidence, and who reported directly to him: Rear Admiral Konrad Engelhardt, the sea transport chief of the Wehrmacht. Engelhardt had previous experience of troop and materiel evacuation and, once given this assignment, he wasted no time. Although acutely aware of the fuel situation, he understood he had to deploy every ship in the Baltic that was still afloat.

Engelhardt had been in the Navy since 1916 and had a well-developed network of contacts. He also had a non-bureaucratic approach that did not always go down well with higher-ranking colleagues. Dönitz, who understood and appreciated his qualities, promoted him to Rear Admiral in 1944 with the words, 'Now you can stand up against the field marshals!'

The *Wilhelm Gustloff*'s career as a hospital ship was a short one. Because of her capacity, it had been planned to use her for the invasion of Britain. When these plans were abandoned, the ship was moored in Gotenhafen.

Now Engelhardt could hand-pick his own staff. Cutting through the red tape, he dispensed with military etiquette, giving those who worked for him the title *Probes Führer* ('Special Leader'). It was not only his pragmatism that got results: Engelhardt was also extremely well-informed. Constantly on the move, he was always seeking to acquire and process new information. This skill was vital in an operation that was eventually to involve a thousand vessels.

Engelhardt's spartan office was initially in Eberswalde, a small town on the railway line between Stettin and Berlin. It was here that he and his subordinates identified which ships could be used. There were in fact a number of large passenger ships that were suitable for use as hospitals, troop transports and refugee evacuation. They included the *Wilhelm Gustloff, Robert Ley, Cap Arcona, Hansa, Hamburg, General San Martin* and all the '*Monte*' ships that sailed to the Americas, including the *Monte Rosa, Monte Sarmiento* and *Monte Cervantes*.

Passenger ships were one thing, but no cargo freighter could be quickly transformed into a people freighter. They needed beds, toilets, fresh water tanks, safety jackets, lifeboats and all things that any passenger vessel would carry. Later, it would turn out, many of these necessities had to be replaced by faith in Providence and prayer for the absence of Russian submarines and Allied bombers.

Many of the big passenger ships had lain idle for several years. At the outbreak of war the *Wilhelm Gustloff* had been converted into a hospital ship – a conversion that was complete by 22 September 1939 – and renamed *Hospital Ship D*. She had left Hamburg on 27 September for Danzig-Neufahrwasser. The *Robert Ley* had similarly been converted into *Hospital Ship B*.

In the spring of 1940, the *Wilhelm Gustloff* had been ordered to sail to Oslo. It may have been with very mixed emotions that Captain Bertram received the order: less than a year earlier he had brought vacationing Germans to the Norwegian fjords; now he was returning to a land his own nation had invaded.

The *Wilhelm Gustloff* had been intended for deployment in the invasion of Britain, but when the British successfully repelled the German air attack in the Battle of Britain, the plan was abandoned and the ship was taken to Gotenhafen-Oxhöft in Danzig Bay. No longer a hospital ship, she became the accommodation and training ship for the Second Submarine

Left: Wilhelm Gustloff's career as a hospital ship was short.

Below: The *Wilhelm Gustloff* moored in Gotenhafen. After a career as a cruise ship she was occupied with transporting wounded soldiers before becoming an accommodation and training ship. (Thomas Rockwell)

School Division. Here the war, for the crew at least, seemed far away and the ship became home to the crew for several years. On 9 October 1943, Gotenhafen was attacked by American bombers. A bomb exploded a few metres from the *Wilhelm Gustloff* and tore a 1.5m hole in her starboard propeller cap. It was clear that the ship would eventually have to go into a shipyard for repair. In a war there are few such opportunities, but in two days they managed to effect a temporary repair.

After the German invasion in 1939, the Polish port of Gdingen had quickly been renamed Gotenhafen. The Treaty of Versailles signed in 1919 had created the independent city state of Danzig, and the Polish republic had sought to develop a harbour that could compete with its rivals. With the help of funds from French and US banks, Gdingen grew from a small village to, by 1938, the largest port on the Baltic. Under the Germans, many of the Poles who had helped create the enlarged harbour were expelled. Some 12,000 were executed. Gotenhafen was turned into a major naval base, where battleships and heavy cruisers were anchored, far from the main theatres of war. And in the harbour lay the giant grey whale of the *Wilhelm Gustloff*.

As the sounds of war came closer and closer, huge numbers of refugees headed for the towns along Danzig Bay, and especially for Gotenhafen where these big ships lay.

While in Gotenhafen, the *Wilhelm Gustloff* was used for training military personnel.

The Wilhelm Gustloff departing Hamburg around 1938. It is worth noting that hardly anyone makes the 'Sig Heil' sign neither on the ship nor on the shore. Far more people were on the last trip, estimates give the number to much more than 10,000 people.

A DREAM COME TRUE

Like all boys in Nazi Germany, Heinz Schön joined the Hitler Youth. It was 1936 and he was not yet 10 years old. There was no choice, but at the time it was as natural as being a member of the church. His dream was to go to sea, but Heinz was found to be near-sighted, so it seemed as if a seaman's career would be denied him. Instead he found a job in the personnel department of the Hamburg South America Line. Then one Saturday in February 1944 his dream came true when he came to the office and was met by his manager, who said, 'Mr Schön, we have a ship for you.'

Schön had been appointed assistant purser on the *Wilhelm Gustloff*. Two days later he was in Gotenhafen and on board. He noted the characteristics of the crew:

> 165 are on board, including 28 women, most employed as stewardesses, washerwomen, ironing ladies, kitchen workers. In addition there are 22 Croats. Most of the German crew are over 50 years old, have multiple ailments and therefore are not 'war useful'. Among the under-18s a mess boy, a ship's boy and the purser's assistant. One man in the crew has a special status: Party Comrade Kaufhold, laundry manager: he is the NSDAP's local group leader, he is the only one who reminds us what it was like before the war.[1]

With the shortage of troops becoming apparent, Hitler was desperate to find more. From 24 September 1944, all 14–15-year-olds and men over 55 were trained to handle weapons and to march – in other words, to become soldiers. On weekends Schön and the rest of the crew were compelled to help build the 'Ostwalle', the defensive line through East Prussia, which they considered would effectively prevent the advance of Russian tanks. But the training officers did not have much respect for their recruits: he called Schön and his peers 'a terrible collection of savages!'.

At the beginning of October, Schön and his colleagues heard the provincial governor Erich Koch on the radio declare firmly: 'No Russian will ever tread in East Prussia!' His delusion was brutally exposed a few days later by the massacre in Nemmersdorf and the sweep of the Russian tanks across the province.

In Gotenhafen, the new captain of *Wilhelm Gustloff*, Friedrich Petersen, was convinced that the ship would never leave the dock, and it was here, he told Schön, they would 'see the end of the war'. This may have been partly based on his assessment of the quality of the current crew: 'With such a crew, I cannot go one sea mile with the ship,' he told Schön, a phrase that lodged in his memory.

However, the situation was changing rapidly. More and more refugees were gathering in Danzig and around Danzig Bay, in Gotenhafen, in Neufahrwasse and Zoppot, at Elbing, Königsberg and Pillau. The hardships they had been through to reach the ports were indescribable. Their hope now was that a ship would save them and take them away to the west, toward Kiel, Lübeck or Copenhagen, from where they would be free to move on, or even just take them to the island of Rügen.

A FATEFUL DECISION

Meanwhile in Berlin, during the night of 9 January 1945, Chief of General Staff of the Army Heinz Guderian explained the situation to Hitler and his colleagues. Without reinforcements from the West, the whole Eastern Front would collapse. He believed that in the next two days, on 12 or 13 January, the Russian winter offensive would be launched. He argued that the Russians were numerically superior: for every ten German infantrymen there were 110 Russians, against one German tank there were seven Russian tanks ... Guderian rattled off his comparisons like a machine gun. He ended with the words:

> Mein Führer, the clock is at five minutes to midnight. On the basis of my presentation today, I hope you will decide to put the necessary reinforcements to the eastern front, and this very night![2]

Refugees in an unknown harbour. Prams were not allowed on board and the quaysides were littered with them. (Heinz Schön)

Hitler went into one of his rages. When he calmed down he retorted:

> No reinforcements to the East! There I can lose ground, on the Western
> Front not at all. The East must help itself![3]

It was one of Hitler's greatest misjudgements, a disastrous decision that
would have devastating consequences throughout Eastern Europe for
between 10 and 15 million people. He seemed to refuse to believe that 3
million Russian soldiers – the largest concentration of troops in history
– had gathered for attack and were on the march into Germany and its
heart, Berlin.

Even though abandoned with no prospect of reinforcements, each
German soldier in the east was still expected to defend every inch of
ground, to fight to the last bullet. Surrender or flight was tantamount to
treason and punishable by death.

In Gotenhafen, the men who trained submariners were considered
of particular strategic importance and their safe transfer to the West
became a priority. Admiral Dönitz issued a decree on 21 January that,
among other things, detailed who would be considered for evacuation
on the *Wilhelm Gustloff*:

> *Wilhelm Gustloff* is to take the families of the Second Department of
> Second Submarine School Division, marine army personnel and a
> fixed number of the serious injured, whose transport by sea is deemed
> urgent, following the guidelines the provincial leadership of the NSDAP
> in Danzig-West Prussia set for non-conscripted citizens. From the area
> Gotenhafen-Danzig: refugees from West and East Prussia who are still in
> Gotenhafen.
>
> Transportation of civilians in *Wilhelm Gustloff* is under provincial man-
> agement: special travel documents in two copies are available. It is the
> responsibility of the regional leadership of the NSDAP to make these
> documents available in different locations in the city.[4]

Other ships that would bring people west were the *Hansa, Cap Arcona,
Deutschland* and *Hamburg*. Since the latter part of January they had started
to take on board the injured and refugees, not just troops destined for the
Western Front.

The *Robert Ley* had sailed with more than 6,000 people on board and had reached the West safely. But for every ship that reached Lübeck, Kiel or Copenhagen, another ten waited in Danzig Bay for an escort. Meanwhile, the situation in Danzig and the communities around the bay deteriorated hourly.

SAVE LIFE AT ALL COSTS

Captain Friedrich von Wilpert, orderly officer to General Karl-Wilhelm Specht, commander of the area around Danzig, saw refugees everywhere and witnessed their despair. He had managed to get his wife and his youngest daughter aboard the *Deutschland* but never forgot what he saw during those days in January:

> The kilometre-long road to Troyl [near Danzig] was characterised by exhausted, desperate people, especially women and children who could go no further who sat on the suitcases and backpacks they brought with them and waited for any help whatsoever. It was a tragedy so shocking that you just heard a quiet complaining. Otherwise, it was just the icy wind howling that was heard.[5]

Horst Woit was 10 years old and lived in Elbing, south-east of Danzig, with his mother, Meta. On New Year's Day 1945 he had reached the magical age that would allow him to be accepted in the Hitler Youth. The previous year he had run behind the young marchers knowing that it would not be long before he was there too, marching and singing. But it was not to happen. He and his mother sat in her kitchen, the only room that was warm in the apartment, when someone knocked on the door:

> It was a fourteen-year-old from the Hitler Youth who said, 'The Russians are in Elbing: you have to pack and make sure that you get away!' Mother quickly packed a suitcase and then went to her friend's to take advice what could be done and what escape route to take. Of course, I was terribly afraid, for we heard only terrible things about the Russians.[6]

They obtained travel permits to go to Gotenhafen and managed to travel there on a small steamer. It was 28 January and the huge Russian invasion had not yet begun. They walked along the Gotenhafen quayside and in the distance they saw the *Wilhelm Gustloff*:

> Then we came to the ship and I had never seen something so big before. Compared to this, the steamer in Elbing was just a matchbox. When Mother had presented all the papers, we were sent into a large hall [on *Wilhelm Gustloff*] where there were already hundreds of people.[7]

People were everywhere on the ship: they stood, lay or sat in every corner. Over the next two days, with a 10-year-old's curiosity, he took the opportunity to explore every nook and cranny of the *Wilhelm Gustloff*. He thought in the end he must have been in every inch of the ship. Every night before they went to sleep, his mother told him not to take off his life jacket. She told him it was important that he got used to it for the forthcoming voyage. Shortly before their departure, they had the good fortune to be assigned a berth with his mother's friend from Elbing, Hildegard, and her daughter. Horst thought it very exciting, even though the cabin had no windows or portholes. But for a small boy everything was exciting.

Horst Woit at the time of the *Wilhelm Gustloff*'s last voyage in January 1945. (Horst Woit)

Inge Bendrich
in 2001. (Inge
Bendrich)

Milda Bendrich's parents had fled from central Poland to join her and her 2-year-old daughter Inge at her house in Gotenhafen. They knew they would not be staying in the town for long. Milda and her parents packed as much as they could: clothing, bedding, books and cutlery and even the carpets in the apartment. Everything was carried down to the central station on sleds and sent westward by train. But very little ever reached Hamburg; ten weeks later all she recovered was a laundry basket, some yarn remnants and a bathrobe. The rest had vanished.

On 27 January, an acquaintance, a *Marine Oberleutnant*, knocked on her door. He asked Milda if she intended to leave for the West. Everyone knew that the Russians were close and everyone was in fear of their uncontrolled hatred that would sweep through East Prussia. He told her that there was talk in Gotenhafen of the *Wilhelm Gustloff* departing not only with troops and the wounded but also with an unknown number of refugees. He also said that he knew the purser on the ship and there would be a chance of obtaining authorisation to travel.

Milda went with the officer to the harbour to meet the purser. He offered two tickets. But this was not enough, she explained: she had her aged parents as well as two elderly neighbours she wanted to take with her. The purser protested and said that he could not hand out travel permits to 'the four unproductive' people: only Milda and her daughter Inge could be counted as 'productive'. But she would not accept this and told him she would not leave her parents, or her neighbours. Finally, the purser relented and Milda returned home triumphantly with seven travel authorisations:

> Then we sat down to assiduously pack the last of our belongings. The 180-centimetre-long sleigh was packed with bags, boxes and packets to a height of 170 centimetres. I know this precisely, because I was 172 centimetres high. He [the Oberleutnant] pulled the sled and I pushed, and I have the image in front of me of the approximately two kilometre-road to the port. It lasted a long time, since we were always getting the sled stuck in the snow.[8]

The only one who thought it was an amazing adventure was 2-year-old Inge, who sat at the top of the sled in a small gap between the bags, safe from the raw January wind.

Once on board, the party split. Milda and her daughter found space in a cabin while her parents and the two neighbours each received a mattress on the floor of one of the ship's lounges. Later the cabin was filled with other women and children and Milda particularly wondered about a woman in her fifties who had fled from Königsberg. She was horribly restless and before the *Wilhelm Gustloff*'s departure she disembarked.

Arvid and Selma Schilder were Baltic Germans who, back in 1939, had left Reval for Gotenhafen. Margit, their daughter, had spent her whole childhood in Estonia but when Poland was conquered the family – and many others – saw the opportunity for a good life in the occupied lands:

> We thought we'd go to Germany but were not permitted. My father was a dentist and it was decided that he take an internship in Gotenhafen and we couldn't decide where to move. We also knew that we could not remain in Reval, because then we would have ended up in Siberia … My father had been a Czarist officer during the First World War.[9]

In Margit's view, Gotenhafen was not an exciting place to be. Everything happened in Danzig. There was, for example, the theatre there: Gotenhafen had nothing. Nevertheless, the family lived contentedly: Arvid looked after the naval officers' teeth and was never called up. But all was to change in 1943 when the Allied bombing began.

By February 1944, Margit had almost completed her education but the progress of the 'total war' had meant that schools were closed. All older children – boys and girls – were compelled to undertake *Arbeitsdienst* (labour service) but Margit managed to avoid it: her father Arvid managed to get her a job in the Torpedo Versuchs Institute (TVA – Institute for Torpedo Testing) in Gotenhafen. There, she became a parts designer. Meanwhile, the front was coming closer and closer:

> We knew that the war was lost; after Stalingrad we knew … it was awful that many did not believe, who did not want to believe it … you could only go 150 kilometres and no more without permission. There were always checks on the trains and if you didn't have permission you couldn't go. We couldn't leave and if we did we wouldn't have received any food coupons.[10]

Margit Schilder around 1945. (Margit Brook)

Arvid, perhaps because he had refused to join the Nazi party, could not obtain permission to leave Gotenhafen, not even as the Russians approached. But Margit was more successful:

Yes, I was employed at the TVA in Gotenhafen, and therefore I knew a lot of officers, and this way I could get two tickets [for herself and her mother]... And they were for Hansa at first, but then we had two cousins of my father, Aunt Grethe and Aunt Trude and they wanted to come too ... but there were no more places and so I changed our tickets to Wilhelm Gustloff because they definitely wanted to sail with us ... But the night before, my father went with me to the two old ladies because they had a large black cat and so my father had to kill the cat with a morphine syringe.[11]

The next day the old ladies telephoned to say that the morphine had been ineffective and because Peter the cat was still alive they couldn't leave him. So Margit and Selma Schilder were left to travel on their own.

They arrived at the dock at midday on 30 January. So many people crowded the gangway that it was difficult to board. But, according to Margit, some control was maintained and those with authorisation were allowed past the barriers. The Schilders had brought all the luggage they could carry but Arvid was not allowed to help them carry it on board.

Margit was surprised that there were so many soldiers, and wounded, and submariners and their officers. She and her mother had no cabin, only a spot on the upper promenade deck. They found large armchairs they could sleep in and so they largely escaped the terrible congestion on the lower decks. They were also grateful that they were inside: 'No one went out, it was freezing cold and windy.'

FOUR MASTERS AND A VESSEL

The head of the second unit of the submarine school, Korvettenkapitän Wilhelm Zahn, pressed for permission for the *Wilhelm Gustloff* to depart. He was aware that his men were urgently needed by the waiting submarines in the West. But he, and all the other officers, knew the risk the *Wilhelm Gustloff* ran if she left without permission: she would have no escort.

The time of departure was not his decision, even though he was the highest-ranking military officer on board. There was also a ship's captain, Friedrich Petersen, who had another two co-captains, as well as the usual complement of deck officers, purser and chief engineer. It was a bizarre command structure (although not unique, as we shall see with the *Goya*).

In addition, there was an onshore chain of command. Lieutenant Commander Wolfgang Leonhardt was head of Gotenhafen's Security Division and so was responsible for ensuring that all outbound merchant ships received suitable and sufficient escorts. Any hopes that Zahn might have had of leaving Gotenhafen without an escort were crushed by Leonhardt.

Korvettenkapitän Wilhelm Zahn. Desperate to get his submariners to the bases in the west in order to strength and continue Germany's submarine war, he pressed both his superiors and Captain Petersen to secure permission for the departure of the *Wilhelm Gustloff*. (Heinz Schön)

'... THEY HAD NO NOTEBOOKS LEFT'

At three in the morning of 25 January, Heinz Schön learned that boarding would commence at eight o'clock. He was almost unconscious with fatigue: the entire crew had been working almost around the clock for days to prepare for departure. The *Wilhelm Gustloff* had been built for 1,463 passengers: 4,000 were now expected.

He was woken roughly at six o'clock by the night steward. 'Get up! It's all breaking loose now!' Looking out of the porthole, he was shocked to see the whole dock was one dense mass of people. He remembered:

> Packed, packed with people and soldiers on the wide gangplank up to the ship. It's mostly women, children and old people who want to come on board. The older boys are the most eager and push the most. Then it turns out that the 'Guidelines for taking on refugees' the party leadership had drafted are not worth the paper they are written on. What will happen to the refugees who get on board and do not have the necessary travel authorisation for *Gustloff*? People who for days have been on the run or come last night on some little boat from Pillau and not familiar with the 'guidelines' and the 'Travel State' in Gotenhafen?[12]

The 18-year-old soldier at the gangway could not possibly stop all the mothers who desperately wanted to get on board without the necessary papers or who wanted to bring their 15-year-old sons, who, officially, should have been taken away to be conscripted. No one could be held back. All the rules and regulations were put aside.

Nevertheless, the accommodation officer Dieter Rauch and his team did their best to organise the boarding and record every person who entered the ship, taking name, address and destination from each and instructing them where to go on the ship. Rauch estimated that by lunchtime of the following day there were already 4,000 people on board.

Two of the hundreds of members of the *Marine Helferinnen* (women naval auxiliaries) who had boarded, Eva Dorn and a colleague, helped with the registration, as well as taking care of wounded soldiers, helping pregnant women get to the infirmary and 'everything that can happen when thousands of people gather':

When refugees really came in large numbers ... they were registered, and I know that the books were full: they had no notebooks left [by the afternoon of 29 January]. I estimated that about 8,000 were on board ... you see, it was so full on board that one could not walk through the hallways. People were put everywhere. In every bed there were two people and all the major halls were full of people. They took anyone on board, they let everyone up ... they came along the gangway in twos or threes. There were very old people; some were carrying dead children they thought were still alive ... and over the wharf area were thousands of people, even those who did not have papers, and they were allowed on board ... There were many children, many with their mothers ....they all came with their children and there were families with eleven children ... [13]

For twenty-four hours after Eva found there were no more notebooks, those who boarded – perhaps another 2,000 people – went unrecorded. Consequently, it is impossible to say how many people were on the *Wilhelm Gustloff* when she finally sailed. Eva estimated just the number of children at 5,000, a figure Heinz Schön thought likely. As the days passed, more and more refugees came on board and the situation became increasingly untenable. Small boats, large boats, barges, ferries and every type of watercraft arrived in Gotenhafen from all over the bay. Everyone wanted to leave and *Wilhelm Gustloff* and the other ships were the only means of saving themselves. There may have been 10,000 people on board, which is not an unreasonable estimate when compared with the numbers other ships carried.

BELOW THE WATERLINE

A few lucky members of the *Marine Helferinnen* managed to get cabins, but the majority – several hundred – were accommodated on mattresses in the large, tiled (drained) swimming pool in the lower depths of the ship. All in all, the atmosphere was still fairly optimistic: they were shortly to head west, they were on a big ship and were seemingly safe.

The *Marine Helferinnen* came from all over Germany. Eva Dorn had been in Gotenhafen for about two years, working in an office in Oxhöft where aerial reconnaissance was analysed. She had boarded the ship before the great crush: her whole department, about ten women, had arrived at the dock on a flatbed truck and were immediately allowed on board. For Eva this meant, among other things, that she had plenty of time to get to know the *Wilhelm Gustloff*: she knew where the stairs led and where each facility lay.

She refused point blank to be accommodated in the swimming pool. Even though it was empty, the fear of drowning because she was so low in the ship was too strong and she put her mattress down in one of the big drawing rooms.

Years later, she described herself as 'the type of person who just cannot sit still'. Eva found that she could help out in the infirmary and she became 'ever more engaged in the work', spending as much time there as she could.

Many women who came on board were pregnant and several gave birth on the *Wilhelm Gustloff*. But the hospital was not as well equipped as they had hoped: improvisation was mandatory. Children with frostbite on their faces were given a dab of petroleum jelly on each cheek:

> But then the Vaseline ran out so we went to the Battalion Chief Physician Richter and asked if he could give us anything to do. We became some sort of self-appointed coffee and tea providers for the entire hospital department … but then Richter said that someone was needed to man the department's telephone and so we got a cabin to sleep in.[14]

For a 10-year-old, being on board such a large vessel was exciting. Horst Woit and his mother had come from Elbing with a friend of hers and her daughter. On 29 January, they were moved from the large lounge where they had been billeted to a higher deck. The crew restricted the amount of luggage the refugees could bring on board so their situation resembled that of most refugees: they had a suitcase – nothing else. Gangways and corridors had become sleeping quarters – luggage would simply cause an obstruction if an emergency arose.

Rudi Lange was a corporal and a radio operator who had been with the *Wilhelm Gustloff* since 1944. He had grown up in Danzig with his mother and four sisters, and he had managed to obtain permission for them all to accompany him on the ship. However:

> My mother said, 'Water is not safe, we will not travel on Wilhelm Gustloff. You will of course, you're a soldier and we will find any other way to get out of here.'[15]

Perhaps the most famous passenger on the *Wilhelm Gustloff* was the renowned marine painter Adolf Bock. Born in Berlin in 1890, Bock had volunteered for the Imperial Navy and come to the attention of Kaiser Wilhelm II during a voyage of the yacht *Hohenzollern*. He had been given a scholarship to study at Berlin's Academy of Arts, after which he spent many years in Finland. He had good contacts with Scandinavian newspapers and had made a round-the-world trip for the Danish newspaper *Illustreret Familie-Journal* (later published by *Allers* magazine). In 1939 Bock returned to Germany: he was one of the few people to become a professor during the Nazi regime. Hitler personally ensured that he obtained a flat in Berlin, which had been seized from a Jew whose fate is unknown. Early 1945 saw him in Gotenhafen, using his contacts to secure a travel permit for the *Wilhelm Gustloff*.

A HAGGARD LADY

A considerable amount of work was needed to get the ship ready. No longer the pride and joy of the KdF, the years at Gotenhafen had taken a heavy toll. The former white hull colour had been replaced by a grey, perhaps better reflecting the seriousness of the moment and of that icy, grey January day in 1945. The ship seemed like a giant grey rock, but nevertheless a rock that would take them away from the Russians that everyone feared.

When the equipment was checked earlier that month, it was found that there were no lifeboats. The large motorised boats had also been removed: they had been taken out into the bay area of Gotenhafen to confuse bomber pilots and never returned. Now the officers replaced them with other boats and rafts, which were stacked on the deck by the ship's crane. First Officer Louis Reese had also discovered that there were no life jackets. He instructed the second officer to secure at least 5,000, but he had not reckoned on the rush to the ship in the last three days before she sailed.

On 27 January, anti-aircraft guns were mounted on the deck. The officers assumed they would now have permission to go: Zahn had already told the authorities that there were 4,000 refugees on board, and that the loading was completed. In response, he received only a short message '*Gustloff* will take on board more refugees!' To the officers, it sounded as

First Officer Louis Reese.

if they could expect few thousand more people; *Deutschland* had already taken 8,000 people; *Cap Arcona* had 9,000 and was continuing to load. Given the *Wilhelm Gustloff*'s size there was every possibility that she would be loaded to the brim.

WHEN WILL THE CONDITIONS BE RIGHT TO DEPART?

As the 27th turned into the 28th the officers grew more and more concerned. They were convinced that the Russians must know that there was a huge accumulation of people and vessels in Danzig Bay and they would have their submarines ready to attack. But still the *Wilhelm Gustloff* had no permission to depart and the despair on those on board was increasing hour by hour, as was the stream of refugees. Every day the risk of an air attack increased. Not only that, unrest was growing on the ship. The thousands of people on board had nothing to do but wait … perhaps thinking that they were waiting only for that airstrike.

But Zahn's responsibility was his men – he had to get them to their new submarine bases in the West. He hoped he could influence Leonhardt to give the *Wilhelm Gustloff* the necessary authorisation to sail. But Leonhardt replied that the risk of Russian submarines made it too dangerous to let the *Wilhelm Gustloff* (and *Hansa* which was also ready) depart unescorted. Leonhardt was unable to provide the escort that in his opinion was needed.

Zahn did not give up. He argued that his submarine division had its own torpedo boats and minesweepers that could act as an escort if Leonhardt could not offer anything better. Eventually, on the morning of the 29th Leonhardt contacted his superiors and it was decided that the *Wilhelm Gustloff* and *Hansa* would depart within twenty-four hours. Their escort would consist of vessels from the submarine division.

At the same time as Leonhardt was informing the officers of their imminent departure, an announcement was made over the ship's tannoy: all submariners were to surrender their life jackets to the new arrivals who were still streaming on board.

On Tuesday, 30 January Heinz Schön woke at six in the morning and through his porthole, looked on what had become a regular scene:

An endless line of people slowly walking aboard. On the way up I have to step over people and luggage in the corridors. The aisles, which must be kept clear as escape routes, is filled in many places with refugees.[16]

Engineer Erich Goering could not understand how so many people could be accommodated on the ship:

It was awful. People, refugees, women and children, they had arrived several days ago. As time went by, they [the officers] on board had no more control over how many there were, I think. Six thousand or seven thousand, it must have been. I did another round and saw how they were billeted in the cabins, in the corridors and in the halls where they once had danced. In the dining room mattresses lay on the floor and everybody was lying there.[17]

The day was the anniversary of NSDAP's foundation, a day that was usually celebrated. But there were no festivities at the dock in Gotenhafen. Massive amounts of food were still being loaded. For the last few days the kitchen staff had been working around the clock as if they were expecting to feed an entire town every hour, day after day.

One of the few who changed their travel plans was Gotenhafen's resident engineer. He had worked on the preparation and provisioning of the *Wilhelm Gustloff* and for him there was, of course, no problem to obtain travel permits for his entire family of seven and a maid:

> When I came home in the evening and described the conditions to my wife with the words 'In three days she's off', strong doubts suddenly came over me. *Gustloff* was too large for a flight over the Baltic Sea. My wife shared my concerns.[18]

That night he went back to the office where permits were issued. To everyone's surprise, he asked to travel on a smaller vessel and was told that there was such a ship:

> 'You can take your family on the *Regulas* but you absolutely must be on board no later than 8 o'clock tomorrow morning!' With this information, I returned home just before midnight. We packed immediately. Yet there was still time. I took my family to the *Regulas*, which sailed in the morning and arrived safely at Swinemünde. So by my forebodings or unknowingly I saved the lives of my loved ones and spared them the death ride with *Wilhelm Gustloff*.[19]

Heli Beneicke was 28 years old and travelled with her mother, two sisters and a niece of just 3 months:

> My father belonged to the fleet in Kiel and had been transferred to Gotenhafen for two years. I was visiting my parents. There were not so many bombs, it was quieter, but then we had to leave when the Russians came. We had a cabin assigned ... My father said that he had arranged a departure for us ... I think it was the 28th when we came aboard the *Gustloff*. And we got a cabin on the upper promenade deck... [20]

However, before they had left home, her father had telephoned and said:

> 'If you want, you can go with a[nother] ship' ... it was called *Oranjefontein* and was already out on the roads and would go to Copenhagen. But my

mother grieved so much that she had had to leave their home … and it looked quiet out there [on *Wilhelm Gustloff*].[21]

They decided to stay on the *Wilhelm Gustloff*. Heli had time to walk around and thought, 'Yes, that's a beautiful ship,' and she felt it was safe. But as the stream of refugees grew and grew, she noted that there was not much left of that beauty.

First Helmsmen Rudolf Geiss belonged to the civilian crew and knew the *Wilhelm Gustloff* well. He had undertaken officer training at the School of Navigation and could substitute for an officer if necessary. The cabin he shared with just one crewman had suddenly become a cabin with seven occupants, as his companion's friends joined them. There was no choice – it was barely possible to find a space anywhere else on the ship.

Quartermaster Rudolf Geiss at the time of the *Wilhelm Gustloff*'s final voyage. He is pictured with his then-wife. (Rudolf Geiss)

Geiss was horrified at the state of many refugees:

> They were frozen when they came on board the *Gustloff* after walking far through snow and ice. It was warm [on the ship], they were cared for, they got food. They thought, 'Now we've done it, now nothing more will happen to us when we are on this ship.' … It was full … especially in the great halls, where they had moved all the tables to the side.[22]

DEPARTURE

Half past twelve on the afternoon of 30 January was the appointed departure time. Barely two hours before this, a command was issued over the tannoy from the military police and the Security Service's counter-intelligence teams on board: all male refugees between 15 and 17 years and all between 55 and 60 were ordered to the upper sun deck. Perhaps, as Heinz Schön suspected, it was an order purely for show – they found no deserters or men who could be conscripted into military service, either on the sun deck or in the corridors and passageways they searched.

The crew took their places. Any passenger without a lifebelt was instructed to go and collect one from the ship's stores. The telephone, power and water were disconnected and a few minutes later the pilot was on the bridge. In these last few moments the purser's office worked at a frantic pace. The passenger lists had to be finalised and handed over to the port authorities before the *Wilhelm Gustloff* departed. According to these lists there were 6,050 people on board, a figure that, as we have seen, must be a significant underestimate, given that refugees had been boarding for more than twenty-four hours without any checks or registration.

The tugs came up to the *Wilhelm Gustloff* and secured their hawsers. The gangway was withdrawn and the mooring lines were thrown off. It was the routine of an everyday departure of a passenger vessel. But many of those on board knew that as the ship moved away from the quayside they would never see their homes again. They were on their way, but towards what future?

Eva had settled into to her work in the infirmary, but she had explained to her superiors that she absolutely must see the departure:

Probably the last picture of the *Wilhelm Gustloff*. All around Gotenhafen refugees knew the ship was about to go and desperate scenes took place when those on the quayside were denied boarding.

> I had never experienced a ship departing, so when we stood up there [on the side of the ship] and looked down, I said that even if you gave me one thousand marks, I would never jump in! And then I saw that the whole deck was like an ice rink. I did not understand it and I asked why they did not put sand down. And all the boats and rafts that were up on the deck were frozen … My friend Tsajko [a nickname] wanted to enjoy a bath in a tub but I wanted to see how we left![23]

Flotsam continuously bumped against the ship's side and initially the *Wilhelm Gustloff* made little progress. It was as if, after all the years of idleness, she was tentative in setting out on the voyage.

According to Winston Churchill, the Second World War was decided by the great ocean liners *Queen Mary* and *Queen Elizabeth*, which had huge transport capacities coupled with speeds that no submarine could match. In her day, *Wilhelm Gustloff*'s strength had also been her speed. But that day had passed. Her old maximum speed of 16 knots was now unthinkable: the bearings would collapse if the engines were pushed to their limit. The engineers informed the bridge that she could go no faster than 12 knots. And at this speed she would be vulnerable to a torpedo attack. Perhaps this was why another order came over the tannoy – all passengers were to put on their life jackets and under no circumstances whatsoever to remove them for the duration of the voyage.

But no such negative thoughts seemed to be in the minds of the soldiers on the open deck: they roared three hearty hurrahs as the *Wilhelm Gustloff* cast off.

The ship was only about 100m from the dock, still under tow from the tugs, when, out of nowhere, a small ship appeared. As it neared, it was clear to those on the *Wilhelm Gustloff* that this ship was packed with people, crammed on deck like sardines in the bitter January weather. They had been sailing all night, when the temperature may have been as low as -20°C. The only heat was body heat and those on board were now exhausted as well as frozen. The small ship was the *Reval*, which had sailed the previous evening from Pillau in the hope of reaching Gotenhafen before the *Wilhelm Gustloff* sailed.

'*Nehmt uns mit, nehmt uns mit!*' ('Take us, take us!') came the screams from the *Reval*. Despite the protests of First Mate Reese – 'We've only space left in the aisles!' – the crew put out an accommodation ladder, opened the door and began to take the *Reval*'s refugees on board.

An unknown ship carrying refugees at Reval.

How many people boarded was not recorded: Assistant Purser Heinz Schön estimated between 500 and 600 people. Who they were, where they were from and where they wanted to go, no one knew. But they were on board: that was enough.

Looking back at the *Reval*, Schön saw that not everyone had been taken off. Those left behind had frozen to death during the night and were now 'pillars, standing here and there on the abandoned deck'.

The stop to take on the *Reval*'s passengers took possibly no more than a quarter of an hour, then the tugs began to pull the giant again. The further she was from the shore, the more people gathered on deck. Many had never been on board a ship, some were farmers with soil still under the fingernails who had seen the sea from afar but had never travelled on it. They stared at wharves and bombed out buildings, at wrecks in the harbour and the coast they would never see again. The dusk light was hitting the beaches and far away they could hear the rumble of war approaching inexorably.

Heinz Schön had also gone up on deck:

During the previous few days I had no time to sleep or even time to go up on deck. The purser's office had been open day and night and we could not complain about being bored. But now all the stress has gone away.[24]

A TEMPORARY STOP

When the ship finally began to move again, relief began to spread. Any melancholy over the departure was muted by the chance to escape the nearing Russian forces. But the feeling was not sustained for long. Suddenly the passengers realised that the *Wilhelm Gustloff* had stopped again. Then the anchor was dropped.

On the bridge Captain Petersen and officers discovered, to their surprise, that the *Hansa*, which had departed ahead of the *Wilhelm Gustloff*, was anchored. Then the order came for the *Wilhelm Gustloff* to drop her anchor, too. One of Petersen's co-captains, Weller, used the tannoy to reassure the passengers that there was no need to worry, they were only waiting for an escort. Tranquillity was restored, everywhere except on the bridge.

Captain Friedrich Petersen. An experienced sailor, he had spent a long time as captain of the *Wilhelm Gustloff* when she was moored in Gotenhafen and didn't believe his ship would ever go to sea again. When she finally did, it was thought that the command on the bridge needed to be strengthened. Consequently, three additional captains were appointed, and all four had to agree on courses of action. (Heinz Schön)

Telegraph officer Rudi Lange was busy at work and realised that there was disagreement about the escort and the order in which the ships would go:

… First around one-ish we were to pass the pier head at Gotenhafen. When we had left the port area, we came out on the roads. There was a variety of vessels drawn together to keep up with the escort, and there would be several large ships escorted by warships westward. Disagreement remained about what ships were to come as an escort with us. *Hansa* had problems and was anchored. We ourselves anchored, but continued on after a moment.[25]

The ship was anchored off the Hela peninsula when a telegram was received ordering her to sail to Kiel and then Flensburg. Kiel was the destination for the submariners, soldiers and *Marine Helferinnen*; the wounded and the refugees would be taken on to Flensburg.

Meanwhile, unsettling news was received from the *Hansa*: she had engine damage that would take several hours to repair. Shortly after, another telegram was received: the land station at Gotenhafen-Oxhöft was asking how long the *Wilhelm Gustloff* would lie at anchor because they wanted another 2,000 refugees to be boarded. This time the ship's officers refused: there were neither life jackets, nor lifeboats nor sufficient supplies for so many more passengers. They also feared that even more requests would arrive if they waited any longer.

Hansa of Hamburg America Line.

The *Löwe*, earlier the Norwegian destroyer *Gyller*.

The promised escort of three ships from the Submarine School Division now materialised into two. One vessel was the torpedo boat *Löwe*, formerly the Norwegian destroyer *Gyller*, which had been seized in 1940 during the German invasion. The second convoy escort was to be a torpedo salvage boat, *TF-1*. These two small vessels would be the escort for the *Wilhelm Gustloff* with its cargo of 10,000 people.

Meanwhile, the weather had worsened; snow clouds were blowing in and the wind had increased sharply. The temperature dropped to -17°C and there was a risk of sea ice. The Baltic was showing its worst side.

The latest information the officers received was that there were no enemy submarines in the area. But a ship at anchor would be a sitting duck for a squadron of fighter-bombers. So, despite the inadequacy of the escort, Petersen, with Zahn's agreement, decided that they would depart, and received permission to do so. However, Petersen believed the ship would be at risk if she went faster than 12 knots, whereas Zahn wanted to squeeze 16 knots out of her. Petersen insisted that this was out of the question: the speed would be 12 knots, as his engineers had advised.

The command structure on the bridge, which had been put together rapidly, was now beginning to unravel. The mixture of four captains and officers from both the Navy and Merchant Navy, which did not share a common training, led to disagreement and quarrels about who was really in charge:

On the wheel was an officer from the Navy, by the machine telegraph was a Marine corporal. Both were commanded by an officer in the merchant marine and a captain who belonged to the merchant navy. The helmsmen who served on the bridge belonged to the Navy and their commander there was Korvettenkapitän Zahn, but they also took the orders of the captain of the merchant marine.[26]

ZWANGSWEG 58

If speed had caused the first disagreement on the bridge, the choice of route provoked an even harsher exchange of words. The officers had two options: either to follow the coast and avoid submarines but risk hitting a mine or to take the deep-water channel, which had been cleared of mines but which would run the risk of a submarine attack. The deep-water channel route, which was used by warships, was called Zwangsweg 58 (Fairway 58). It meant taking a course closer to the island of Bornholm.

The interiors of *Wilhelm Gustloff* were light and welcoming.

The *Löwe* and *Wilhelm Gustloff*, on an unknown date possibly in Gotenhafen.

This time it was not Zahn and Petersen who argued: it was First Mate Reese who was adamantly opposed to taking the deep-water channel. Even though there was the risk of mines, if the ship struck one, the passengers would have more chance of survival if the ship was close to the shore, and the ship could be run aground. Most importantly, the coastal trough was only about 10m deep – too shallow for a submarine. But Zahn and Petersen believed that Zwangsweg 58 was faster. Moreover, they feared an air strike was more likely along the coast.

Captain Petersen finally ruled that they would take the deep-water channel but rejected a proposal for the ship to zig-zag to avoid submarines: the *Wilhelm Gustloff* was not built for such manoeuvres, and, top heavy as she was, her wind resistance would put her stability at risk.

With speed and route now decided, discussions on the bridge turned to the calmer topic of the weather. The wind was west-north-west, and its speed had increased to between 6 and 7 m/s (Force 4 – a moderate breeze) with occasional heavy snow showers.

Everywhere on *Wilhelm Gustloff* the non-seafaring passengers were seasick. The air in the great halls and the drained swimming pool was a mixture of vomit, stale breath, the odour from people who had not washed in days (or perhaps weeks), screaming toddlers nobody could quieten and the excruciating heat from thousands of people who found themselves tightly packed. Milda Bendrich was not exempt:

It was not long before the first seasick passengers hung above the sinks. The attempt to reach the toilets in time was impossible because corridors and stairs were filled with people, mostly women and children. Of course,

I also became seasick. Rough seas in combination with the stench from the cabin could not save a strong stomach such as mine.[27]

With the air temperature now down to -18°C and the decks like ice rinks, seeking relief on the open deck was not an option. A few sailors tried to hack the ice off the anti-aircraft guns but they did not succeed: within a few minutes they were completely frozen again.

As if there weren't enough problems, *TF-1* announced that she had a leak in a weld. Water was coming in, so she requested permission to return to Gotenhafen. The *Wilhelm Gustloff's* officers could not refuse. As *TF-1* turned, Zahn remarked sourly, 'A dog leads a giant through the night!' Now they had just one escorting vessel.

Margit Schilder had settled down with her mother in the armchairs, even though the life jackets were so large and bulky she could hardly sit. Eventually, becoming restless, she left her mother for a short while:

I went around to see if I had any schoolmates [on board] and I found some. But at nine o'clock I came back to my mother who was waiting for me.[28]

The snow swirled and at times the wind blew in squalls. 'The entire upper deck was icing up,' Mate Rudolf Geiss recalled. He was not afraid that they were sailing virtually alone. He had heard rumours of Russian submarines, but he felt that they were indeed only rumours. He saw the *Löwe* from the bridge: 'She looked like a small rowboat – and she would protect us!' The bridge was 16m above the water, from which the torpedo recovery boat looked like a small toy.

A WELL-ORGANISED BATTALION DOCTOR

In contrast to the chaos on the bridge, the physician Helmut Richter showed immense professionalism. He had served as chief physician to the Second Submarine School Division in Gotenhafen and he had actually just moved its hospital on board. He, along with other healthcare professionals, knew very well that the patients would be among the most vulnerable if something happened. Therefore, he had carefully planned what to do if they were subjected to an air or a submarine attack. Richter had also trained his staff: every detail had been gone through to determine everyone's role in an evacuation, and how to do it quickly.

Richter also had to ensure that all births took place on board without complications. The mothers were given a special certificate where place of birth was stated as 'MS *Wilhelm Gustloff*' along with the latitude and longitude at the time.

At six o'clock in the evening a telegraph was received announcing that a convoy was heading towards Gotenhafen. It was a minesweeping patrol in open formation making 12 knots. There was a considerable risk of collision as the *Wilhelm Gustloff* was completely blacked out. Petersen suggested putting out lanterns: First Mate Reese responded that this would mean advertising their position to the enemy.

Second Officer Paul Vollrath was also opposed to using lanterns and again an animated discussion ensued. But as Petersen had not received notification of any submarines in the area he still considered it safe to light the ship in this way. The decision was that lanterns would be lit. None of the minesweepers in the convoy was spotted and at 19:30 the lanterns were extinguished.

Alfred Wiegand, one of the sailors training in the Second Submarine School Division, was on watch that evening. Around half past eight, he saw something he could scarcely perceive, it looked like a 'wink':

> There was no light, more like a shimmer. I thought it could be the peri-scope of a submarine, perhaps a Russian submarine. I immediately reported my observation to Gustloff's bridge. The answer was, 'Don't worry, [it's] a German submarine!'[29]

In fact, a submarine warning had been transmitted, but atmospheric interference had prevented it being received by the *Wilhelm Gustloff*. To complicate matters further, *Löwe*'s telegraph worked on a different wavelength to that of the Ninth Security Division in Gotenhafen that had sent out the warning. But even if the message had been received, it may have made no difference – *Löwe*'s submarine-locating devices were completely iced up and so were useless. The 'eyes' with which *Löwe* was equipped were closed.

In contrast to the telegraph, Hitler's speech broadcast on the radio to commemorate his seizure of power was perfectly audible. He said that it was exactly twelve years since providence had put the German people's destiny in his hands. Then the provincial governor Erich Koch spoke:

> The Führer's thoughts are with us in this hour. He will never abandon East Prussia. His best divisions will defend East Prussia and new trained armies and new weapons will drive the Bolshevik hordes back behind the Urals.[30]

Heinz Schön walked past a cabin where the door was ajar, and listened to both Hitler and to Koch. 'No,' he thought, 'I will go back to my cabin and have a brandy.' He took out a glass and looked at his book: he was reading a novel by the German writer Pelz von Felinau, *Der Untergang der Titanic* (*The Sinking of the Titanic*).

The same thought crossed the minds of the officers on the bridge. They had gathered in the cabin of First Mate Reese to drink a brandy and then eat; the last hours had taken a heavy toll on everyone, but the tension had subsided and everything was calmer.

THREE TORPEDOES

Indeed, a general calmness had settled throughout the *Wilhelm Gustloff*, even in the ship's hospital, where a young woman from Elbing was in labour and the staff knew would give birth in a few minutes, but Dr Richter was fully prepared. Among the sick and injured, a spontaneous orchestra had formed, using borrowed instruments.

Around the ship, people relaxed. Some defied the order and took off their life jackets, as it was very uncomfortable to sleep with them on. Heli Beneicke later recalled the intense cold. As everything was quiet and still, she and her family were about to lie down:

> My sisters had already gone to bed and I was talking to my mother. We looked through these large windows, as we were on the upper promenade deck and you could see out over the whole ship.[31]

Rudolf Geiss stood in the chart room, calculated the ship's position and laid his ruler on the chart. It was blowing so hard that the ship was rolling and he had to grip the table to stay upright, although this did not bother an experienced sailor.

Heinz Schön leaned back in his cabin, smelled the brandy in the glass and began to sip. He could feel the strength of the alcohol through his nostrils and he enjoyed being at peace and escaping the stress that had gripped him and the rest of the crew over the last days and nights.

It was a quarter past nine in the evening. Eva Dorn, in her uniform, was still in the infirmary. She wasn't wearing a life jacket:

> The room we were in was a large room with a large, round sofa. There was a large round table and the room was used for meetings when everything was normal. There was also a desk where I wrote a letter to my mother … when I helped at my first birth.[32]

Eva Dorn, or 'Dörnchen' as she was nicknamed by the doctors, held the hand of the woman from Elbing, 'to give her courage'. Then she went into an adjacent room, where she was joined by Richter:

> He came in and said, 'I can tell you Dörnchen that you do not have to worry about yourself. In three quarters of an hour we will be outside the Russian submarine area.' Then the nurse came in from another door and said, 'Herr Doktor, the head of the baby is appearing!' At that moment the first torpedo hit.[33]

5

THE SEA OF DEATH

23:08 Three torpedoes exploded against the target's port side. All hits. Distance 400–600 metres.

23:09 The target begins to sink.[1]

The *Wilhelm Gustloff* was going down, but all was not well on board the submarine that had attacked her, as torpedo operator Vladimir Kourotschkin recalled:

> We had four torpedoes ready … when the commandant gave the order 'Fire.' I fired four torpedoes. But only three torpedoes came through *S-13*'s tubes. The torpedo in Tube 2 with the inscription 'For Stalin' had inexplicably stuck … It was very dangerous for us because I knew that the slightest shake could activate ignition and then in the next moment we would be in heaven – or hell. I pushed it thoroughly and finally I thought I knew what to do. But nothing happened. The bastard was activated and the drive motor was running … I began to sweat because it was very dangerous. We were lucky … the torpedo motor stopped.[2]

On the *Wilhelm Gustloff*, one of the infirmary doors slammed shut so hard from the impact of the first torpedo that it was damaged. When Eva Dorn tried to open it, the handle came away in her hand:

> Then I heard a huge crash … and with the second torpedo, I stood with the door handle in my hand and with the third torpedo the door opened. We immediately had such a list that you couldn't walk properly anymore … In a large glass case stood a skeleton, like in schools … and we had such a list that it fell with a mighty crash and everything went into pieces … but it was in front of the door so we had to push the door open by force, shoving all the

glass aside and I and everyone else had to step over the bones and shards and everything. And then I said 'If I can walk over the dead and manage then I will survive,' and so it was.[3]

Wilhelm Zahn and the others were being served brandy by Petersen's steward Max Bonnett when the *S-13* attacked. Later Zahn stated that the low speed was partly responsible for what happened:

During the conversation, about 21:20 [sic], three detonations came within two to three seconds. The lights went out. Our emergency diesel engine immediately started and gave sufficient emergency lighting. The ship had about a 5° port list. There was no fire. The fo'c's'le was somewhat lower than normal. All the officers gathered on the bridge. The refugees were given instructions to get to the upper deck, not to panic.[4]

All the crew had lost a close relative or friend at the Siege of Leningrad. Their fighting spirit was as strong as their desire for revenge. (Heinz Schön)

The swimming pool was quickly transformed into a deadly inferno. Splinters from the torpedo were mixed with fragments of tiles and glass shards from shattered wine bottles in the nearby wine cellars. (Heinz Schön)

The clock on the bridge showed 21:16 and it was here that the detonation of the first torpedo was very noticeable, as it was almost directly above where it had struck. Captain Weller immediately pulled on the telegraph to order the engine room to stop the engines. Then came two more explosions. Zahn said to Captain Petersen, 'There we have it!' Immediately they could see and feel that the *Wilhelm Gustloff*'s bow was going down. Water was already flooding the forecastle.

DEATH IN THE POOL

Many of the *Marine Helferinnen* quartered in the emptied swimming pool probably never realised what had happened. The first torpedo exploded here, killing them instantly. In an adjoining cabin was Ursula Schneider-Pautz, a 20-year old from Berlin. Her inability to find a place in the pool was her salvation. Earlier in the evening she had looked out and seen her comrades very seasick, but she had finally managed to fall asleep:

> A terrible blow threw me high into the air and then came a second and a third blow. It was like iron discs fighting against each other with a violent force. We did not understand what had happened. Suddenly we heard a girl screaming shrilly, 'Airstrikes, they are throwing gas bombs!' An extremely strong smell of gas filled the cabin so that I could hardly breathe. In the dark, I groped for the gas mask. When the emergency light came on I saw the devastation.[5]

Water was already coming up to the cabin door. Ursula looked out and saw a hodgepodge of massacred girls, some drowned, others crushed. The torpedo had not only blown up the swimming pool, but the adjoining wine and liquor stores, and the force of the detonation turned thousands of bottles into shards of swirling razor-sharp projectiles.

Those still able ran up the stairs toward the watertight door, but this had already been closed from the bridge. They were trapped. Ursula heard screams from everywhere for help, for God and for mothers:

> Another comrade next to me had found a knife somewhere and screamed, 'If God won't help me, I'll do it myself!' And she cut open the artery on each arm – her blood mixing with the water that was pouring in all the time … No help was given to us, we all seemed wedded to death. Then suddenly a comrade next to me, Sigrid Bergfeld, shouted, 'There must be an emergency exit on this side!' And then she stepped right over the screaming crowd. I did that too and followed her. She showed me a narrow door in the wall. With our last strength we pried the door open and pushed through the small gap and saw the narrow stairs. It was the emergency exit up from the engine room. Unimaginable forces awoke within us. In order to save our lives we went up the steel stairs as fast as we could – we wanted to survive![6]

In the moments before the attack, Second Engineer Erich Goering was thinking about *Löwe*, 'the little scab', which he felt was the reason the *Wilhelm Gustloff* was going so slowly. He was off duty and had taken off his shoes, and, despite the order, his life jacket as well. However, the jacket, and a flashlight, had been carefully placed on a table beside his bed within easy reach; he knew it was important to be prepared:

> Then came the first detonation. And then I jumped high: A mine! It was the
> first thought. With my shoes on [I went] directly down to the engine room.
> Then came the second detonation. I thought, 'This is not a mine.' And then
> came a third. In the engine room, it was black, you could not see, only [hear]
> the bubbling water that gushed from the outside into the engine room.[7]

Being off duty had probably saved his life, although he did not realise
this at the time. An emergency exit on the starboard side took him up
to the upper promenade deck, where he saw Chief Purser Peter Martin
Jensen about to throw a rope ladder along the side, and then he started
throwing floats in the water. It was a difficult job and the two men helped
each other. Finally, they had all the floats in the water. The two men then
parted: Goering never saw Jensen again.

THE DOORS CLOSE

On the bridge the order had been issued to close the watertight doors.
A large part of the crew was quartered forward of the watertight door,
which would hermetically seal this part of *Wilhelm Gustloff* from the rest
of the ship. Heinz Schön was aware of this: his cabin, far forward, was on
the 'wrong' side of the bulkhead:

> I grabbed my uniform jacket, threw my coat over it, put on my hat and
> tried to go out – but the door was stuck. The ship had already list to port
> [sic]. With all my strength I pushed the door open just enough so that I
> could squeeze through the gap. I think it was a matter of minutes.[8]

He came out into the corridor and threw himself through the still-open
bulkhead door as he heard the unmistakable buzzing sound, which meant
that the door was about to close. Safely through, Schön heard a steward
running behind him collide with the now-closed door. The steward and
an unknown number of crew and passengers were trapped. They would
either drown or, if the bulkhead held, suffocate from a lack of oxygen after
a few days in total darkness.

The painter Adolf Bock, as a prominent person, had a cabin all to himself on the boat deck – the Führer's cabin:

The time was just after 21:00. I was reading in my little 'chamber' when suddenly a sharp blow made the vessel tremble, and I flew off the chair and was hurled against my bunk. Within short intervals two further shocks followed. The lights went out, and the ship began slowly to lean over to port ... In the faint glow of the emergency lighting, which still worked, I hunted for my coat, hat and gloves with great haste and hurried onto the deck. An icy wind blew against me.[9]

Milda Bendrich in her cabin couldn't have been asleep for more than half an hour, with 2-year-old Inge between her and the cabin wall. The first torpedo explosion threw them out of the bunk and a few seconds later they felt two more explosions. Milda was a landlubber, she knew nothing about the sea, but she knew something terrible had happened: something had rocked the ship and that meant danger. The cabin light was not working but when Milda looked out into the passageway, she saw the emergency lights were on. They had to get out and up onto the deck, that much was clear, but every corridor, stairway and stairwell was clogged with people:

This staircase from C Deck to B Deck consisted of two flights, and between the two stair sections was a small square landing, which in memory I climbed past countless times in the following years ... struggling to cope with the wave [of people] behind me and the women in front of me. They, like me, had no strength left to move on. Those who gave up were another obstacle for those who came after. I had almost given up on the second flight when a woman behind me who, with the words 'For God's sake, do not fall', pushed me forward.[10]

Finally, they arrived on the open deck. She saw snow lying there, took a handful and washed her face with it. The cold seemed to do wonders: she straightened up with the baby in her arms and tried to think clearly. She found the room where her parents were quartered. It was virtually empty: everyone had fled to the boat deck. Milda saw that the list was now almost 30 degrees, but she took herself back out onto the deck, clutching baby Inge tightly in her arms. Little Inge was strangely silent, thought Milda; she seemed not to care about what happened.

Nineteen-year old Helmut Zokolowski from Danzig worked in the laundry department on the *Wilhelm Gustloff*. He had managed to secure

The sundeck of the *Wilhelm Gustloff* during her time as an accommodation ship. The storm had made the sea wash the deck, which turned it into an ice rink. Many later testified that it was almost impossible to move over the decks since they had become so slippery. (Heinz Schön)

travel permits for his parents and five siblings, his grandfather, his aunt with three children and several other relatives, a total of fourteen people. It was quite a crowd and everyone was enormously grateful to Helmut because he had given them a chance of escape. They were not in one of the dormitories: Helmut's comrades had moved out of their accommodation so that the family could stay together, in the forward part of the ship. By chance, Helmut had been on deck when the torpedo came. As he worked on board he knew the procedures – the watertight doors would be about to close. He rushed down the gangways, not even hesitating as he rushed past an armed guard, but finally he came to a closed door. The watertight door was closed. Those on the other side of the door had no chance of escaping. They included his entire family.

Margit and Selma Schilder had been sitting in their chairs and trying to relax and ignore the rise and fall of the ship as she sailed through the waves:

Then suddenly 'bang' and within minutes the ship started to lean … and we were lucky that the slope was like that – we ended up on top of a pile of furniture and lounge chairs and potted plants and table … the worst thing was that the lights went out … so we had to grope our way to the nearest door.[11]

Many who thought they had been fortunate to be allocated a berth in a cabin discovered the opposite when cabinets and all the other moveable furniture fell and blocked the doors. Heli Beneicke and her family found themselves trapped:

We talked to each other … then there came a shock, the ship shook, there could have been a mine or something like that … but then directly came the next shock and we screamed and woke the baby right away … and then the next shock arrived and instinctively, I knew [the ship] had been torpedoed.[12]

The cabin was small and there was a stand-alone cabinet that, when the ship started to heel, fell and blocked the door. They managed to move it and because they slept with their clothes on they went straight out into the corridor, wearing their life jackets. The corridor was dark, but then the emergency lights came on and it was soon filled with people:

Like a swarm, they came from the deck below … and even then I saw how people got on top of each other … men who just stepped out, climbed over the women to get to the exits … and all pushed from behind. My mother and I went first, my sister with the baby barely three months old was in the middle and the sixteen-year-old came last. I paved the way for them so we could stay together.[13]

They made it out on to the deck but Heli's youngest sister was pushed away. Now she noticed how slippery the deck was, and the ship's very obvious list.

NO RADIO

The situation in the telegraph office was desperate. Despite the emergency electricity being on nothing was working. The tubes in the radio

The 'Little Dog', as Korvettenkapitän Zahn had nicknamed the *Löwe*, was the first vessel to reach the *Wilhelm Gustloff* and began the rescue of people from the sea immediately. The storm made it impossible for the *Löwe* to get close to the *Wilhelm Gustloff* and rescue anyone from the ship herself.

equipment had probably been crushed by the explosions, which had also destroyed the accumulators. The emergency batteries that should have been hooked up in Gotenhafen had not been, and now it was too late.

Luckily, Rudi Lange the naval telegrapher had brought portable radio equipment on board and he used this to get a message out:

> In an emergency, I could break radio silence, but only if there was the imminent danger that we would go under. I had managed to convey to the Löwe that the ship had been hit by three torpedoes, and I, as a trained ship designer, already understood what was going to happen.[14]

'The Dog', as Zahn called *Löwe*, received the message and because the *Wilhelm Gustloff*'s radio was out of action, it fell to her to transmit distress signals to the outside world.

Rudolf Geiss, who had stood at the chart table and taken the ship's position when the torpedoes hit, was ordered to work with the signal seaman and send up flares:

> When the torpedo explosions came, I found myself as the officer helmsman on the bridge. After I carried out the order to launch flares, I went down below deck to see if I could do something and help … By the stairs to C deck I and some friends pushed the dead or half-dead to the side to make a clear path for those who wanted to come up from below.[15]

For a while the *Wilhelm Gustloff* seemed to hold steady. Then she shook convulsively and her bow dipped lower.

One of the few who bore the situation with the utmost calm was the doctor, Battalion Chief Richter. He had already trained his staff, over and over again, about what must be done in an emergency – and now he knew that he had not wasted his time. When he, Eva Dorn and the others came out of the infirmary, stepping over the broken skeleton and the glass shards, he quickly organised his team. 'It all happens according to the plan,' he called to one of the sergeants. 'Sure,' he replied curtly.

Richter went to the woman from Elbing who was about to give birth. 'Calm, just calm,' he reassured her. He gave her a soothing injection that temporarily stopped the birth. She was wrapped in blankets and carried to a lifeboat.

Because the infirmary was close to the boats, Richter was able to evacuate his entire department – staff and patients – into the boats. It seemed that all they had ever done on the ship was train for an evacuation, so in the event it took only a few minutes. Richter could breathe out: he'd got them all out, even the woman from Elbing. But he did not know whether she would survive the night. In the event, she was in the first lifeboat to be lowered, which was one of the few to get away cleanly.

THE LITTLE DOG

Löwe, 'the little dog', would prove to live up to her proper name ('lion') when rescuing people from the sea. Her commander, Kapitänleutnant Paul Prüfe, knew, however, that while *Wilhelm Gustloff* had thousands of people on board, *Löwe* had room for no more than 500. But he put such thoughts aside as his ship approached the stricken giant. The *Löwe* came so close that they could see the holes made by the torpedoes in the ship's side. Trying to aid the *Wilhelm Gustloff* was out of the question: the men on the *Löwe* had to concentrate on saving those in the sea. Their searchlights played over the *Wilhelm Gustloff*'s side and picked out a lifeboat being lowered, but which for some reason had its bow higher than its stern.

When Eva Dorn went from the infirmary to the boat deck, it was a quicker journey than she had anticipated: she slid all that way. Once there, she saw this same lifeboat:

> The boat hung on its davits, it was full of people and it was about to be lowered … And then it moved to the right side, it jarred – and all the people fell into the water, women, children, everyone who was in the boat.[16]

The ropes had failed to run smoothly through the pulleys because the mechanisms were iced up, and when the left davit ran but not the right davit, the lifeboat tipped suddenly and mercilessly tipped everyone into the sea. It all happened so quickly that no one had time to react. Dorn was sure that they would meet a certain death. In the heavy weather, she did not even hear anyone scream. No one on the *Löwe* heard anything either but she was not close enough to see if anyone from the boat could be saved.

Torpedo boat *T-36* was 105m long with a maximum speed of 34 knots. She was only a few months old when she received her baptism of fire. Put into service in December 1944, she had been in Danzig where important engine parts and other maintenance supplies had been loaded, along with 250 refugees. It was unusual for a torpedo boat to be turned into a refugee transport, but the crew did the best they could to help their passengers. But now she was also serving as an escort for the cruiser *Admiral Hipper*, which was following in her wake.

The *Admiral Hipper*, at 13,900 tonnes, was one of the last major warships Germany had in the Baltic. Overloaded with refugees, munitions, shipbuilding equipment from the shipyard in Elbing and other goods, she had passed Hela where a number of ships had gathered in anticipation of the escort. The master of the *T-36*, Kapitänleutnant Robert Hering, had noticed that *Wilhelm Gustloff* was not there.

RADIO WAVES IN THE NIGHT

The message that the *Wilhelm Gustloff* was sinking began to spread through the German ports on the Baltic. One of the last to hear was Korvettenkapitän Wolfgang Leonhardt, head of Gotenhafen department's security division. It was only later that he realised precious time had been lost because his division used a different wavelength to *Löwe*'s failing radio apparatus.

Leonhardt put his hopes on the *Admiral Hipper*. Not only was she in the vicinity, she also had the capacity to carry out a massive rescue operation. Unless more torpedoes struck the *Wilhelm Gustloff* she should be reached in time – 22.00 by Leonhardt's calculation. It comforted him that the *Admiral Hipper* must be on her way, or possibly had already arrived.

His assumption was correct. The *Admiral Hipper* could make 32 knots – twice as fast as the *Wilhelm Gustloff* – and a submarine would never catch her. The cruiser had left Gotenhafen a few hours after the *Wilhelm Gustloff* and kept the same route as the KdF ship. But the cruiser did not receive the *Löwe*'s message about the stricken ship. It was not until about 22.30 that the navigation officer on the *Admiral Hipper*, Boden, saw a falling red star. His fellow officers initially assumed this was an exercise signal, but Boden was of a different opinion:

> These are no exercise signals, they are distress signals. It became abundantly clear to everyone on the bridge. They hovered right ahead, straight ahead of the *Hipper*'s route and then they went out. There were new [ones] all the time. Over the horizon a silver gilt shimmer appeared, like a narrow streak of lightning bugs on a dark night. It's a ship, a fully-lit ship where all the shields had been removed from the portholes.[17]

To the *Hipper*'s officers a vessel no longer shielding its lights could only mean that there was no longer anything to hide. Only minutes later the cruiser picked up the *Gustloff*'s distress call and with *T-36*, sailed at top speed toward the ship. Hering put his crew on high alert:

> I went at top speed toward the horizon where *Wilhelm Gustloff* was occasionally visible and reached her after half an hour. Meanwhile, the crew put together all the supplies needed for the rescue with feverish speed, chopped

the ice away and made everything clear. The doctor and even the kitchen were prepared, as those on a warship have always been trained.[18]

Patrol Boat *1703* had come to Stolpmünde from Libau that day and the crew were exhausted. Captain Hanefeld wanted everyone to rest and take the next day off. In the mess hall the men sat and shared a bottle of rum, two accordions had arrived and the atmosphere was good. But the party did not last long before the alarms began to sound. The crew were ordered to take their places: the *1703* was to depart immediately. When the crew heard about the *Wilhelm Gustloff* they understood the gravity of the situation. However, the ship was 12 nautical miles from Stolpmünde and *1703* was not the Navy's fastest boat. She had to be pushed to the limit.

Unlike the *Wilhelm Gustloff*, the *Admiral Hipper* had received a submarine warning. Captain Hans Henigst now had to balance the danger to his ship, the 1,500-man crew and almost as many refugees, against the fact that there was room on board for several thousand more who would be likely to die if the cruiser did not reach them.

A torpedo boat similar to *T-36*. The low freeboard enabled the quick recovery of people from the water. Pairs of crewmen lifted victims from the water and passed them to sailors behind, who in turn lifted them onto the deck. As the rescue was under way, a Russian submarine was trying to torpedo the boat.

Meta Woit at the time of the *Wilhelm Gustloff* disaster. (Horst Woit)

Meanwhile, a double tragedy was playing out on the *Wilhelm Gustloff*. It was dawning on the officers that there were not enough sailors either to lower the boats or to man them: so many had been trapped behind the watertight doors. There were many submariners, but they had little or no lifeboat training. The consequences were catastrophic.

Panic now began to set in. Ten-year-old Horst Woit understood that the very loud explosions meant that something serious had happened. He and his mother, Meta, ran out of their cabin – Horst without his shoes – into the corridor and down the nearest stairs:

> Then a fire extinguisher went off. The stairs were like soap. Mother fell down all the stairs and I stood at the top and screamed all the time, 'Mother, where are you? Climb up again!' Eventually she found the handrail and pulled herself painfully up. But I did not stop crying. Mother screamed all the time 'Horst! Horst!'[19]

They struggled on to the deck on all fours but managed to keep up with Meta's friend, Hildegard, and her daughter, Christa. There were many others there:

We got pushed from behind when we came out; we were the same level as the lifeboats. Rockets shot up, people yelled and shoved, then we had to descend a staircase. Mother held me firmly by the hand and we pushed ourselves against the railing, Aunt [Hildegard] and Christa were close to us.[20]

Earlier, Rudolf Geiss had noted that in the vast public rooms all the tables and chairs had been pushed aside to make room for mattresses. When the ship began to list, everything movable now began to shift and these same large and heavy tables moved like projectiles through the halls, crushing everything in their path. In trying to avoid them, many people ended up on the port side of the rooms where there was no chance of reaching a stairway or finding the nearest exit.

THE JUMP INTO FREEZING WATER

Before the emergency lights came on, Margit Schilder and her mother, Selma, had managed to grope their way out of the cabin. They came to a stairwell and pulled themselves up along the handrail. Reaching the sun deck, Margit saw the panic as people fought for the few remaining life jackets:

We stood at the top, it was the sun deck, and then someone who did not have a life jacket on ran and tore off my mother's life jacket, so she had no life jacket when we got into the water.[21]

Getting to the boat deck was impossible, so they stayed on the sun deck, but in the confusion, Margit lost sight of Selma. She asked an officer for help, but he replied that there was nothing that could be done:

Half an hour later the officer said that now we had to jump, otherwise we would go down with the ship … he took my hand and it was terrible, and [we] jumped into the icy water … It was the worst moment when we jumped … then one knew that it [the ship] was close to its end … Lumber and people, all screaming. But this officer held my hand the whole time. And then we swam to a rescue boat and it was full of people. We tried to keep hold of that boat, but they hit us with oars. They shouted that we would all go under … Well, then we had to let go of the boat; there was not a chance.[22]

The *Wilhelm Gustloff* during her short career as a hospital ship. Armed soldiers were stationed by the lifeboats to prevent anyone unauthorised from entering. Disastrously, many of the wires by which the boats were lowered had frozen in their blocks, and, with no time to thaw them, the boats could not be launched.

Heinz Schön knew he must get to the boat deck quickly, to the lifeboat he had been ordered to command. Everywhere people were jostling and screaming in panic. Those that stumbled and fell did not get up again: they were trampled underfoot. Someone tried to pull off Schön's coat but managed to get hold of only one arm. Schön also lost a shoe in the melee. When eventually he reached the open deck he saw flare after flare being fired. He understood that any attempt to conceal the ship by hiding her lights had been abandoned – they were now calling for anyone to come to their aid.

TO SINK A RESCUE SHIP

From a safe distance, Marinesco on board *S-13* watched the results of the successful torpedo strikes and the frantic rescue efforts. Hitler's men were getting what they deserved, he thought. He and his crew were convinced that they had sunk a troop carrier.

As he watched the rescue work, he considered sinking the rescue vessels as well. He wanted as few Germans as possible to get away alive, and he knew that this sinking would be regarded as a triumph by his superiors ... and would give him and the crew glory and honours on their return to the submarine's home base.

But *S-13* was not the only Russian submarine in the waters around the *Wilhelm Gustloff*. One or more torpedoes were later fired at *T-36*, but not by *S-13*. Which submarine it was has never been discovered.

Schön pushed his way forward towards his boat, No. 5. It was guarded by two officers and four sailors, all holding cocked pistols. A soldier with a bandage on his head, deciding he did not care about the order of 'Women and children first', decided to step in the boat. A dull shot and a scream followed:

> The infantryman falls into the gap between the upper deck and the boat railing and splashes into the water. After seeing him fall, some of the women in the lifeboat put their hands over their eyes.[23]

The incident was effective in deterring others from storming the lifeboats. Schön understood that Lifeboat No. 5 would be launched with only women and children. A single officer was organising the loading. When Schön informed him that he was in command of this boat, the officer replied coldly, 'Anyone can say that' and threatened to shoot him if he attempted to board. So the boat was lowered with no seamen on board to handle it. It is possible that the officer thought that there were enough men in the water already who would be able to scramble on board and take control.

Schön had the same experience with other lifeboats, and was on the point of giving up. But then he remembered the rafts stacked on the deck: these could give him a chance of surviving the night.

A HUMAN AQUARIUM

Some sort of order was now restored to prevent a rush on the lifeboats. SS officers guarded the exits and people gathered on the starboard side of the long glass-enclosed lower promenade deck that ran around the ship on A deck. Undoubtedly they prevented a mass panic and possibly an even greater loss of life. They may still have hoped that rescue vessels would arrive.

The windows in the enclosed promenade decks were fitted with armoured glass and were impossible to break by hand. They turned the decks into a death trap where perhaps 1,000 people were quickly engulfed by the rapid inflow of water.

The lower promenade deck was 166m long, and now filled with perhaps 1,000 people who had nowhere to go. But as the bow went down further and further, the port side also sank deeper and deeper and those on deck realised that they were in a death trap: caught between a glass wall and a rising water level.

Some tried to smash the glass with shoes, with anything they could find. But the armoured glass was designed to be almost unbreakable. Then there was a heavy thud, and *Wilhelm Gustloff* lurched again: probably an engine had left its bed and had slid down to the ship's side. To many up on deck it felt as if a giant had struck the ship. Someone shouted, 'The water is coming! The water is coming!' This was the cue for an uncontrolled panic.

One of the trapped was Maria Kupfer. She saw men banging on the armoured glass with their fists as the water rose. One after another they fell back into the water and disappeared, their screams mixed with the roar of the inflowing water. Then finally, a giant wave surged though the promenade deck and smashed one of the windows. It took Maria with it, pushing her up to the surface. She was the only survivor from the lower promenade deck.

Eva Dorn was standing at the davits where the boat was being lowered:

I was in uniform, I was a soldier, I need to help … And then a man came along with suitcases and said 'I must get in the boat, I must get in the boat!' When a sailor asked him, 'Why should you be allowed in the lifeboat?' he replied 'Well, I'm on special assignment for Himmler, I have important papers and I have to be rescued!' The sailor answered, 'Get into the water and swim!'[24]

She heard gunshots but did not see if anyone was hit. But Heinz Schön found himself on the aft deck superstructure and saw a senior officer:

… in the brown party uniform with a swastika armband, with his wife and two children, and his wife yelled at him, 'Put an end to this!' He shot his two children and his wife. After that, he wanted to shoot himself in the temple, but there were no bullets left in the chamber. He shouted at me, 'Give me your gun!' But I cried that I had none. Then he lost his grip [on the rail] and slid away after his wife and children. I also saw naval personnel who opened up their arteries … they chose death voluntarily because they had a fear of death by drowning.[25]

Much later, stories were told about the officers who guarded the exits shooting down anyone who made a run for the lifeboats, but there is no reliable evidence that this happened. Perhaps the infantryman was one of the few who were shot in cold blood. The other pistol shots that survivors witnessed were either to discourage the lifeboats being stormed, or 'suicides' such as that Heinz Schön had witnessed.

Milda Bendrich stood with her back pressed against the deckhouse, her daughter held tightly in her arms. The list of the ship was too great, the deck was too icy, so she could move neither forwards nor backwards. An officer beside her also seemed be in a dream but winced when they heard the sound of gun shots. He ordered a soldier to help Milda into a lifeboat:

> The soldier held onto the railing and offered me a hand while the officer lifted me up as far as he could. Pushed and pulled, we reached the railing and I was lifted into the lifeboat. While our boat was being readied, another was launched, but it swung around and lost all its human cargo.[26]

Adolf Bock had only himself to look after. He tried his best to locate any remaining lifeboats while trying to stay away from the crowds, realising that they could become dangerous if panic took hold:

> I tried to get myself away from the throng so that if we had to go into the water I would be able to swim freely. I fumbled my way along the leaning superstructures aft, where a number of large rafts were piled up. Then in the pale moonlight I discovered, half hidden by the bulky rafts, several lifeboats intended for warships, and now I recalled they had been brought on board by floating crane in Gotenhafen. They lay like dark shadows, and in the distance could be taken for deck superstructures, completely iced over and covered by snow. There were even the oars, and the boats were therefore quite workable. Quickly, I threw my document bag, which contained my papers and valuables, into one of the boats.[27]

Heli Beineicke made it to the deck with her family. Her 16-year-old sister gave her life jacket to another family member, then went to find another. She was not seen again. The crowd pressed, so Heli made her older sister grip the railing. They couldn't see any lifeboats. The *Wilhelm Gustloff*'s list was accelerating and as they were on the starboard side, they climbed over the railing to avoid slipping down the deck:

> My mother was not so agile, as it is when you are fifty years old, and she had left the baby to me … and my mother tried to climb over the railing, but it wasn't possible, I tried to keep hold of her [and the child] but then they [including her sister] fell into the water among all the people. And then I was alone, completely alone, everyone in the family was gone …[28]

She held on to a rope and managed to lower herself down towards the water before dropping the last few metres into the sea:

> I swallowed a lot of water, but I knew I could come to the surface because I had always swum in the Baltic Sea in October … There were no lifeboats on our side, they were on the other side.[29]

More and more people jumped in the water but many others were terrified by the horror of a black sea. No one had a clear picture of what was happening, only the minutiae of their own circumstances. But everyone saw the flares that were continuously being sent up. Eva Dorn understood what rockets at sea meant:

> … then I saw the rockets … and then came a sailor came up to me, 'You too get into the boat!' Yes, I stepped into the boat, I was the last one and I got to sit at the helm a lot. I'm clinging on because of the high sea … normally there would have been about forty-five people in the boat, but now it was obviously packed … it was rough seas and we were all completely soaked.[30]

By now the torpedo boat *T-36* had arrived and Kapitänleutnant Hering assessed how he could begin the rescue work:

> It was not possible to get optical contact with the bridge; I went once around the sinking ship to find a place where we could go up alongside her. Now, it was noticed that the vessel was sinking quickly and getting more and more of a list and this made it impossible to board her. So I was lying a few hundred metres aft of *Wilhelm Gustloff*.[31]

Eva Dorn photographed in 2001.

TIME IS RUNNING OUT

It was with some surprise that First Mate Louis Reese saw several lifeboats hanging empty on the port side while people hurried past, towards the stern and up to the starboard side, which was furthest from the water. The problem was that he had so few sailors available to man the boats. He found one of the boats ready to launch but with just one of his crewmen on board he told the man to wait: he had to find someone who could lower the boat. On the sloping deck he climbed up and found himself at the height of the funnel when the *Wilhelm Gustloff* gave another lurch forward and downward as perhaps another piece of machinery broke loose or a bulkhead gave way. Reese lost his footing and tumbled rapidly down to the lifeboat again. He struck the railing with a huge force. Fortunately he was recognised and they called out to him to get in the boat, as there was little time left. 'I think I've broken something!' he shouted back.

He had not expected to be rescued, but now he was carried into the boat. Suddenly a wave lifted the boat and carried it away from the ship. Reese realised that his tumble down the deck had saved his life.

HORST WOIT'S PENKNIFE

Horst Woit saw the rockets shoot upwards. When he reached Boat 5, he and the other children were loaded first, followed by their mothers: there were only a few men on board. However, as the boat was lowered, it was discovered that the ropes were frozen solid and the lifeboat could not be freed from the tackle:

> When the boat was being lowered and near the water, suddenly someone began yelling, 'We do not have a knife! We have no knife! Who's got a knife?!' Now, it so happens that my uncle was an officer in the German army, and he had left his summer uniform in the apartment we stayed in. And you know, kids get into everything, and I had looked in his trunk and I had seen his pocketknife. I stuffed it in my ski pants before we fled and there it stayed. And as we sat in the lifeboat and they started scream-ing 'Knives! A knife! We cannot get free!' I had the knife and I gave it to a soldier. They cut the ropes and that's how we got loose.[32]

As the lifeboat rowed away from the *Wilhelm Gustloff* those in the water tried to climb on board, grabbing the gunwales. But they were knocked off by those in the boat, who feared their own lives could be in jeopardy. Horst was too young to quite understand what was happening, but it was something he never forgot.

It was clear to everyone that the *Wilhelm Gustloff* had very little time left. Captain Petersen gave the news to the crew via the ship's whistle, which blew incessantly as if they were sailing in fog. But with hardly any boats left, how could those still on board possibly save themselves? The air temperature was -18°C, the water almost zero and the conditions practi-cally a storm. Petersen knew that few could survive in the water for long.

Fifteen metres away from where he stood, Heinz Schön saw a lifeboat still hanging in the davits. It was in the process of being loaded: maybe there was room in it for him. But the same thought went through several

Even if one had managed to get into a lifeboat and it was launched successfully, the danger was not over. The boat could be hit by falling equipment or simply entangled on the ship's side and dragged down with her. This picture was taken during a rescue operation undertaken by the *Wilhelm Gustloff* in April 1938.

other heads and in a few moments a large number of people had gathered around the boat. Any chance Schön might have had was gone. He watched as the boat was lowered. It almost reached the water when an anti-aircraft gun on the deck begun to move. It went over the side with a bang, and a second later it landed exactly on top of the lifeboat, crushing it. All that was heard on the deck were a few muffled screams.

Fifty minutes after the torpedoes had hit, the ship was listing 28 degrees to port. Some of the ship's officers were still on the bridge. There was not much they could say to one another, but when the bow went deeper and deeper and the water was approaching the windows, Zahn declared it was time to leave. He climbed towards the aft deck to see if there were any floats left. As an experienced sailor, he was able to manage the awkward life jacket, but the angle of the deck was too great even for him. He lost his footing and slipped quickly in the water.

Zahn's life jacket now changed from an encumbrance to a life saver. But this was not true for everyone. The jackets were designed for adults, not for children for whom they were too large and had too great a load-bearing capacity. Survivors would testify that they had seen many children in the water with life jackets, their legs sticking up in the air and their heads under water.

JOSEPH GOEBBELS' TOTAL WAR

Telegrapher Rudi Lange had given his life jacket to a woman with three children who had not been able to get hold of a single one. He wondered for a moment if his life would end that day. He thought of Goebbels' question in a speech just after the defeat at Stalingrad: 'Do you want total war?' and the enthusiastic response it had brought. He and everyone else on the *Wilhelm Gustloff* were now in this total war but no one was cheering now. He tried to release a raft at the front of the bridge on the starboard side, but it was stuck. Everything seemed to be against him. He returned to his wireless set:

> The ship went deeper and deeper and my set also slid away. I could no longer get anything away with my portable transmitter and I did not know if I was even being heard any more or if my batteries were still working. I let it go and as if by a miracle, I noticed that the waves had torn the raft free. Now I could hope.[33]

He clung to the raft as the water rose. But as it swung in front of the bridge, something caught Lange on the head and knocked him off. Suddenly he found himself underwater. When he came up the surface, the raft had gone. He trod water then looked around and saw something white – a life jacket:

> In the life jacket a child, a girl that was maybe ten years old, was hanging. I saw that she was in the life jacket with open eyes, but she was dead. I did not have the courage to take the lifebelt from the dead … It was simply awful to see how the child had lost her life in this way.[34]

In the distance Lange spotted several people on a raft. He called out, but received no reply. Working his way towards it, he managed to clamber up and then understood why he had had no response. The people were frozen: they were all dead. The cold and wet night had killed them. Lange said a prayer, thanking God that he was still alive:

> I saw the moon every now and then through the tattered clouds. My raft drifted through a ruined field, a mass grave of dead. Again and again I screamed and cried, but there was no one to answer me. Then I noticed how the cold had made my uniform stiff. I began to be afraid.[35]

So as not to freeze to death like the others, Lange slid back into the water to soften his clothes, while holding onto the raft. An eternity went by. Then Lange saw a searchlight playing across the water. He waved his arms, but he did not think he had been spotted:

> Then suddenly the searchlight stopped: the men from the *Löwe* had seen me. Our escort boat now became my rescue. They came close. At the side of the vessel several rafts were hanging and suddenly there was a soldier there. He reached out and pulled me over several empty life rafts on board the torpedo boat *Löwe*. But then I lost my strength and collapsed.[36]

The *Wilhelm Gustloff*'s watertight compartments kept her afloat longer than anyone imagined, even though safe construction was the hallmark of her Hamburg builders. She had not capsized despite the huge holes in her side. However, just before 22:16 water penetrated sufficient compartments to make her unstable. More and more people threw themselves into the water. It was clear that there were only minutes before the *Wilhelm Gustloff* would disappear.

On the aft deck there were three large lifeboats that had been among those that had been loaded in Gotenhafen. Now people took refuge in them, hoping that they would be floated off by the sea as the ship sank lower and lower. A sailor cut the rope that lashed the boats together. The first shot down the deck like a projectile and capsized when it hit the water. The second boat never reached the water: it was crushed against the railing. In the third boat sat Adolf Bock, two friends of his and Captain Petersen. This one was lifted by the waves and thrown into the Baltic. Luckily for the occupants, such was the momentum that it was carried a good distance away from the ship, yet too far for them to offer any assistance to those left on board. However, Adolf Böck was not sure whether he and the others would survive:

> Our boat was lifted high up by the swirling waters and hurled with a crash against the falling funnel. Another wave threw us against the davits still visible above the water so that the small boat creaked in its joints. With horror, we saw how the whole transom on the other boat was smashed and the waves washed the people out and into the water.[37]

One man had taken refuge in the funnel, but only as a place to die. He was the 19-year-old laundry assistant Helmut Zokolowski, whose fourteen relatives were now trapped behind the bulkhead in the forward part of the ship. Helmut had lost the will to live, and had decided to go down with the *Wilhelm Gustloff*. He waited for the water that would push him down into the bowels of the ship and was ready when the first wave reached him. But instead of being pushed down the wave sucked Helmut out. He had no chance of holding back, so in a few seconds he was out in the open water, some distance from the *Wilhelm Gustloff*.

PEOPLE IN THE SEA

Assistant Engineer Goering climbed up along the starboard side of the ship. By this time the *Wilhelm Gustloff* had largely turned over and only a part of the stern on the starboard side was still above the water, so, as he later described it, it was rather that he climbed down until he was near the keel. Part of the vessel was already on the Baltic seabed: the depth was only about 40m and the ship was more than 200m long. The last thing Goering did on the *Wilhelm Gustloff* was to take off his shoes, fold his arms and look up at the sky:

> And the next wave washed over the ship. I just jumped away from the ship and swam … On 30th January, at approximately a quarter to eleven, in a freezing cold sea. My uniform is on and over it a khaki jacket: you must have this if you jump into cold water. And then I swam. When the cold water reached my throat it felt as if a knife had cut it. And then I swam thirty, forty metres, I'm not sure. And suddenly I got hold of one of these

rafts [...] Peter Martin Jensen and I had thrown overboard ... there was still room on a raft and I heaved myself up with my arms. There were already people on the thwarts, it was densely crowded. Then I saw arms sticking out of the water which I grabbed. They clung to me, the heads were under water, just arms stuck up. Then they disappeared before my eyes.[38]

Eva Dorn and the others in her lifeboat had their hands full in keeping the lifeboat afloat and keeping themselves in it. The boat was loaded far beyond its official capacity and there was no room for a single extra person:

This was when it was worst for me personally. It was the people who clung to the lifeboat and who were pushed away. Even today, I have on my retina a man's face. He looked at me ... and I could do nothing. He was also rebuffed ... There were so many people in the boat and everyone wanted to save their own lives. He was not the only one, but the only one who stayed in my memory ... It's because I cannot forget his face. It was a long one. He was thin, he had a beautiful face, a noble face, he looked like a professor.[39]

He said nothing to Eva: he only looked at her for a few seconds but she felt it was an eternity.

They were hailed by cries from another lifeboat: it had no oars and was drifting. Although they were not far apart, the waves made it difficult for Eva's boat to reach it. She heard another shout: was a doctor in their boat? A woman was about to give birth. It was the woman from Elbing who was waking up from the anaesthetic. From Eva's lifeboat came the reply: 'We have a doctor!' It was Battalion Chief Richter who replied; he could hardly believe it was the same woman. The boats were only a few metres from each other as the waves pushed them apart. Then someone shouted that they had sighted a ship. It was the torpedo boat *Löwe*.

Meanwhile, Margit Schilder and the unknown officer had been forced to let go of the lifeboat to which they clung:

... so we started to swim, we two ... [He] was like a guardian angel for me. Then we saw a rubber raft go past us and he was so strong, he ploughed after that life raft and jumped in and pulled me up. I would never have been able to pull myself up. And then we sat, we two, in that raft. How long we were there, I do not know. We talked all the time to each other to calm down. Sometimes the moon came out, so we saw a little bit.[40]

To those in the lifeboats, the rafts, rescue boats and even those in the water the *Wilhelm Gustloff* looked like a clumsy grey whale that was about to dive. The searchlights lit up the darkness, the moon occasionally broke between the clouds: the ship herself wanted a grand finale. No Wagnerian opera could match this closing scene: thousands of people were struggling to survive in the water as she slid down.

DEATH ILLUMINATED

In her final moment, as if by a magic hand, every light on what was left of the ship above the water was suddenly on. The funnel bases were illuminated and each davit and mast glimmered. Someone thought it looked almost comical. Then her siren roared a final farewell cry and the *Wilhelm Gustloff* disappeared.

In her lifeboat, Eva Dorn was battling with an oar:

The vessel was behind me and then someone said 'Now *Gustloff* is going down' and I turned around … I saw she was completely lit up and then she turned suddenly and went under.[41]

That same magic hand now turned all the lights off. It was 22:18.

It took only a moment for the ship to disappear. With her siren now silent, the cries of those suddenly thrown into the water now rose above the noise of the storm and waves. Eva would recall it for the rest of her life:

The cry from the thousands of people who were there, this one cry, because everyone knew that now it was over – I'll never forget. It rings always in my ears. It was probably the hardest thing of all. It was known that there was no salvation [for those in the water], it was over, finished … But we saw rescue vessels and then a large warship passed. It was *Hipper*, but everyone was distraught when *Hipper* just flew by.[42]

As the cruiser *Admiral Hipper* reached the site of the disaster, there were fears that a submarine was in the near vicinity. To avoid risking the lives of those she had on board, the *Hipper* left almost immediately, to the despair of those still in the water.

As the giant shadow of the *Admiral Hipper* appeared, those in the water thought she looked like a high cliff. Her bank of searchlights seemed to bathe the whole Baltic in light. On the bridge, Captain Henigst had not received warnings of submarines in the area, but he knew that even in daylight a ship would have been a perfect target, but a ship at night with her searchlights playing across the water would be impossible to miss.

During the dash to the *Wilhelm Gustloff*'s last position, Henigst gave an explicit order to his crew: 'Not a word to the passengers.' He did not want alarm to spread among them, particularly when he could not be sure that the area was free of submarines.

Meanwhile, on *T-36*, Kapitänleutnant Hering was approaching the wreck site:

My ship still had some momentum without her engines running and slid into the swimming mass of people screaming for help, and barely ten minutes later my men began the rescue effort with all possible means.[43]

The crew sailed slowly around the wreckage, a lookout on the bridge constantly shouting out what he could see while on deck people were pulled from the water. Hering later recalled the difficulties of the rescue:

Anyone who has ever been at sea and experienced rough seas in winter can imagine how difficult it is to get a man over a two-metre high freeboard … Everywhere the sea was covered with screaming people, mostly women and children, and they were so weakened by the cold that they couldn't move or hardly climb the high side of the ship. Across the boat, several metres apart, accommodation ladders were hung with sailors on the bottom step who stood in the water and secured each person, who was then pulled up onto the deck by three or four sailors. You could barely bring in women who had fur [coats] because of the furs had become so slippery and wet.[44]

The whole crew worked frantically. Some pulled people from the ladders, others threw ropes to those in the water. Even the refugees who had been taken on board in Gotenhafen helped as best they could, taking the rescued below deck – usually to the engine room or another warm part of the ship.

Korvettenkapitän Zahn had managed to find one of the rafts that had been torn from the *Wilhelm Gustloff*. A seaman pulled Zahn on board, who soon discovered that the raft had no bottom. Suddenly the sailor said: 'What about the woman?' Zahn stared and was horrified to see a woman's head sticking up with her body in the water, trapped between lifebelts in the raft. Neither of them had a knife to cut the straps and pull up her up. Zahn told her to try to dive under the raft and get to the other side where he and the seaman would be able to pull her up. To help her, the sailor lay on his stomach and managed to push her head down. But the woman had no strength left: she vanished under the water.

A lifeboat drifting close by now captured Zahn's attention. He threw himself back into the water and swam over to it. As he climbed on board he realised that it was full of water: it was a wreck with, again, no bottom. Later he saw yet another lifeboat, this one with people inside. He managed to get their attention and screamed: 'Take me with you!' They dragged him into the boat and a few of those on board recognised him immediately. He was in the same boat as Adolf Bock and Captain Petersen. The two commanders were reunited, but they did not exchange a word.

Eva Dorn thought that the sea had a remarkable shimmer:

The water was fluorescent: it was silvery grey and glittered … torpedo boat T-36 had a searchlight and I sat in the back of the boat and was obviously afraid of not being picked up. From up there [on the bridge] came 'Hurry up! Hurry up! We run the risk torpedoing by the Russians!' through the loudspeakers … And they let down ladders that you could crawl up on.[45]

From her boat she saw a dead woman floating right next to the rescue ship:

> She had a very pale face and a ring of pure black hair around it. She lay on her back. That was why I noticed that the sea was so bright because I could see her. With each wave that broke against the ship the woman's head struck against the hull too … I can see it in front of me today. There are moments in life when everything stops and there will be images that you will always have on your retinas.[46]

The lifeboat in which Petersen, Zahn and the others sat drifted round the mass of shrieking and crying people, and debris of what had once been a beautiful passenger ship. After the initial shock subsided, Alfred Bock began to feel the terrible cold. They had pulled up so many passengers from the water that they now sat with their feet deep in icy water. He tried to keep warm by rowing:

> Many of those floating in the water were clinging to the oars and prayed for us rescue them. We took a few more women into the boat, though we ourselves were close to falling into the sea, as the waves were often washing over the sides.[47]

They then saw the outline of a vessel that turned out to be *T-36*. The lifeboat managed to get to the leeward of her and they shouted for a rope to be thrown down. As they neared, they could reach the top of the torpedo boat's railing on the top of the wave, but in the trough they were in danger of being crushed. Yet – and despite Bock now having lost all feeling in his legs because of the cold – everyone managed to climb on board *T-36*.

Third Engineer Erich Goering was also rescued by *T-36*. He had spotted one of the smaller rafts that he and his fellow crewmen had launched from the *Wilhelm Gustloff*, jumped into the water, swam to it and climbed onto it. As he paddled with his hands, he could see a black outline in the distance. It was the *T-36*. As he came closer he saw a man at the bottom of the accommodation ladder:

There was a seaman. 'Jump!' he said. And just when I was on the crest of a wave, I jumped and he caught me. Then I was on board the T-36 thanks to this raft that we [the crew], possibly myself, had thrown overboard.[48]

Heinz Schön had taken refuge in a raft he found on the deck. But when the raft was washed off the ship Schön was thrown into the water. His lifebelt supported him, as he knew exactly how it should be worn. As he drifted through the peaks and troughs of the sea, he saw the wreckage of lifeboats and rafts everywhere. And cutting through everything, above the roar of the wind and the sea, were the screams of those in the water:

Next to me a raft suddenly appeared. I stretched out my arm and screamed like everyone else who wanted to be taken up onto the raft. A military medic bent over the edge of the raft, took me under both arms and tried to pull me up but my lifebelt complicated this significantly. But with a last effort he managed it.[49]

Schön and the others on the raft sighted a partially flooded lifeboat, which they made for. Transferring to it, Schön, exhausted and seasick, hung his head over the boat's gunwale. Luckily they were spotted by *T-36*, which immediately came to their rescue. A rope was tied around Schön and he was hoisted aboard, barely aware of where he was. Everyone else in the boat was also rescued, except one. The man who had pulled up Schön out of the water, Werner Schoop, waited patiently to be the last to be taken on board but suddenly he saw that *T-36* was departing, leaving him alone, standing knee deep in water.

When Schön eventually recovered, he wondered what had happened to the man who had saved his life. It would be in 1997, fifty-two years later that, by chance, he saw Werner Schoop again.

Heinz Schön was liberated from the armour of ice that his clothes had become. Someone massaged him and gave him rum. When the alcohol began to revive his body, he started to look around. Hearing a shout, he looked up and realised that he was in an impromptu delivery room. One of the women who should have given birth on the *Wilhelm Gustloff* was now in labour on the *T-36*. Ship Doctor Schlipköter was making his very first delivery.

Once Schön had fully recovered, he began to walk around the torpedo boat in search of anyone he knew. There were not many of the *Wilhelm*

Heinz Schön and his saviour Werner Schoop.

Margit Schilder in her home, 2001.

Gustloff's crew, but eventually he learned that three of the ship's captains were on board: Friedrich Petersen, Wilhelm Zahn and Harry Weller. They found it hard to talk to each other, perhaps because each was mentally debating who was responsible for this disaster: a sinking that would prove to be the worst in history.

Margit Schilder and the unknown officer had watched the *Wilhelm Gustloff*'s final moments in horror, even though they were on a raft a good distance away. Margit could not understand why the whole ship had suddenly lit up:

> How long we had been sitting there together, I do not know. But suddenly, he [the officer] was gone. I'm thinking, he's had a heart attack or has lost his sense of balance, suddenly, he was gone. And then I sat alone in that rubber raft – and then I got scared, really scared![50]

She saw a lifeboat that somehow didn't look right. The bow and stern were intact, but the centre was missing. Nevertheless, there were people in it:

> Then I got hold of myself and jumped from my raft and swam there [to the lifeboat]. I did not want to be alone. It was just too eerie ... In the middle [of the boat] were those who already had drowned and died. I asked a man ... to help me into the boat, but he said he couldn't, because then they would sink ... eventually, he was so kind that he helped me. But then I had already understood that there was no hope of life anymore ... And then we sat huddled to keep the heat up a little, I saw three or four [people alive].[51]

Margit realised that the men in the boat were soldiers of some kind. They told her that this was the worst they had experienced during the war. They now had to try to stay warm and to keep the boat balanced. The boat was so low in the water that there was a considerable risk that they would be tipped into the sea. In the distance they had seen the *Admiral Hipper* sailing past at high speed and shortly afterwards they felt the wake of the depth charges she had dropped to ward off enemy submarines:

> Then suddenly it was quiet. We had reached the point where we saw neither people in the water nor flotsam... And then we saw far away from us a silhouette, but by then it was already quarter past one; we had been sitting

for almost four hours. And then a seaman or an officer who sat in the bow yelled that he had one more flare in his gun. 'Now I'll fire it so that they can see we're here. But it's my last so if they don't, then it's the end of us.' Then he fired a flare and in that way caught the attention of a minesweeper that there were some who were still alive.[52]

It was the minesweeper *M-387*, under the command of Oberleutnant Brinkmann, that had spotted them. Rope ladders were thrown down. Margit saw the first person who climbed up lose his footing, fall backwards and disappear into the water. She could not see how she could manage it herself:

> One by one they climbed up, but I could not. I was so frozen stiff, and when I tried to get up, I was frozen in place. There was water in the lifeboat … I said that they should leave me alone: I did not want [to try] any more. And I was so frozen stiff that I felt like it was suddenly hot. And then I fainted. I do not know how they got me up … Then I woke up and I was lying in a bed. Then I was given a very large schnapps. But it was light when I woke up.[53]

It would be two days before Margit stood on solid ground again, when *M-387* reached Swinemünde. All the time she was confined to her cabin: the officers were afraid that she might kill herself. Another survivor, a young mother who had lost her three children, had already thrown herself back into the water.

During the voyage to Swinemünde, the officers on *T-36* tried to compile a list of those rescued, but even they did not fully grasp the enormity of what had happened.

THAT OTHERS MIGHT LIVE

The problem for the *Admiral Hipper* as a rescue vessel was her enormous freeboard: unlike *T-36*, the height of her huge sides made it impossible for the crew to pluck people from the water and deposit them on the deck. One lifeboat from the *Wilhelm Gustloff* managed to reach the *Admiral Hipper* and tie up: it became a magnet for people in the water. Then suddenly the lifeboat was torn from the ship, so quickly that no one grasped what was happening. The lifeboat swung around, upended and came to rest with its keel upwards. What happened to those who had been in the lifeboat no one knew, but it was now obvious that the *Admiral Hipper* was leaving.

The reason was that the hydrophone operator on the *T-36* had heard the unmistakable sounds of one or perhaps two submarines and had immediately informed Kapitänleutnant Hering, who in turn relayed the message to Captain Henigst on the *Admiral Hipper*. Henigst knew that another 3,000 lives were at risk if he kept his ship stationary: he wished the *T-36* success in her rescue work and ordered his ship to depart at full speed.

Many survivors in the water who saw the large warship suddenly and unexpectedly take off at high speed later described their shock and horror: they could not understand why they, who were fighting for their lives, had been abandoned.

A Russian submarine was still there and, with the cruiser gone, it now concentrated on the *T-36*. Robert Hering was undergoing his toughest test. Using soundings of the submarine, he had to manoeuvre his boat to present the smallest possible target:

A Russian submarine tried to torpedo *T-36*. Lieutenant-Commander Hering continuously manoeuvred his boat so that the submarine could not get a broadside. By such actions he twice avoided being hit. (Heinz Schön)

To be on the wreck-site together with a Russian submarine one had to steel oneself. To attack the submarine was out of the question as my crew didn't have the training to do it. ... So there was no other way for us than that of 300–350 metres facing fore or aft so that we avoided the slowly circling submarine and so we do not suffer the same fate as *Wilhelm Gustloff*. The rescue operation wasn't interrupted by this [manoeuvring].[54]

With his hydrophone operator interpreting the submarine's signals and Hering manoeuvring constantly so that the submarine could not get a broadside to aim at, the two vessels played cat and mouse as the rescue proceeded. But then the operator began to suspect there were two submarines there. Hering was thoughtful: the crew was exhausted, there were well over 500 survivors on board, and the boat had almost been hit by one or more torpedoes. A mixture of skill and enormous luck had preserved the *T-36* so far, but Hering did not want to tempt fate much longer:

The situation became, at a stroke, untenable and I took the most difficult decision of my life, which was to immediately abort the rescue operation ... The ship travelled rapidly away, swerved and had just got up to speed when two torpedoes that were intended for us passed on our starboard side.[55]

At this moment, Eva Dorn was down in *T-36*'s engine room, soaked and freezing:

I had undressed and lay on a control panel ... and then it got too hot there ... and when I was up there on the control panel, I heard a whoosh! And the sailors said only that it was another torpedo ... It was very close and they told us that it was only two metres away.[56]

Meanwhile, Adolf Bock sat on the floor below deck, exhausted to the point of indifference:

Then suddenly the propellers began to operate at high speed, and the boat heeled sharply, I noticed that we had made a strong turn. Soon after the ship was shaken by explosions. Everyone sprang up, their faces painted once more with fear and anxiety. And an officer appeared and announced that a hostile submarine had fired a torpedo against the *T-36*. The torpedo's path had been seen from the bridge – it had passed close behind the stern. T-36 immediately went at high speed in the direction of the submarine and threw depth charges.[57]

Robert Hering had no choice: he had to prioritise saving those on board even though it meant abandoning those still in the water:

> Many of my brave crewmen had gone out a few metres from the ship on rafts during the rescue. Two of them had not come back by the time we left, it later came to light. Despite all the research I did later, I could not find them, and one has to assume that they had sacrificed their lives.[58]

Hering estimated that in addition to the crew of 200 men and the 250 refugees they brought with them from Danzig, they had taken 564 survivors from the *Wilhelm Gustloff*. He now had four times as many people on his ship than she was intended to carry. They sailed at top speed westward, to Sassnitz on Rügen Island, where they arrived just after midday on 31 January.

The rescue work was now left to the *Löwe* and to the other vessels Hering believed were coming. On the *Löwe* the men worked frantically to save as many as they could before the cold killed them. But Heli Beneicke, in the water, was unaware of the possibility of rescue:

> I did not know that the rescue ship was on its way … [there were] just a lot of dead people clung to each other. But I took myself further and further away, so that I would not be sucked down: there were many who were drawn into her [when the ship sank]. There was a raft … and, thank God, it was not snowing anymore.[59]

She climbed up on the raft, where there were already others huddled. She could not recall exactly how long, but it was several hours before she was rescued by the *Löwe*.

BORN ON A TORPEDO BOAT

Even though *T-36* had dropped depth charges to try and chase the submarine away, the *Löwe* was running a huge risk as she continued to rescue survivors. The lifeboat with Battalion Chief Richter on board was spotted and everyone was hastily brought on board.

Among those saved was the pregnant woman from Elbing. Everyone was desperate to get her on board the *Löwe* before the baby was born, and she was quickly taken below deck to get warm.

On the *Löwe* the survivors began to thaw out. Wet and frozen, the reality that he had been saved finally dawned on Dr Richter. Now he heard that there was a desperate search throughout the ship for a doctor. He found a dry coat and went to find where he was needed:

> I was not a little surprised when I saw the pregnant woman: it was the same woman I had given an injection to stop the birth in the labour ward on the *Gustloff* and wrapped in blankets carried by two of my men into a lifeboat. When the young woman saw me, she started crying. During the next few minutes, half standing and half lying, she gave birth in the cramped cabin to a boy. It was challenging, without any aids, just with my hands, everything else was gone, nothing was left. According to the mother's wishes, the boy came to be called 'Leo' because he was born aboard the *Löwe* ['Lion'].[60]

Heli Beneicke photographed on the fiftieth anniversary of the *Wilhelm Gustloff* disaster.

Werner Schoop, recovering from his shock at not being rescued by *T-36*, spotted another lifeboat. It was mainly occupied by men, who had miraculously managed to stay dry. One of them had a flashlight that he constantly played up and down: as a result the *Löwe* was able to find them.

Many others, whether in the water, on rafts or in lifeboats, lost heart when they saw *T-36* disappear. They could only see their immediate surroundings and even if this included the *Löwe*, making towards her in the choppy sea was not easy. And although *Löwe*'s searchlight played constantly over the surface of the sea, it was easy to miss people in these conditions. The crew knew that as time passed the chances of finding anyone in the water still alive were reducing rapidly. The Baltic was taking more victims minute by minute. Those who had jumped into the water from the *Wilhelm Gustloff* lightly dressed had little chance of survival in the 4° water. But some might have been able to hold out longer had they known that the *Löwe* was not alone. Among the drifting lifeboats, survivors thought a convoy was approaching, which gave them new hope.

In fact, several ships were on their way. Motor Vessel *Gotenland* was among them, even though Captain Heinz Vollmer and his crew did not know they were heading towards the *Wilhelm Gustloff*'s last position. The *Gotenland* had sailed from Pillau on 30 January with more than 3,300 refugees on board. She was not a large ship, simply a freighter of 5,266grt and not built for carrying passengers. She was now in a convoy with two minesweepers, *M-341* and *M-387*. These naval ships were also laden with refugees, and equally had no idea they were sailing towards the site of a major disaster.

They had chosen Fairway 58, perhaps for the same reason as Captain Petersen on the *Wilhelm Gustloff*. Their destination was Swinemünde and their 'cargo' was regarded as extremely valuable: the vast majority were women with young children.

Shortly before reaching the position where the *Wilhelm Gustloff* had sunk, a lookout on the *Gotenland* spotted flotsam and reported that he was seeing boats and rafts ahead, adding: 'You have a ship that has gone down!' The *Gotenland* slowed and the closer they came to the wreck site, the clearer it became that something terrible had happened. Not only was there flotsam, rafts and lifeboats everywhere, cries for help were coming from all directions. It was difficult to work out what had occurred, but from the number of drifting boats and rafts Captain Vollmer realised that the ship that had been sunk must have been a big one.

The *Gotenland* was already packed – 'there was barely even room for a mouse' – but Vollmer had a duty to follow the law of the sea and save whatever lives he could. At the same time he knew that in doing so he was subjecting the convoy to great danger: evidence of the havoc Russian submarines could wreak was right in front of him.

On all three ships the men began to prepare as best they could to accommodate the survivors, the refugees already on board squeezing themselves together even more tightly and joining in the rescue work. It was well past one o'clock in the morning when the search began. By this time no one floating in the water was still alive: any survivors would be on a raft or in a lifeboat.

It was later discovered that atmospheric disturbances had prevented messages about the *Wilhelm Gustloff*'s fate being received. The steamer *Göttingen* knew nothing about the disaster but just happened to sail straight to the *Wilhelm Gustloff*'s last position. She too was in convoy, escorted by the minesweeper *M-375* and the torpedo recovery vessel *TF-19*. *Göttingen*, at 6,200grt, was slightly larger than *Gotenland*.

The *Göttingen* had been anchored in the Hela roads because of the weather and had only departed at six o'clock in the evening on 30 January when the escorts arrived. It was terribly crowded on board: there were 2,436 wounded soldiers and 1,190 refugees at Hela, so with the air-defence troops, medical personnel and crew, there were more than 4,000 people on her. Every deck was packed, with many of the wounded lying in beds. Captain Fredrich Segelken knew that it would be incredibly dangerous to stop, so he was greatly surprised when First Mate Braumüller knocked on his cabin door at half past two in the morning and announced that several other ships had been sighted ahead and were reducing speed:

> When I threw myself up to the bridge, I saw a huge oil slick straight away and then I could hear faint cries for help and these grew rapidly in strength. I immediately stopped the engines and ordered 'All hands on deck and make both rescue boats ready!' I promptly informed my escort leader and put the ship upwind. The entire crew along with the air defence soldiers immediately understood the situation and both lifeboats were launched into the sea without problem, although the davits and the blocks were iced. We made full advantage of our new searchlight. I was totally convinced that

I did not have to worry about how the vessel was manoeuvred right then and worried only about saving the greatest number of people.[61]

The rescue boats rowed quickly into the debris field of rafts, damaged or intact lifeboats and all conceivable flotsam from the *Wilhelm Gustloff*. They also saw many life jackets: all empty.

The searchlight played over the area but as the minutes went by fewer and fewer people survived. For every ten people they found, only one was still alive. They had stumbled into a floating graveyard, driving corpses before them. The rescue boat from *M-375* found fifty people in half an hour but only one alive. So as not to lose sight of its own boat, the mine-sweeper picked its way slowly through the field of bodies while keeping a constant eye on their own men.

Winfried Harthun was a 7-year-old whose mother had put him on a raft on the *Wilhelm Gustloff*'s deck. But the raft had hit the railing and as it dangled between the ship's side and the sea Winfried was thrown in a huge arc into the water. Luckily, someone spotted him and he had been dragged onto another raft. This was eventually spotted by *T-36* and everyone was rescued – except Winfried. He was not fast enough, and when Robert Hering gave the order for his torpedo boat to leave, the boy was left alone:

Hour after hour I was entirely alone in the freezing cold night at sea. Somewhere I came in contact with a lifeboat and there were sailors and a woman [in it]. But because there was no rudder on the boat they could not help me and bring me over. In between, a man took hold of the end of the rope on the raft, but I could not help him. He died, and followed me everywhere, with his head hanging in the water all night. Slowly I became more tired and fell asleep.[62]

Eventually, one of the *Göttingen*'s rescue boats had spotted Winfried's raft. It is likely that the crew thought he was already dead, but a rope was thrown anyway, and this movement of the rope half-awakened him. He had been on the raft for nearly six hours. About four o'clock in the morning he finally reached the safety of the *Göttingen*.

The *Löwe* had taken on board 472 survivors. When the commander, Paul Prüfe, quickly inspected his vessel, he was forced to conclude that his torpedo boat was way over capacity. There were people in every corridor, in every cabin and every corner space. Prüfe knew that with so many people on board and the danger from submarines he must depart as quickly as possible. It was two o'clock in the morning when he gave the order to sail for Kolberg on the North Pomeranian coast, leaving the search to other ships.

Sigrid Bergfeld, who along with Ursula Pautz had survived being trapped in the *Wilhelm Gustloff*'s swimming pool on the lower deck, was on a raft until the faint dawn broke. One by one, the others on the raft first lost consciousness, then they lost their balance and finally they fell into the water. She began to fear this would be her own fate. However, she became more and more tired, closed her eyes and these thoughts slipped away.

When she opened her eyes she was lying on a berth on the torpedo boat *TF-19*. At first she was bewildered but it was explained that she had been found at the last possible moment, when she was almost completely frozen – 'stiff as a board' as she described it later.

With the dawn came a considerable improvement in the weather, but the merciless cold remained. On the rescue ships they realised that there would be no more survivors, but they still had only a piecemeal knowledge of the number who had been rescued. Eight vessels had participated in the search and they went to four different ports: Gotenhafen, Kolberg, Sassnitz and Swinemünde.

A BUNDLE IN A BLANKET

Patrol Boat *1703* was the last vessel to arrive at the scene. Her searchlight played over the area but they saw only empty boats, drifting rafts, wreckage and the dead. Approaching one lifeboat, Boatswain Werner Fick jumped down just to check if anyone was alive. He found the corpses of a woman and a girl, which he and Mate Fünrock took on to the patrol boat. He then jumped back into the lifeboat to see if he could find anything that might identify the two. The bottom of the boat was covered with snow but he could see that there were clothes there. Someone on the patrol boat shouted to him to look in the stern.

For some reason a rolled-up blanket caught Fick's attention. It was stiff with ice and partly covered with snow, but he picked it up and found to his surprise that there was a baby, about 1-year-old, inside. He was shocked to discover that the baby was still alive – surely it was impossible that anyone, let alone an infant, could survive for that long in the cold. He quickly carried the little bundle to the ship and rushed into Captain Hanefeld's cabin, where he put the baby on the table. News spread around the ship like lightning and seconds later, the Navy doctor Fleischer came in, just as amazed as the others. Fleischer was uncertain whether the baby would survive: he was extremely cold. But then the baby boy opened his eyes and looked at the men: he was clearly a survivor.

Fick and his wife Marie had sadly never managed to have a child themselves and now he believed that divine providence had sent this child to him. He decided on the spot to adopt the child. 'The boy will be called Peter,' he told his shipmates.

The baby was the last survivor to be rescued from the *Wilhelm Gustloff*. There was nothing more Patrol Boat *1703* could do, so she finished her search and returned to Gotenhafen. As soon as she arrived Fick sent a telegram to Marie:

 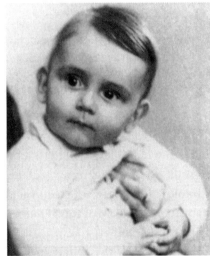

Above left: Boatswain Werner Fick on board his patrol ship *1703*. (Heinz Schön)

Above right: The last survivor recovered from the *Wilhelm Gustloff* was a 1-year-old boy. Werner Fick, who found him, adopted him, giving him the name Peter. For many years a custody battle raged around Peter and his identity but this was never conclusively proven. (Heinz Schön)

We've had a child. I have found a one-year boy in the Baltic Sea. I'll take him with me. On 5th February I will be in Swinemünde. Please come and fetch Peter![63]

Later, however, a battle over paternity was launched that would last for years. It was never resolved but it is possible the boy was actually Frank-Michael Freymüller, the son of Hermann Freymüller, a commissioned officer in Danzig who had sent his wife, daughter and son on the *Wilhelm Gustloff*. Hermann never gave up hope that someone in his family had survived.

At the end of the war Fick was held in a British detention camp for some time but then released. When applying for a passport for the child, the authorities started to ask questions, and wondered if they should seek his true relatives through the Red Cross search service. Fick declared that he had no intention of returning the boy and the family travelled back to their home, which was now in the Eastern Zone. Hermann Freymüller lived in the West and began an unsuccessful custody battle that lasted the rest of his life. The Iron Curtain came to separate them and Peter Fick grew up in the German Democratic Republic, becoming a captain in the East German merchant marine. He never met Hermann Freymüller.

ARRIVAL

T-19 sailed to Gotenhafen. For the survivors, this was the last place on earth to which they wanted to return. Only two of them had the strength to walk down the gangway unaided. One was the 19-year-old Helmut Zokolowski, whose fourteen relatives were at the bottom of the Baltic, trapped in the bow of the *Wilhelm Gustloff*.

Just after half past seven on the morning of 31 January 1945, the *Löwe* docked at the wharf in Kolberg. In better condition than those on *T-19*, 472 survivors silently staggered down the gangway and began to walk towards the places where they were to be quartered. Someone described it as 'a train of misery': some barely had clothes on their bodies, others walked without shoes on the icy cobbles. Stunned by the shock of their experiences, not one of them could answer questions about what had happened.

The same scene played out in Sassnitz when *T-36* arrived at the railway wharf just before two o'clock in the afternoon. The sick and those who were too weak to walk, along with women and children, were guided to an ex-Danish steamer.

Eva Dorn's clothes had dried during the night and in the morning she had been able to dress again. She went around *T-36* to see if she could recognise anyone:

> There I saw Chief Doctor Peters ... He had seen how his wife who was seven months pregnant had perished. It was not easy ... but I was very happy that he was alive.[64]

The day after the rescue she found a tailor's shop, which mended her torn uniform. Now she felt relatively smart:

> And so I went out. There was a beautiful park and then came a gentleman who approached me and asked, 'Could you possibly give me an answer, were there any Marinen Helferinnen rescued from the Gustloff?' I answered, 'Yes, I'm one of them.' 'You? You don't look like it!' And it was ... the painter Bock. And he wanted stories from the accident because he wanted to make a drawing of it ... But I wanted to go to Chief Peters because I knew what condition he was in and how bad he was feeling ... I got in there and there was a lady and [he said] 'Dörnchen, my Mary is alive!'[65]

Karl-Heinz Peters and his wife had jumped almost simultaneously into the water but they had become separated and Peters had assumed that his wife had died. But they had an agreement: if they were separated in one way or another, they would tell one of his schoolmates in Stralsund. That was how they were able to find each other again so quickly.

Heinz Schön was one of the last to leave *T-36*. After descending the gangway, he went down on his knees on the dock, feeling the cobble-stones with his hands. Some thought he was mad, but Schön could hardly believe that he had survived. That afternoon he went to the post office to send a telegram to his parents. After he had written the words 'I'm still alive!' the shock finally overcame over him and he began to weep. Some seemed to take offence at this crying man – because the news of the loss of the *Wilhelm Gustloff* was yet to be made public.

The wreck of the *Wilhelm Gustloff* on the seabed today. (Jonas Dahm)

Milda Bendrich and her daughter were also saved by *T-36* but her parents were gone and so too were the two old neighbours for whom she had struggled to get travel permits. For the rest of her life she lived with the guilt that if she had left them in Gotenhafen they might have lived. After landing in Sassnitz, she and Inge made their way to Plön (a district in Schleswig-Holstein) where she had friends. By the time they reached them, the news of the wreck had broken:

Of course, Nanni told their friends and acquaintances in Plön about Wilhelm Gustloff's sinking and she also told them about me. A few days after our arrival, the doorbell rang and there stood two Hitler Youth. They threatened us with terrible reprisals unless we stopped our chatter about the sinking immediately. As things were then, we naturally chose to be cautious.[66]

'A GREAT HAPPINESS'

Rear Admiral Konrad Engelhardt received the news at his office on the morning of 31 January. As the day went on, and more and more details emerged, Engelhardt and his staff had a great deal to discuss. He could not understand why the *Wilhelm Gustloff* was allowed to sail with such an insufficient escort as just the *Löwe*. Engelhardt was well informed about his ships and he considered this had been pure folly. The *Löwe* could not even defend herself against aircraft and apparently even less against submarines. The Rear Admiral thought it was indefensible. Engelhardt also soon realised that the *Wilhelm Gustloff* had not been under the Ninth Security Division's protection and, what is more, the Tenth Security Division never received the message that the ship had been sunk. Nevertheless, he told his subordinates that they had to learn from the disaster.

Engelhardt informed Dönitz, which resulted in a meeting being called in Berlin. Adolf Hitler attended, it being felt important that the Führer was informed of what had happened. The minutes noted:

> The Commander in Chief of the Navy reported the loss of passenger ship Wilhelm Gustloff by a submarine torpedo north of Stolpe Bank, adding that in relation to the extensive transport across the Baltic Sea one must initially take losses into account and, despite the painful tragedy, which still is a single occurrence, it is considered as great good fortune that there have not been more losses.[67]

Perhaps it was a meeting with no purpose; perhaps Adolf Hitler had far greater disasters to worry about than the more than 9,000 people who disappeared with the *Wilhelm Gustloff* on 31 January 1945. However, these dry minutes now seem too complacent, given what was to happen four months later.

Engelhardt imposed what he considered to be a sensible measure: ships with large numbers of passengers were to have a sufficient escort before they would be given permission to depart. Unfortunately there were not always enough warships to form escorts and within days misfortune and coincidence played their parts in undermining his good intentions.

The depth charges from the *Wilhelm Gustloff*'s rescue vessels had not destroyed Alexander Marinesco's submarine, although they came close.

S-13 had escaped by a hair's breadth and although shaken she came away unscathed. Marinesco was convinced that he would be rewarded for his actions, but he had two month's supplies on board so there was no reason to return to the base in Turku just yet.

What he did not know was that his report about sinking a vessel of 20,000 tons was received with the greatest scepticism by Captain Kurnikow in Kronstadt. He had experience of Marinesco's exaggerations and, not being able to pick up anything on German radio traffic about such a large ship being sunk, he dismissed the claim as yet another of his overstatements.

When Marinesco reported to his base that *S-13* had sunk a very large ship, his claim was taken with a pinch of salt. News of the sinking of the *Wilhelm Gustloff* had been suppressed by the German media and therefore the Russian interception stations heard nothing about the disaster. Here a torpedo is being loaded on board a Russian submarine. (Heinz Schön)

S-13 continued to patrol Danzig Bay, cruising the waters while waiting for the next bite. During the day she was under water, surfacing at night to recharge her batteries. More than a week passed without spotting anything of interest: Marinesco did not want to waste torpedoes on the small vessels that passed by; nor did he wish to draw unwanted attention to his submarine.

In the evening of 6 February, with the sea calm, First Mate Jefremenkow was on watch when he saw another submarine surge past barely 5m away. It moved very quickly but Jefremenkow could hardly believe it: a German submarine had passed by without noticing them.

Two days later, again in the evening, *S-13* was on the surface and Marinesco was scanning the horizon with his binoculars. He saw a light and thought it might belong to a German cruiser. It was a convoy: he readied his crew for the attack. At that moment one of the convoy suddenly swerved and was heading straight for them. Panic almost erupted on the *S-13*. Quickly, the submarine dived. For an hour she remained perfectly still. To minimise the risk of detection, Marinesco decided to fire while the vessel was still underwater. He edged closer and when 400m away, Marinesco gave the order to fire two torpedoes. Both hit and exploded. A third explosion on board followed. The ship sank quickly. Shortly afterwards, Marinesco proudly telegraphed his base to announce that once again he had sunk a big ship and had sent a great many of Hitler's men to the Baltic seabed.

6

THE BEAUTIFUL WHITE *STEUBEN*

In the bathroom, during the voyage I tried to wash seven-day-old blood from my face and the dust and dirt, and eventually, I was feeling decidedly better. I lay down again but I could not really fall asleep, then there was a terrible groaning and moaning around me and I also noticed that the [nursing] sisters went now here, now there, covered a person up and said that someone has died again. At twelve o'clock at night I slept well and woke up only when I was shaken by a terrible blow about ten to one on the morning of 10th February.

Franz Huber[1]

Many passenger ships had been converted into hospital ships at the beginning of the Second World War. Even before the outbreak, such an eventuality had been considered as part of the preparations for Hitler's long-planned intentions. In 1937, twenty-four merchant ships were listed as prospective hospital ships. By 1939, this fleet included the *Robert Ley* and *Wilhelm Gustloff*, but in fact their careers as hospital ships were short. The *Wilhelm Gustloff* was anchored in Gotenhafen for most of the war while *Robert Ley* was moored in Pillau.

As the war neared its end, the increasingly critical situation for the German armies in East Prussia became clearer with each passing day. The number of wounded grew dramatically in parallel with the swelling number of refugees. More vessels were required for evacuation of the wounded, and of German civilians desperate to evade the advancing Russians.

Ships painted white with large red crosses indicated to submarines, aircraft and artillery that they were carrying the wounded, and as such should not be attacked. Both sides were aware of this but during the last

General von Steuben before she was painted white.

year of the war the Baltic was no longer a 'sea of peace' but a maritime battleground, where ships of all descriptions – including hospital and refugee ships– were fair game. Aware that a red cross no longer guaranteed protection, after the sinking of the *Wilhelm Gustloff* no German hospital ship was allowed to sail without an escort.

Stuttgart, originally owned by Hamburg Africa Line, had enjoyed a career in the *Kraft durch Freude* fleet but had been converted into a hospital ship in Hamburg. She made a number of transport voyages in the Baltic, as well as to Kirkenes in the far north of Norway before finally sailing to Gotenhafen. In a huge aerial offensive against the port on 9 October 1943 the *Stuttgart*, even though she was clearly marked as a hospital ship, was not spared. She received several direct hits and in minutes was transformed into a blazing ball of fire. The inferno spread so rapidly that many on board were burnt alive. So little was left of the ship that she was towed out to sea and sunk, with many of the bodies still on board. The number of lives lost is unknown.

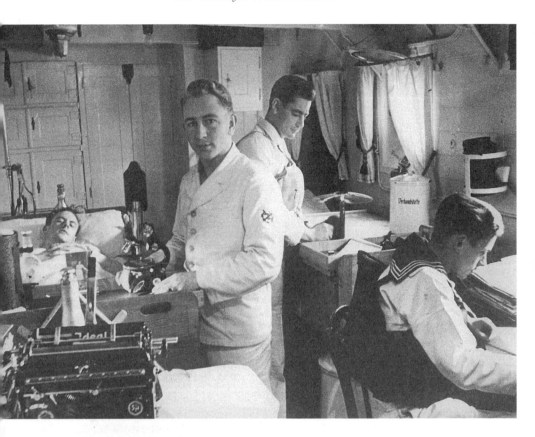

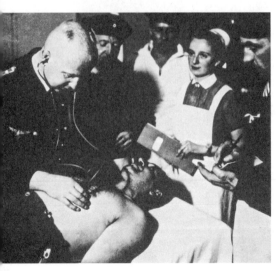

Above: As the demand for troop transports grew so did the need for hospital ships. Many passenger ships were turned into floating hospitals or simply transporters of the wounded. During the latter part of the war, the non-combatant status of hospital ships became less respected and they ran the same risks of being hit as a military vessel.

Left: Examination on a hospital ship – note the badge on the doctor's uniform.

General von Steuben was a popular passenger liner. This picture shows her in Valletta harbour, Malta.

The *Steuben* before she was painted white. At the outbreak of the war she was used as a transport for the wounded but later she was designated as a hospital ship, with all appropriate equipment. Even major operations could be performed on board.

General von Steuben was originally named *München*, and belonged to the North German Lloyd of Bremen, from where she sailed the North Atlantic. She was the first German merchant vessel to arrive in New York after the First World War and so came to signify a new beginning for the German merchant fleet. She had been intended to become a cruise ship taking tourists to Spitsbergen but on 11 February 1930, while in New York, a fire broke out on board. She was carrying a cargo of potassium and peat, which self-ignited. Luckily no one was killed but the fire was so devastating that the ship had to be completely rebuilt. Fortunately, the engines were undamaged and she was able to return to Bremerhaven for the repairs to be carried out.

She was rebuilt in a contemporary style and at the same time converted from coal to oil. Her name was also changed to the *General von Steuben*, after the eighteenth-century Prussian soldier who became George Washington's chief of staff. For most, the name was too much of a mouthful, and they chose to call her just the *Steuben*.

THE FLAGSHIP OF THE CRUISE FLEET

When cruising as a leisure activity began to take off in earnest, passengers demanded comfort, and particularly en suite facilities. Many ships were too old fashioned to meet such demands and were decommissioned but the *Steuben* was perfect for the trade. She was marketed as the 'beautiful white *Steuben*' and became very popular. In a North German Lloyd advertisement she was called the 'flagship of the cruise fleet', and the beauty of her lines was highlighted in a Swedish brochure:

> At the sight of some vessels, it happens that even old experienced sailors stand still to quietly admire the ship's shape and lines, its hull, masts and funnels. Their eyes slide almost caressingly over the ship, calmly and majestically before them; they nod hardly noticeably and mumble 'a beautiful vessel'. How often are these words said at the sight of the world-famous and universally popular white Steuben … Yes, everyone rejoices to see the beautiful, white General von Steuben, built with so much care and devotion.[2]

An interesting detail is the davit, made by Welin in England, which was similar to those used on the *Titanic*.

She was refitted again around the turn of the year 1937/38 with even more stylish interior fittings. Another promotional leaflet described *Steuben* thus:

Standing at the top of what the art of our time and technology can perform … Life on board is a constant source of pleasure and recreation, cheerful activities follow one another on the white ship, which constantly carries its passengers to new destinations, to foreign ports.[3]

Passengers who travelled first class could not complain about the comfort and the beautiful decor. She reflected the spirit of the times, when skilled craftsmen made everything on board.

After 20 December 1938, she came to be called the *Steuben* semi-officially. Suspected of being gay, the old general was out of favour with the Nazis and although the name on the ship was not removed, 'General von' was dropped.

Like many other merchant vessels, she was requisitioned when war broke out. From 4 December 1939, the *Steuben* was the command vessel in Danzig-Neufahrwasser and was later to be taken as a *Verwundetentransportschiff* (transport ship for the wounded). This was not quite the same thing as a hospital ship. The latter, painted white and with red crosses, would be protected by the Geneva Convention, but transport ships for the wounded were painted grey and fitted with anti-aircraft artillery. As the war progressed, it became an academic point: international conventions were ignored. Indeed, just after the German invasion of Russia in 1941, the Russian military command frankly declared that they did not care about respecting German hospital ships when the German government had already committed systematic abuses of international agreements. The bombing of the Soviet hospital ship *Armenia* by Axis aircraft on 7 November 1941 with the loss of an estimated 5,000 lives shows how little conventions were respected.

The *Steuben*'s transformation required a great deal of work. Much of her loose interior fittings disappeared, although many fixtures remained. This meant the injured lay in a field hospital surrounded by hand-made panels and stucco decorations.

In the autumn of 1944, she sailed between Swinemünde, Pillau, Riga, Gotenhafen and other ports to collect and ferry the wounded. On a few occasions she was attacked by Soviet aircraft, but her anti-aircraft guns successfully warded them off.

As with any other on-board hospital, there were a large number of medical personnel, from doctors and specialists to nurses and assistants. Indeed, the civilian crew of 160 was outnumbered by the 270 members of the military medical team. Relatively advanced surgical procedures could be undertaken, and once the *Steuben* began to evacuate refugees as well, it was so common for children to be born on board her that a maternity section was established.

In January 1945, East Prussian stocks of supplies, including fuel, began to drop to a precarious level. This made the situation for the small port towns along Danzig Bay even more desperate, unprepared as they were for the huge influx of refugees caused by the advancing Soviet troops.

On 23 January, the *Steuben* loaded large quantities of medical equipment and supplies in Danzig for the trip to Swinemünde via Pillau. On the return journey, the ship was ordered to change her course so she could participate in the search for survivors of the *Wilhelm Gustloff*, but when she reached the site in the morning on 31 January, all search operations had already been cancelled. In the freezing weather, there was no longer a chance that anyone could still be alive.

At the same moment in Swinemünde, another hospital ship, *Berlin*, was manoeuvring to join a convoy, but drifting ice forced her to bump against a mine that promptly exploded. The officers decided to ground *Berlin*, which they managed to accomplish successfully. She partially sank but only one person was killed. The *Berlin* was left semi-submerged for the remainder of the war.

When the *Steuben* returned to Pillau after another trip to Swinemünde, the supplies she had ordered had not been delivered and she now had very limited resources with which to perform the most urgent surgery, let alone take care of the thousands of people who would shortly be coming on board.

The story of the *Wilhelm Gustloff*'s sinking had travelled like wildfire all along the Pomeranian coast. Even though many Germans were now putting all their hopes in a rescue by sea, it was a stark reminder that the voyages were anything but safe. The captain of a corvette in Pillau by the name of Schön later recalled that:

In the harbour all types of vessels were crowded. Dreadful scenes were played out. The people were like animals. Most of the refugees were not aware of the dangers of the journey across the sea. Yet no refugee ship that had gone from Pillau had been sunk by mines, torpedoes or air strikes: all the ships had come through and everyone had been saved. On 1st February, however, some refugees and the people of Pillau had a shock, but thank God there were not many, perhaps a thousand or more. At night, two mine-sweepers entered the harbour and anchored and the rumour of this spread quickly. Immediately apartments, gathering halls and barracks came to life. They ran to the harbour, just in order to be able to board.

The vessels did not carry refugees. Guards were standing to keep the refugees back. Then the trucks came up and the ships were emptied of their cargo. Refugees' surprise turned to dismay: from minesweepers stretchers were carried ashore, one by one, and those carried were dead. Stretchers were carried to the trucks and loaded on, they came back, came back, back again. This happened on both ships and it lasted a long time. One of the stretcher-bearers then revealed the truth: these were 123 corpses the minesweepers had recovered from the Baltic: the dead from *Wilhelm Gustloff*.[4]

For those witnesses waiting for a berth on a ship it was an eerie reminder of what could happen. The bodies were buried at the cemetery in Pillau without any of them being identified.

The injured to be evacuated on the *Steuben* had, in many cases, been brought directly from the front with wounds that had not been tended for several days. They were bloodied and dirty; they were hungry and frozen after being transported along bomb-damaged roads. Many were completely exhausted after several nights' lack of sleep. But the rate of loading them on board the *Steuben* was frantic, as is shown by the complete lack of passenger lists or even lists of the wounded. The exact number of people who were on board has never been established. Time was scarce: the luxury of the week taken to embark everyone on the *Wilhelm Gustloff* could no longer be enjoyed.

Anti-aircraft Captain Franz Huber had been wounded in the head by shrapnel. He had also been in a vehicle collision and was suffering severe bleeding in the genital area:

With these injuries, I was taken to the field hospital in Pillau and was medically treated. My friends later told me that they removed shrapnel in my head cavity with strong magnets. Early in the morning of 9th February 1945, I was part of a shipment to Germany. I was sent in an ambulance a few hours earlier on extremely rough roads through Pillau to the harbour. Because of my six-day-old injury, I had a high fever and almost unbearable pain. The journey to Pillau's harbour where we were loaded on to a vessel felt like an eternity but in the end we were carried aboard *Steuben*.[5]

Bavarian that he was, he had never been on a big ship. At first he could not see much from his stretcher, but quickly discovered that she was like a small town.

Another of the wounded was Corporal Alfred Burgner, who belonged to a company of grenadiers. He had a severe arm injury sustained during fierce fighting in which his unit had retreated after heavy losses. After scanty bandaging he was sent to a temporary hospital in Heilsberg, but it was impossible to stay there because of the Russian advance. His journey continued to Pillau, the final leg completed in a small boat:

Those who couldn't walk were lifted on board on stretchers. They were usually placed in the lower parts of a vessel, leaving them almost no chance of escape if the ship should begin to sink. (Kurt Gerdau)

Here we were billeted in a large barrack room and a man stood watching for the next hospital ship that might take us from Pillau to Swinemünde. The announcement [that we were to be evacuated] was received with joy. When, however, we heard about the *Gustloff*'s sinking, and some victims had been brought to Pillau to be buried, we understood that our transport by a ship westward was not as safe as we had initially thought, and that escape by the Baltic Sea had its risks even in a large ship. As there was no other escape route my comrades and I put our trust in God that luck would stand by us and we were overjoyed to come aboard *Steuben* on the morning of 9th February 1945.[6]

When he saw the ship in the dock, he decided to stay on deck during the entire voyage. He reasoned that should something happen he would have a chance to make it to a lifeboat. However, a medic found Burgner and ordered him below. The deck, he said, was intended for the refugees: the wounded should stick to their respective infirmaries:

The orderly took me two stairways down and after I got a blanket and a mattress I took a place in a hallway right next to a toilet door. All places in cabins and corridors were already totally full, because I was one of the last to come on board.[7]

REFUGEES AND THE SICK

The refugees were taken aboard a vessel that was never intended to be an evacuation ship and the huge influx of refugees caused the collapse of all bureaucratic accounting. This was also true of the convoys that accompanied the *Steuben*. Russian troops had broken through the defensive lines at Königsberg; the front was approaching rapidly and relentlessly, increasing the pressure on every ship that was able to depart. Despite some 800 refugees being taken on board the *Steuben*, the quayside in Pillau was still densely packed, and when none of these were allowed to embark there was near panic.

Thick clouds hung over the harbour as the ship departed. Along the quays people stood still hoping for a ship to take them westwards. Probably some imagined that the *Steuben*, one of the largest vessels in the Baltic, would be back in a few days – after all, she had been back and forth many times.

The ship's elegant ballroom was transformed into a hospital ward. As many sick and wounded as possible were packed in, but refugees were also allowed to board. The latter were mostly lodged in the upper parts of the ship.

TRUSTING IN PROVIDENCE

Some doctors counted their patients just before the ship departed, but in the confusion that prevailed it was not possible to establish precise figures. Approximately 2,800 injured were on board, 800 refugees, 100 soldiers, 270 employees of the fleet and the medical staff and 160 crew members, additional medical staff and air-defence troops, so the total was around 4,260 people. This was far more than initially planned. There were insufficient supplies for a long trip with so many people, and insufficient equipment in the event of an accident … and there simply were not enough staff to evacuate so many people safely and effectively if an accident occurred.

Neither Captain Hermann Hohmann nor his Second Officer, Johannes Grage, had any idea of how, if the ship was attacked, they could possibly deal with this number of people, but they knew that there was not enough life-preserving equipment. The maximum capacity was just under 4,000 but the latest estimates they heard had shown that they had far more than that, but Hohmann kept his worries to himself: 'they don't lead anywhere'. There was nothing he could do.

Once the pilot from Pillau had left, *Steuben* steered out to sea towards Hela where the escort was waiting. This consisted of torpedo boat *T-196* and the smaller *TF-10*. On board *T-196* were about 200 refugees from Königsberg and with this extra load the vessel was not as easy to manoeuvre as usual.

The *Steuben* was a steady ship, built for the North Atlantic. She had been through all kinds of weather and therefore the crew thought the 'duck pond' of the Baltic was not much to worry about. She was also a relatively fast ship, able to zig-zag to avoid a submarine. But convoys are governed by the speed of the slowest ship, and that was 12 knots.

A deceptive calm settled over the ship, but soon after the convoy left Hela, two Russian aircraft were spotted. They immediately attacked *T-196*, which returned fire and drove them away. The incident raised concern throughout the convoy, although no more aircraft were seen. By the afternoon calm was restored. On the *Steuben*, none of the passengers seemed bothered that there were more passengers than lifeboat places, nor that if anything happened to one of the ships in the convoy, there was virtually no room on any of the others to take them. If anything did happen, then surely there were other ships in the vicinity. The refugees were further reassured when the out-swung lifeboats were swung back in. But those in command knew that the sea has no mercy. The water temperature was too low for anyone to survive for long, even with a lifebelt. As a precaution, even the doctors had been issued with firearms, just in case panic broke out.

But how would someone unfamiliar with the ship ever find their way up on deck where the lifeboats were? The *Steuben*, with her long corridors, halls, lounges, stairways and numerous decks, was like a steel maze. To get to know her, one would have to be on board for several days, to learn how to get from one of the lower decks up to lifeboats. For the bedridden wounded soldiers, this was academic: they would not be going anywhere.

Corporal Heinz Portmann, a signaller, had no such worries. It was the first large passenger ship to which he had ever been assigned and he greatly enjoyed exploring and getting to know it:

And it was not long before I had explored everywhere on board, put myself at ease and got somewhat used to such a large vessel. I was surprised on one of the first days on board when I was met [by] some Chinese people, who in answer to my question gave me to understand that they belonged to the civilian crew and worked in *Steuben*'s washing area.[8]

The doctors were not able to take time off. As on all their voyages westwards, they were preoccupied with complicated operations, assessing patients' injuries and prioritising care. They worked intensively, whatever the hour of the day.

A PUFF OF FLAME AND SMOKE VISIBLE

The dog watch came: time to change the officers on the *Steuben*'s bridge. As they did so, they noticed with alarm that sparks were flying from the chimney of *TF-10*. Her stokers were burning as much fuel as they could to keep up with the other two vessels but they were using too much charcoal laden with coal dust. This, in combination with an elderly furnace, was the cause of these sparks. And they were making *TF-10* very visible.

The officers were right to be worried. Shortly before midnight, Alexander Marinesco and First Officer Jefremenkow on the *S-13* watched the strange sparks on the horizon in amazement. The submarine's hydrophone operator reported that he could hear the vibrations of ships' propellers clearly. Marinesco now knew that he had found a German convoy. The long days of idleness were over: he ordered his crew to be ready to attack.

Then suddenly one of the convoy's escorts changed course and headed directly towards the submarine. Marinesco thought for a moment that they had been discovered. They dived immediately but continued to track the convoy. Half an hour later, the submarine resurfaced close to the big ship, which Marinesco thought could be a cruiser of 20,000 tonnes. To attack immediately was risky and therefore he decided instead to try to fire on the ship with his stern torpedoes.

At 00:53, the first torpedo struck the *Steuben*'s starboard side, just forward of the bridge. The second torpedo struck amidships. A huge column of water shot up, almost reaching the tops of the masts. The bridge windows were briefly hidden behind a huge wall of water, but once they were clear, Captain Hohmann could see that the anti-aircraft battery in the bow had been tossed away like shuttlecocks. There was nothing left of the anti-aircraft crew: they had all been washed overboard. Hohmann ordered the immediate halt of the engines and relayed

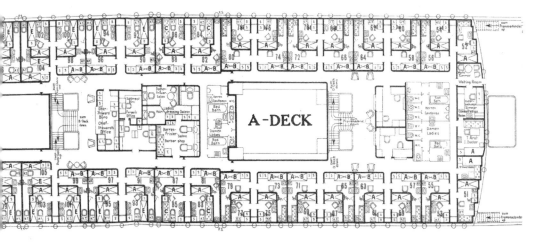

For a landlubber the layout of a ship is always confusing and it usually takes a few days to find one's way around. The *Steuben* was filled beyond capacity with people and the narrow corridors became death traps during the evacuation.

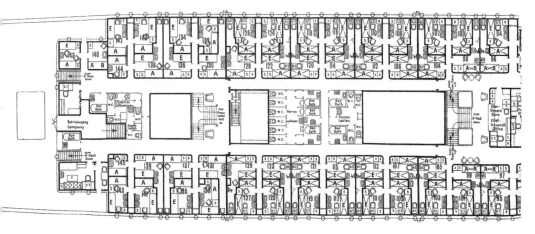

to the escort what had happened. He also announced that given the speed of which the ship was capable, there was a chance that he could take her to the shallow water of Stolpe Bank, 12 nautical miles to the south-east of Bornholm, and ground her. He was, however, being optimistic – his officers had not yet had time to assess the damage the torpedoes had caused.

Anti-aircraft Captain Franz Huber had had about an hour's sleep before being roughly woken by the powerful explosions. The world seemed to be imploding:

The first torpedo hit a little forward of the bridge; the second hit her amidships between the funnels.

> The whole body of the ship trembled and shook, and one had the feeling that it would burst any minute. In every room people screamed and yelled. Medics and nurses stood in the doorways as the ship violently flew back and forth. The wounded standing upright were immediately thrown against the walls. The rest of the wounded fell over each other. We fell again and were hurt again as if we hadn't been hurt already.[9]

Everything not fixed down on *Steuben* was thrown around or toppled by the explosions. In the large dormitories all the cabinets, tables and other furniture fell on those who lay on mattresses on the floors. Many of the injured immediately assumed that they had been hit by torpedoes or by mines.

Further below in the ship, water poured in through the two openings created by the torpedoes and the *Steuben* soon had a marked list. The water rose quickly – too quickly for the injured who had been placed down there. Almost immediately the two escape routes were clogged by people desperate to escape the lower decks.

Second Officer Grage had been thrown out of his bunk, but he quickly got his coat and lifebelt on and went directly to the bridge. Here he saw Captain Hohmann give the convoy a progress report. Grage could not quite grasp how the man could be so calm: it was as if he was exchanging pleasantries about the weather.

A SOVIET HERO

Alexander Marinesco had reported to his base that he had sunk a large vessel of perhaps 20,000 tonnes. He felt that he now led the 'tonnage gang' among Russian submarine captains and that he himself might be honoured with the title 'Hero of the Soviet Union'. *S-13* would be named the 'Flagship submarine' and his crew would be honoured in both Turku and Kronstadt. He estimated that he had drowned perhaps as many as 10,000 fascists, the equivalent of an entire division: he had sent Hitler's soldiers and submariners to where they belonged. No one in the crew gave a thought to the possibility that there had been anyone on the ships they'd sunk other than soldiers. Marinesco himself never knew. Only a few of the *S-13*'s crew reached old age and discovered, more than fifty years on, who was actually on board the *Wilhelm Gustloff* and the *Steuben*.

The *Steuben*'s engineering officers now notified the bridge that they no longer had control of the ship. One of the torpedoes had damaged a bulkhead and water was about to flood the engine room. All ability to manoeuvre was lost. Captain Hohmann now realised he had to send distress signals immediately and request any assistance that there was. With no fear of further submarine attacks, he ordered the signaller, Heinz Portmann, to fire flares with his signal gun.

On the upper decks panic had not yet erupted, but down below it was a different story. One of the medics, Corporal Adolf Ruppert, who had a cabin on D deck, had, like everyone else, been abruptly woken by the torpedo strikes. But the cabin lights were still on, and despite

The Russian submarine *S-13*. Her commander, Alexander Marinesco, was not certain precisely what he had torpedoed but knew it had been a very large ship, and believed he would be decorated as a 'Hero of the Soviet Union'.

Marinesco (left) and two other Soviet submarine commanders.

the loud explosions, everything seemed normal. But when he looked in a stairway he saw about fifty women and children struggling to get dressed. Because of lack of space they had been sleeping on the floor and, despite the explicit prohibition on undressing or removing lifebelts, they had done so. There was complete chaos with everyone trying to dress at the same time, taking life jackets from wherever they could be found. Ruppert went up to A deck, where he met one of the doctors and asked what had happened. The doctor told him dismissively that nothing had happened: the best Ruppert could do was to go down and try to calm the screaming people.

Another of the doctors, Dr Sachse, made his way to the starboard side of the boat deck. Pressed against the railing, he saw in the darkness that some of the lifeboats had got away, but there seemed to be no time for any systematic evacuation. All that mattered was being lucky, in the right place at the right time.

Then suddenly the *Steuben* lost stability and the list to starboard became a list to port. Those who had jumped from the port side were now crushed by the ship. Sachse, who seconds earlier had been pressed against the starboard rail, suddenly discovered that he was now hanging from it. This lasted only a few moments, then he lost his grip and slid down towards the port side, which was now a few feet from the water. What was worse, all loose fittings on the ship now began to rain down on him.

Boxes, floats, benches whizzed past and slammed into the railing: miraculously, he was not hit. Then he saw a lifeboat hanging in its davits: the boat was swung out and it was full of people. They begged him to lower the boat but Sachse had never done this before and had no idea how it was done. It all looked very risky and he thought that a raft would be safer than a lifeboat.

The list increased more and more. It was becoming harder and harder to move about the ship. Second Mate Grage realised that the ship would soon go down, and, with a few other sailors, he tried to free one of the large boats on the starboard side. A crowd quickly gathered round, suddenly seeing a chance to be saved. Grage did not think they would have time to lower the boat: however, it might float off when *Steuben* went down. The boat filled rapidly and everyone waited to see what would happen next. It was struck by a number of strange, long projectiles, but not damaged. As the ship was going down, the boat was caught up in the suction but Grage threw himself

Most of the wounded were lying down below and were doomed from the moment the torpedoes struck. Survivors later talked of pistol shots – probably fired by soldiers below who wanted to end their lives quickly rather than wait to be drowned.

out, found a boat hook and pushed the lifeboat from the ship's side with all the strength he could muster. On board three sailors also pushed with all their might to free the boat. Eventually they succeeded and at the last possible moment Grage made a giant leap back towards the boat, where the sailors grabbed him and hauled him aboard.

PASSING PROJECTILES

Up to this point everything had happened so quickly that Grage had had no time to think. But in the lifeboat he now began to ponder the strange projectiles that had struck the lifeboat when it still hung in its davits. There had not been one; there had been several of them. Then he realised what these projectiles were: those who had died on the journey from Pillau had been placed on stretchers in the drained swimming pool. Frozen stiff, they had shot like elongated cannonballs past the lifeboat. They splashed heavily into the water and disappeared into the night.

Franz Huber had his coat and lifebelt on but in his panic he had not dared to stop to put on socks or shoes. He came up on the freezing deck barefoot:

> I saw hundreds of wounded, doctors, nurses and medical staff who jumped into the water and I tried to reach the ship's highest place and hoped that this particular part would go under last. I sat alone for a long time in the darkness, listening to the screams on the vessel. I heard the Lord's Prayer read by a voice in a way one had never heard before and may never get to hear again. I heard the screams in the water and saw that the ship was burning with something and it created silhouettes in the water and on the ship. I saw many people squeezing out of the various openings and then throwing themselves into the water. I waited and really didn't know what I was waiting for until I heard a voice next to me [which] said, 'Now we have to jump, otherwise it will be too late and then the suction will come.' These words convinced me ...[10]

Huber jumped as far out as he could and lost consciousness for a few seconds. He thought later that he jumped from 20m as he sunk down deeply. The water shocked life into him and he flew up to the surface like a ball.

A few minutes earlier, one of the medics, Corporal Stobe, had tried to reach the cabin on D deck to retrieve his lifebelt. He ran down the stairs and reached only C deck, where the water in the corridor was already half a metre high. Everything below was awash and filled with floating dead bodies. There was nothing to do but get back up as quickly as possible. As the water rose, survivors could hear screams from the lower decks, but these gradually became fewer and fewer. Some testified to hearing gunshots fired by wounded soldiers who did not want to drown, preferring to free themselves quickly from further agony.

There was little the escort ships could do for the Atlantic steamer, although their searchlights continued to play across the water and, despite the lack of space on their own vessels, they did their best to pick up people from the water.

Searchlights on the *TF-10* picked out a lifeboat that was being launched on the port side of the *Steuben* with as many as thirty nurses on board. The boat had barely reached the surface of the water when the ship's list became too much for the forward funnel. With a deafening roar, it crashed on top of the boat. Everyone was lost in a cascade of water and the noise of metal being torn apart. No one could do anything but witness this awful drama played out under the strong beams of the searchlights.

Medic Adolf Ruppert, along with a crew member and one of the injured soldiers, made his way to the starboard side of the boat deck. He had no idea what to do: he hoped that a vessel would come up to the *Steuben* and take the people off directly, but the chances of it happening soon shrank rapidly. It seemed as though most of the people had already thrown themselves into the water because this part of the boat deck was almost deserted. He had seen them jump only to be killed against the side of the ship, so he understood the risks.

The fateful swimming pool. Around this dead bodies were stacked during the last voyage.

The *Steuben* sank bow first; the stern rose and then descended like an enormous lift. It was thought at the time that the ship broke in two. Many who jumped were impaled or smashed on to the rudder or propellers.

Ruppert and the two men looked around in the hope that there were still some rafts on the deck. Eventually they were successful, finding one clamped to the edge of the swimming pool. Joining forces, they freed it and began to lift it over the rail on the port side. Just then an ammunition box fell down towards them and crushed the injured soldier. Ruppert and the crew member managed to get the raft into the water and jumped but seconds later he could see neither the raft nor the crewman. It all happened so quickly and he was now surrounded by hundreds of screaming people, but he knew that it was dangerous to be too close to a sinking vessel. Luckily he found a large basket floating by, a basket that had probably belonged to a passenger, into which he managed to climb. Then he saw a small flotilla of rafts drifting towards him. He climbed up into one of them and tied three rafts together. More and more people came swimming by and climbed up, but none of them said a word. Everyone was numbed by the horrors they had seen.

Another medic, Kurt Dammann, and his friend Hans Köhler had tried to launch a lifeboat but, like Dr Sachse, this was the first time they had encountered a davit and neither of them understood how the mechanism worked, so they left the lifeboat where it was. They looked around: somewhere there must be more rafts. But the rafts that had been thrown into the water drifted away very quickly, as many who had jumped into the water expecting to find them discovered too late. But for any chance of survival in the cold February sea, one had to be on a raft or in a lifeboat.

Links: Das Schlauch-boot, das den Män-nern eines Kampfflug-zeuges zur Rettung dienen soll, falls sie in Seenot geraten, wird vom Gerätewart im Rumpfrücken des Flugzeuges zusammen mit Leuchtpistole, Kompaß, Notproviant und einem wasser-dichten Seenotsender sorglich verpackt

PK-Aufnahmen
Kriegsberichter Schödl
(Wb 3)

Rechts: Durch eine „Generalprobe" über-zeugt sich der Geräte-wart, daß die auto-matische Einrichtung zum Klarmachen des Schlauchbootes in Ordnung ist. Die Be-tätigung eines Griffes am Instrumentenbrett des Bordfunkers muß genügen, um das selbsttätige Aufblasen des Schlauchbootes durch Preßluft auszu-lösen. Damit der Fahrt-wind im Ernstfall das Boot nicht sofort mit-reißen kann, wird es mit einer Leine am Flugzeugrumpf fest-gehalten

Schlauchboot-Generalprobe

Links: Das Schlauchboot nach der Füllung. Die in Seenot befin Besatzung findet in ihm alles Notwendige vor, um auch längere Z zur Rettung durchhalten zu können

An article in the October 1942 issue of the German magazine *Der Adler* showed how a rubber boat opens automatically. This type of device was the salvation of many in the water.

As the ship sank, an anti-aircraft gun crashed into the starboard gunwale next to them. This was followed by an avalanche of sand: it was the sand to be used to put out fires on the deck. They understood that they could not wait much longer, they had to get away from the ship or the suction would probably pull them under. Then they spotted a raft tied to the railing and together they got it into the water. Throwing themselves in after it, they managed to get up onto the raft. They pulled up others until there were fifteen people aboard. But they had not thought about untying the raft and now it was getting critical. Fortunately, someone with a knife leaned against the railing and cut the rope: the raft was free.

There were no paddles, and they seemed to be getting nowhere paddling with their hands. Meanwhile, the stern of the *Steuben* rose higher and higher – so high that they could see one of the propeller blades was cracked. The men on the raft realised that if they did not get away from the ship in her death throes very quickly, it could go very badly for them. When a piece of planking passed by serendipitously, one man picked it up and, by using it as a paddle, they sped away from the colossus in its final seconds.

STEUBEN DISAPPEARS

The bow of the 168m-long ship probably hit the bottom of the sea at a point where the water is less than 100m deep, which would have put an enormous stress on the hull. Despite the darkness of the night, the medic Dammann thought he saw the vessel had snapped in the middle. Concidentally, several survivors of the *Titanic* disaster in 1912 gave accounts of the ship breaking while she was still above the surface. In fact, neither broke at this point in their respective sinkings. Dammann also said he saw the bow suddenly pop up again, perhaps a metre above the water, then sink once more. The stern pointed straight up and he saw people clinging to the stern deck railings shouting in panic.

Just before the *Steuben* disappeared, Second Engineer Karl Kollwitz climbed up on the stern. Searchlights from the escort vessels played upon him. In their glow he saw desperate people who had been standing beside him jumping out into the water, away from the ship. But Kollwitz knew it was certain death to do this. He was right. He saw them dismembered when they hit the stationary propeller blades. He closed his eyes. Kollwitz crouched down and waited until the ship reached a point closer to the water where he could jump safely.

When the ship disappeared there was in fact no suction but, as with the *Wilhelm Gustloff*'s final moment, there was a millisecond of silence before the air was filled with screams. Survivors later testified unanimously that the screams were something they would never forget.

The *Steuben* disappeared at 01.26. Relatively few of those on board escaped, partly because the sinking took only half an hour and partly because most were injured or bedridden.

TO SAVE THEMSELVES IN THE NIGHT

Franz Huber had been pushed up to the surface but was still dangerously close to the sinking *Steuben*. He swam away from the ship like a madman, away from the suction he believed would come, away from the masts and rigging and other things that might easily drag him down. He heard a strange gurgling sound close by. He could now see that the water was penetrating the large vents on the deck. He knew that if he survived this 'spectacle', as he later called it, he would never forget what he witnessed. He hardly saw where he swam, but away he went, into a sea of screams. Suddenly he heard a female voice next to him, someone shouting for help. It was a nurse and Huber told her that maybe they could help each other if they swam together:

> And she said to me that you also will go under and that she wanted to go
> home to her mother. I then said to her, either we both drown or we will
> both get out of here alive. She swam for a while with me and I noticed that
> her strength left her. I laid her head on my wounded body and told her that
> she must move and help herself not to become numb. I also gave her my
> mother's address if she happened to survive this.[11]

The next moment they heard swearing and some incoherent voices nearby, and Huber assumed that there was some kind of fighting going on. He was correct. They saw one of the large lifeboats that had been launched in time, filled with people:

The Baltic's temperature was around 4°C. It was impossible to survive for long in such waters. Many of the wounded and the refugees were already very weak after what they had been through, which further diminished their chances of survival. (Kurt Gerdau)

> And the soldiers clung to the outside of it and they were heavily beaten by those who were in the boat. They fought with rifles, pistols, with hard objects and one cannot imagine worse self-preservation.[12]

The two pushed on. Huber tried to keep moving, the whole time reassuring the woman that they needed to survive together, while also thinking that it was probably pointless because they were so far from land. But then his fingers met something he first perceived as soft, maybe a human or an animal. The next moment, he had a rope in his hand and at the end of it was a small inflatable boat designed for two people:

> Like a miracle this inflatable boat came drifting past and we had no strength to climb up in it. For a long time I tried with all my might until I discovered another survivor on the other side who also tried to get up. I thought that if more survivors try to come up on the other side there is probably no place for

me in the dinghy. The other comrade was able to climb up and I prayed and begged him to help me and this nurse, a Red Cross nurse who after all really had done so much good for us. But from the comrade came not a sound.[13]

Huber finally managed to climb into the dinghy, and after what he thought was an eternity he got some of his strength back and he tried to pull the woman up. He threw his arms around her and started pulling. Then she threw her arms over her head and slid down into the water again. Huber did not give up; he was determined to try to get her up:

> I encouraged her to redo the experiment. So I asked her to at least hold on to the rope that ran around the boat. We rested for a little while and then tried again to get her up in the raft. I sat on my knees, leaned far over the edge of the boat and tried to get my arms around her and pull her up, but this failed. When she reached the point she threw her head back and fell back into the water.[14]

He'd had no help from the other man on the raft, who seemed bereft of speech: he had still not said anything. But Huber still did not give up. He had promised that he would save her and perhaps it was this promise that also saved him. He simply could not be defeated.

Then another swimmer approached, a man who was among the injured with a bandage across his chest. It turned out that this man was a corporal: when the *Steuben* was going down, a large piece of metal had fallen on his hand and severed several of his fingers. But now the two men would work together: Huber would get back into the water and they would jointly try to get up the woman into the rubber boat.

It was a very tedious process. Huber was tied with a rope to prevent him drifting away but after what he thought was another eternity they finally got up the woman on the raft. Huber thought he had no strength left but somehow managed to get himself up into the boat:

> Now we were four in the rubber boat: The mute stranger who has not yet given a squeak, the nurse, the corporal and me. So, when I calmed down, I noticed how a violent chill came over me, I could once again feel the injury to my head and my stomach hurt. The efforts of the last hour had obviously been too great. And the cold was clearly felt. I said to my fellows in the boat that we should get close together on the rubber boat to retain

body heat and prevent cold damage. I insisted that everyone would follow my advice. Then for the first time I heard the voice of the stranger in the middle of the rubber boat and he explained that he absolutely did not intend to do this. He was doing just fine where he lay. I told him that if he did not immediately follow my orders and sat in the boat like we three, we would jointly throw him from the raft.[15]

The silent man yielded without the least protest, but the atmosphere was tense. It did not improve later when they saw the light beams from searchlights on the horizon. The silent man, who proved to be a sergeant, thought they were the lights of a Russian submarine and what awaited them next was imprisonment in a Russian camp beyond the Urals. Huber told the sergeant that it was stupid to talk that way and told him to keep quiet.

The vessel with the searchlights came closer and they did everything they could to attract attention. A whistle on a life jacket failed do the job, so instead they tried to shout. Still, it did not seem as if they would be spotted. Then suddenly, as if they were in the centre of a stage, they were in the middle of a searchlight's beam and they started screaming madly.

They had been discovered by *T-196*. But Huber could go on no longer: he lost consciousness. The four were taken on board the ship and given coffee, tea and brandy – anything that would restore the heat to their bodies. It was brandy that revived Huber and once it was poured into his mouth, he woke up with a jolt:

For a moment I didn't feel the injuries to my head and stomach at all. It was just the legs that ached terribly and I thought I had frostbite. One corporal from Munich, a young man and a crewman on T-196, immediately showed concern and massaged me like his own brother, he sweated properly over it, but the pain in my legs became constantly greater. Then a doctor came and gave me some injections and I fell asleep and didn't feel them for the moment. Before that I had heard that T-196 had completed the rescue and had now set course for the port of Kolberg.[16]

Adolf Ruppert remembered he was taken to a room that was very hot, and someone gave him a stiff drink. He began talking to the nurse he had saved, who was resting in the same room. She told him this was her fourth shipwreck.

A picture taken on the morning of 10 February 1945 when the search for survivors was still going on. By then there was no chance of finding anyone alive in the water, so the search concentrated on looking for floats and lifeboats. But in most cases, the people found had already died. (Kurt Gerdau)

Both *T-196* and *TF-10* had done what they could to save as many lives as possible. But it was a cold and clear winter night and everyone knew that there were no more than minutes to rescue people from the water. When Dammann woke up he was lying completely naked in the engine room of *TF-10*.

Someone gave him hot red wine and cigarettes. Eventually he learned that of the fifteen who had been on the raft, only five had survived. He remembered that in the horrible freezing conditions someone had sung sea shanties, someone had slapped their arms around his body, and someone kept striking out in an effort to keep the cold from killing him. They had been on the raft for more than half an hour and the cold had taken most of them.

The *TF-10* also rescued Second Officer Grage's lifeboat. But Grage disembarked his passengers and then, with two sailors, returned to the mass of dying people to see if there was anyone who could still be saved.

They worked as quickly as they could and as long as they had strength left they went back and forth. They rescued nearly 200 people, after which they were completely exhausted.

When Grage came aboard the *TF-10*, he was asked to take a watch on the bridge so that other officers could continue the rescue work. As he stood there, he had much to ponder. This was his second shipping disaster: two months earlier, on 4 December 1944, he had been on the steamer *Seeburg* when she sank. On that occasion Grage had fallen into the water, so he knew exactly how it felt to swim in the Baltic in winter. What he could not know was that within a week he would experience his third shipwreck: he came to be appointed as second officer on the pilot boat *Ditmar Koel* in Swinemünde, which on 14 February struck a mine and once again he had to experience the biting-cold water. But Johannes Grage was a lucky man: he survived again.

THE SOVIET HERO

Alexander Marinesco was now absolutely convinced that he would get the award of 'Hero of the Soviet Union', but his superiors remained suspicious of him. They had certainly noticed reductions in German shipping, but Marinesco's earlier behaviour and exaggerations were still held against him. Although he was given a triumphal arch and a dinner was held in honour of him and his crew, the finer distinctions were withheld. He was awarded the most ordinary medal, 'Order of the Red Banner', and *S-13* received a Red Banner award.

Marinesco was not given a new commission and the *S-13* was laid up. It was not until May that she next ventured out. In the meantime, Marinesco wrote a dissertation about the submarine war in which he criticised his superiors – a risky thing to do in Stalin's Russia in 1945. When the *S-13* eventually came out again, the war was effectively over and there were no more heroic feats for her. Neither Marinesco nor his crew participated in the victory parade in Moscow and it was obvious that he had been passed over. He was forced to resign from the fleet because of allegations of alcohol abuse and indifference to his work. In 1946 he took a job as a warehouse man in a construction organisation. When Marinesco pointed out that the party bosses exploited the system to their own advantage, including getting building materials privately through bribery, the revelation was unwelcome. The Security Service had opened a file on him and he was sent to a camp in Siberia. When he was finally rehabilitated, he was a very sick man. Only after his death in 1963 was he properly recognised in Soviet military circles as the most successful submarine commander of the war. Today, the Submarine Museum in St Petersburg is named after him and there are monuments dedicated to him in Kaliningrad, Kronstadt and Odessa.

SMALL LOSSES

Early on the morning of 10 February, the ever-well-informed Konrad Engelhardt received the news of the *Steuben*'s sinking. The office in Hamburg noted that the disaster was one of the biggest during the evacuation, and that only the sinking of the *Wilhelm Gustloff* had claimed more lives. Of the nearly 4,300 on the *Steuben*, only 659 people were rescued. *TF-10* had saved 512; *T-196* rescued 147. Around 3,600 people had perished.

The numbers were terrifying: Engelhardt and his staff knew they had to find a better way to protect the evacuation ships. He noticed that there were parallels between the *Wilhelm Gustloff* and the *Steuben*: both had left the harbour too quickly and not enough attention had been paid to the importance of a strong escort. There had been such a hurry to evacuate people, but now they had to ask themselves if such a hurry was really sensible. In the space of just under two weeks, nearly 13,000 people had lost their lives in the two maritime disasters. And nothing boded well for the future.

In the Führer's headquarters, the news was received rather differently. The loss was to be lamented but it was not in any way to delay the transport of injured servicemen. The hitherto rapid and successful evacuation must continue:

> It is correct to deploy all available resources for the transport of injured and thereby occasionally take losses in the bargain, rather than waive away transportation of large numbers of casualties. So far, a total of 76,000 injured have been shipped from the Baltic region, and the losses amount to only a small percentage. The Führer agreed.[17]

Although strictly speaking this was an accurate assessment, the problem was that the number of refugees was not reducing. On the contrary, it was rising rapidly. Alarming reports were being received from Königsberg of a huge increase in the number of people making their way westward. In mid-February between 50,000 and 60,000 people were waiting to be transported. This task fell on Engelhardt and his staff. As if that was not enough, the shortages of food and fuel was making themselves increasingly felt. When Engelhardt was ordered to provide Gotenhafen, Königsberg and Danzig with supplies for three months ahead, he began seriously to wonder if the General Staff had any contact with reality at all. It was abundantly clear to him that their understanding of what was happening was not consistent with what was actually taking place. Engelhardt was, however, flexible and together with his colleagues, he tried to adapt to the situation, even though it was continually altering.

The wreck of the *Steuben* on the seabed today. (Jonas Dahm)

As the pockets of German resistance on the North Pomeranian coast decreased, town after town and port after port were evacuated. One example was Stolpmünde, between Hela and Kolberg. Engelhardt had to organise a rapid evacuation of the outflanked town. Some 100,000 people had already been transported from Stolpmünde by ship to the West but with Russian troops and artillery advancing quickly, Engelhardt had to act to rescue the remainder. He sent all the vessels he could – fourteen of them – to Stolpmünde. They were not ships of any great size but in two days, between 6 and 8 March, more than 18,000 people were evacuated. When Russian troops finally entered the town they found it virtually deserted.

The destination for many of these ships was Swinemünde. As a result, there was often a large concentration of vessels in and around the port area, which was very appealing to Allied bombers. On 12 March it was subjected to an intense raid – 700 bombs were dropped in a matter of minutes. Although a relatively small number of ships were actually sunk, little of the medieval town was left standing.

That same night, parts of Hamburg were bombed. Engelhardt's office at Alte Rabenstrasse received a direct hit. Engelhardt was in Cuxhaven at the time but returned immediately. Not much was left of the office – the bomb had been followed by a devastating fire. Virtually all the documents had been destroyed, so the painstaking task of reconstructing the evacuation organisation began. They had to improvise even more: including using the steamer *Malaga*, which had an engine so badly damaged that she could not be sailed as his new office. She was towed to Flensburg on the Danish border and it was from this ship that Engelhardt continued to organise the evacuation of the East Prussian ports for the few months that remained of the war.

THE FINAL BATTLES

In early March the situation in Kolberg also changed dramatically. It had become yet another in a series of outflanked towns, where the Russian forces severed all land supply and evacuation routes. More than 80,000 people waited here desperately for some form of maritime transport. When the ships eventually came, they were more or less stormed by the refugees. Meanwhile, the remaining German soldiers put up a bitter resistance. When the evacuation was nearly completed, there were still about 1,200 people left at the dock. Most were women and children. But there was only one destroyer left, *Z-34*. As the fighting came nearer and nearer, block by block towards the port, people were ferried furiously out in small boats until finally, everyone had a place on the destroyer. She was so densely packed that the only people who had any room to manoeuvre were the air-defence troops on the deck: they had been able to respond to any attack. But it was successful – the ship left Kolberg before it was taken by the Russians.

The small pockets held by German resistance along the southern Baltic coast were quickly filled with despairing refugees. Their only hope was a passage by sea, and any vessel that floated was good enough for evacuation. (Heinz Schön)

Now the final battle of Danzig was approaching. On 23 March, the whaler *Walter Rau* started taking on board refugees. There were bunks for 300 people but they had prepared themselves for between 5,000 and 6,000. On the dock, however, there were more than 10,000. Everyone wanted to be on the *Walter Rau*. Ship doctor Jesse could not believe his eyes:

> On the dock stood a countless number of desperate people, women and children, of whom *Walter Rau* could only take a fraction. The events that took place when the ship left was terrible, but most of the unfortunate knew this was the last chance for them ... There was not enough food, especially fresh milk ... As the intention was for the ship to take only healthy refugees, the equipment for the sick was totally inadequate. The staff consisted of one nurse and two military medics that would cover more than six thousand people ... On the whaling ship's icy deck and in the holds were refugees: women and children, wounded and dying, brain injured who screamed and died alternately. In between wild sexual orgies unfolded between desperate people.[18]

The *Walter Rau* made it to Copenhagen and any plan to return to Gotenhafen was abandoned. The city fell in late March. Almost simultaneously, Danzig was taken and the old Hanseatic town that was once likened to Venice lay in ruins. The loading port for refugees now moved to Hela. This narrow sandbar was defended for the remainder of the war and became the bridgehead west for hundreds of thousands of people. In fact, the German units at Hela held out until 14 May, six days after the rest of the German forces had surrendered.

The sinking of the *Steuben* was followed by more disasters in the Baltic Sea. The steamer *Neuwerk* sailed from Pillau on 9 April with some 1,050 people on board. It did not have an *Erkennungssignal* – the signal light of a specific colour code, which was changed every day and identified the vessel as friendly, but as she was travelling in convoy this did not seem to be a problem. Tragically, the *Neuwerk* lost her escort in the darkness and lost her way. She was found by the motor torpedo boat *S-708*, which assumed her to be an enemy vessel and at four in the morning sunk her. When the torpedo boat came nearer, they realised the terrible mistake that had been made. More than 950 were killed and only seventy-eight people were rescued: a disaster that hardly anyone has ever heard about.

Twelve hours later, the cargo ship *Moltkefels* was attacked by Russian bombers as she lay at anchor off Hela with some 4,000 people on board. She received several direct hits and caught fire. Several bombs were timed to detonate when they passed through a deck or hit a cargo hatch. The Second Officer Henry Lange later wrote of the hell that broke loose:

> From the burning bridge deck, we took the wounded soldiers who were still alive. Our third officer climbed with a rope around his belly down into the smoking lower Cargo Bay Two. However, when the severely injured but still armed, who had no more hope of salvation, started shooting at him, he had to save himself. The forecastle was strewn with charred bodies, dead and wounded. Everywhere, everywhere you went – people. Between the dead and those who were still alive, you could hardly see any difference … If anyone was alive and screaming we threw them overboard to the ships around us, who saved whoever could be saved from the Moltkefels.[19]

Despite the inferno and the number of people on the *Moltkefels*, about 3,500 people were saved. Nevertheless, between 400 and 500 died in the flames.

The evacuation continued at a breakneck pace. Many freighters had been ordered to Hela and one of these was the motor ship *Goya*, one of the larger cargo vessels. She could make 16 knots and at this speed no submarine could catch her, so she was regarded as safe.

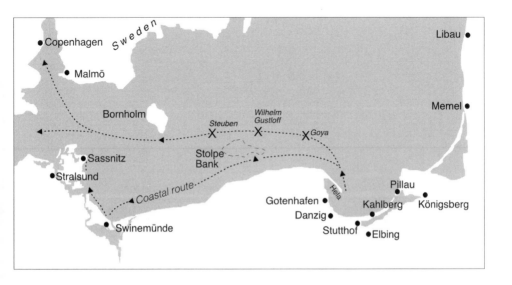

7

THE MOTOR SHIP *GOYA*

What we really heard is hard to describe. I think it was the screams from the steamer *Goya*, which seemed to have gone under in seconds. Our ship chased the Russian submarine, but without success. When we got back to the accident we saved one survivor …[1]

Like so much else, including many other ships, the *Goya* was seized when Norway was occupied by the Germans in 1940. She had just been launched – on 4 April – and when five days later the German troops occupied Norway, outfitting had only just begun. The ship had been ordered by the Ludwig Mowinckels shipping company in Bergen from the Oslo shipyard of Aker Mekaniske but she was never delivered. However, her sister ship, the *Bolivar*, was denied to the German navy thanks to tactics that caused her not to come into service until 1946.

The *Goya* was designed as a strong and fast ship, a workhorse of the sea. She was 141m long, more than 17m high and 7.7m wide with a gross tonnage of 5,230grt. Two seven-cylinder Burmeister & Wain machines gave her 8,400hp and a maximum speed of 16 knots.

But the war changed everything, and the *Goya* was not the civilian cargo ship she was intended to be. After the German navy took her, she kept her name but was modified several times and ended up in the fleet of the Hamburg America Line. She was fitted with the obligatory anti-aircraft defences and in January 1942 camouflage-painted in Hamburg and given more ballast to improve her stability. She became an accommodation ship and a target ship for submarine training in Königsberg. The civilian captain was Otto Plünnecke, who was to remain with the vessel to the end. The *Goya* was transferred to the 26th Submarine Flotilla and was to be stationed in Memel, where the trainees tested dummy torpedoes against her.

The motor ship *Goya* was launched in Oslo 4 April 1945. Five days later, Norway was occupied and *Goya* was a welcome war trophy. She was a strong and fast cargo ship but she had never been built to take more than 6,000 people. (Norsk Sjøfartsmuseum)

All this ended on 8 September 1944 when the transportation of troops, military equipment and refugees westwards began to pick up speed. As she was one of the faster motor vessels the Germans possessed, there was great confidence in her. In 1944 she carried more than 15,000 refugees and injured soldiers from Memel and Libau to Gotenhafen and Swinemünde. When a ship carried so many wounded, they were loaded on pallets in the various compartments in the hold and often hoisted into place on their stretchers. As a freighter, she lacked a normal passenger vessel's arrangement of stairs, but instead had vertical iron ladders leading up to the main deck. In an evacuation, few would have a chance to climb these, and definitely no one who was bedridden. However, so far *Goya* had not been subjected to submarine attacks and her speed was trusted to get her through.

Considerable quantities of food could be shipped in the *Goya*'s cold storage rooms, and she made two trips from Memel, where large amounts of supplies were kept. But these voyages were exceptional: she was soon exclusively a human transporter. One obvious sign was the makeshift wooden toilets on the aft deck, which were built when she was in Danzig-Neufahrwasser. This was also the time when newer cannon and anti-aircraft guns, taken from submarines, were fitted.

PEOPLE IN THE HOLD

On one occasion, the *Goya* had sailed as a ferry between Gotenhafen, Libau and Danzig-Neufahrwasser. When carrying supplies to the army at Courland (in Latvia) she ended up loading wounded soldiers. But in March 1945 her role would be entirely refugee transportation. One person on the *Goya* was Charlotte Dölling, who fled with her two children and her mother. After many hardships, they managed to reach Hela. They rejoiced when they finally saw the sea, as it promised deliverance, but they also saw that the whole place was full of people:

> But another horrible sight met us: women and children lying on each other in large halls; they sat on their knapsacks, they waited, they argued, they were exasperated, it was really miserable to see. Hardly anyone was clean and neat; they had already been waiting here for days for a chance to find a ship.[2]

Charlotte and her family had had the sense to obtain travel authorisation, which many had not. She had obtained this from a man in Hela and he now waited impatiently for them at the ship. They were almost besieged by a mob because they had managed to acquire this coveted certificate, which was the only way to get on board. For Charlotte, a sea voyage was something very unusual; she had rarely seen the sea and ships:

> We had to climb a very steep stairway and the ship rose hugely in front of us up to the sky and suddenly I lost the courage that I could get up there with my mother and the children. But we managed with the help of the sailors; it went pretty well. And then we were on the deck. It was *Goya*, a fairly large floating structure, a former freighter, but now she was probably used as a troop carrier. So we looked to find somewhere to sleep and were carried by the sailors into the ship.[3]

They climbed down into the hold, but everywhere there were people, sitting, standing or lying. When they finally found a place where they thought they might sleep, the air was so bad that they could hardly breathe. On top of this, every new person was regarded as a usurper taking up space and so added to the tension of the atmosphere. Charlotte looked at her mother and they agreed that it was too crowded, musty and dark, and they took their luggage and lugged it back up the ladder on the deck again. They met a sailor who offered them a place among the crew; when they were on duty Charlotte and her children could have their bunks:

> So we did not have to sleep down there among all the people; they'd only the deck planks to sleep on. Instead, we came into the crew accommodation spaces and we could stay in their dining room; we were able to sit properly at the table and sleep in their bunks when they were on duty. But what did we care? We knew where we would go and we had a much better situation than most refugees on this ship.[4]

Charlotte Dölling thought there were 3,000 refugees and 300 severely injured soldiers on board. She remembered that they departed on a Sunday, but no sooner had they weighed anchor than the alarm went off. 'Russian aviator', she heard and felt a panic inside. They had come so far and now she wondered if everything would be lost. But for once it was a false alarm and calmly she went back to bed:

> The vessel departed quickly. It was quiet everywhere. On deck, I met our escort again. We could not bring him down with us. The sailors had not agreed to this as they had taken down two wounded soldiers who needed special care … so we got our assigned bunks. Of course, we could stay there all night. Whoever was on duty, left the berth for anyone coming in. We had been able to sleep very well, if we could stop ourselves thinking what would happen if the ship would go down. At every jolt, every sound from the machines, we jerked awake.[5]

Charlotte had thought that the *Goya* would go to straight to Copenhagen but to her disappointment she discovered that instead they were anchoring elsewhere. She did not know where it was: it was night and she could see nothing. When daybreak came, she realised that the ship had dropped anchor in the roads off Swinemünde. No one was allowed to go ashore because the day before the town had been flattened in an air raid. More and more people gathered on deck and Charlotte was filled with a great foreboding when she saw that the *Goya* was not the only ship that lay at anchor:

> More and more ships anchored out here. A wonderful attack target for enemy aircraft and submarines. All day we lay at anchor at sea and all we could see was the coastline, and nothing happened. Conditions on board the ship were catastrophic. Supplies ran out; in the end there was only oatmeal that was cooked in water. Drinking water was getting short. For those injured it was particularly difficult, because there were no dressings or any medication left, moreover, in their department there was an air that you could not breathe. The refugees were not much better, as there were no toilets and such facilities for this type of human assault. Conditions were simply indescribable.[6]

Finally they went ashore, with the help of small boats. The *Goya* then returned to Hela, where she took aboard 3,000 refugees. Some were taken to Swinemünde; the rest were taken onto Copenhagen, where the city was reaching the limits of what it could deal with. The Danes did not appreciate that their city was becoming more and more like a refugee camp, increasing in population every day as more ships arrived and disgorged their cargo.

TO SURVIVE AT ANY COST

The *Goya's* work as a mass-transport vessel seemed to be endless. On 5 April at Hela, after unloading ammunition brought from Swinemünde, the ship took more than 5,000 people on board. On 12 April, even more boarded at Hela and together with the crew there were about 5,500 on board when she sailed with a strong escort to Swinemünde. No bombing had taken place this time, so the ship could moor at the quayside. Back the *Goya* went to Hela and on the morning of 16 April she anchored at its southern tip. Four hours later, she was ready to take on the next batch of refugees. The officers knew to expect a combination of desperate people and constant bombardment, either from shore or from the air. They also had no delusions about the danger from submarines.

During an escorted evacuation from Pilau and Hela led by the minesweeper *M-256*, *Goya* and another ship, the *Askari*, transported around 7,000 wounded from the battlefields. *Goya* can be seen on the horizon. Around two weeks later she was sunk. (Günter-Ernst Hahn)

Despite the government's attempts to silence them, rumours abounded about the *Wilhelm Gustloff* and the *Steuben*: it was widely known that a very large number of people had perished. However, the refugees who had already made their way across the ice and along roads under continual attacks from the air, had seen dead people along all the way, seen dead infants simply thrown from wagons, had seen the maimed and injured everywhere, experienced hunger, thirst and the numbing cold, so now they probably cared little about fresh dangers. Many were simply stoic: if God wanted them to reach their destination, they would do so.

Among the refugees were Anna Treter and her three children: Ruth, who was 16, 15-year-old Horst and a 5-year-old daughter. They had lived not far from Danzig and she and the others in the village had fled on the evening of 28 March. They went on foot, but they saw many who travelled with carts. Every trailer was full of people and luggage but on occasions they were able to ride with soldiers who came with a horse and buggy. Now and then they stayed overnight with farmers who had stayed put. Finally they reached Stutthof:

We stayed there for three days, then all the refugees had to leave. Stutthof was evacuated too. So we kept moving on constantly. We slept in stables, in bunkers or wherever we ended up. Soldiers gave us food, then we had to leave again. Soldiers then took us to a small ship that took refugees. The ship then went in the direction of Hela. It was 14th April 1945. Hela was already a heap of ruins. It was terrible. There were no residents left. Here all the refugees could rest a while. We found some stuff in the ruins which we were able to camp with. Soldiers gave us supplies. Then early in the morning on 16th April, all refugees were loaded onto small boats and then they went to ships that were to take them to the Goya. There was such a throng, everyone wanted to take with them what they had. So it was that my two children went aboard Goya while I with my five-year-old child did not. Nobody else could get on board. The families were separated when Goya was overloaded. My husband had been in a Russian prisoner of war camp since 1943.[7]

Refugees could take only hand baggage. The soldiers were ordered to line up with their arms. They were from the 35th Armoured Regiment and would become reinforcements on the Western Front.

Straw was strewn on the bottom of the holds, and here soldiers who were leg or arm amputees were placed. But on all the lower decks soldiers in various states of injury could be found. Erich Sasse was one of those who boarded the *Goya* that morning. He had been wounded four times, and after the fourth injury, which partially destroyed his left shoulder, he was demobilised. As he was boarding, the ship was attacked by Russian aircraft:

> It took place in brilliant sunshine – a rain of bombs from Soviet aircraft. On deck, it looked like a slaughterhouse. I crawled down to the bottom of the ship and lay on the fine sand put there as ballast. The bombs exploded on the deck, which I had rightly assumed, but despite this it was a terrible display of horror, which I had not yet experienced during the war. Unfortunately, the modern submarine detectors, which few ships had, were damaged [in the raid].[8]

It was the first air strike that morning. The clock had just passed seven when the bombs began to fall. It was over in minutes.

Boarding recommenced at eight, but half an hour later all hell broke loose as Hela was yet again attacked by Russian planes. The many ships gathered off the peninsula offered an easy target. Boatswain Heinrich Rothlübbers was responsible for the three anti-aircraft guns in the bow of the *Goya*:

> They came in waves of six and nine. We immediately opened fire. The first bombs detonated near *Goya*. They had a severe shrapnel effect. The third or fourth wave hit between the forecastle and the bridge. Several of my men in the front line of defence were taken out of action by injuries. The upper deck of the *Goya* was torn open and Captain Plünnecke threw himself into his cabin on the bridge with a bleeding wound to his face.[9]

On the port side, parts of the forward bridge had also been damaged. The crew surveyed the damage and found that there were some leaks in the bow, but more seriously the submarine detection equipment was now completely destroyed.

Plünnecke had been sick with a fever for some time: and therefore the officers decided that he would have two extra captains. One was the Korvettenkapitän Felix Hahn and the other Kapitänleutnant Paul

Wounded on stretchers were placed in the lowest parts of the *Goya*. Most had leg or arm amputations. The lack of medical supplies, fuel and nearly everything else turned many of the crew and support staff into masters of improvisation. (Kurt Gerdau)

Siegmund. Captain Plünnecke saw this as an attempt to take away command from him, and the atmosphere on the bridge was somewhat tense. But given his condition, there was little Plünnecke could do about it.

DEATH ON THE ICE

One of the refugees who put her hope in the *Goya* was 14-year-old Christel Balsam. Together with her stepmother and her brother Horst, she had left her home village of Argemünde by horse and wagon in October 1944 with some fellow villagers. Leaving their farm and animals behind, they took only the essentials. Everywhere Christel looked there were refugees. After a few days on the road she had the opportunity to stay with a beekeeper in the town of Sargen. There they stayed until January 1945, the entire time waiting for the chance to return to Argemünde. Then the front became perilously close and they could no longer remain. They left the horse and cart in Sargen and, with an aunt who had left Argemünde with them, they finally reached the coast at Frisches Haff, the 'inland sea' that is part of Danzig Bay:

We now escaped towards Braumsberg and over Frisches Haff towards Kahlberg. The whole lagoon was frozen, over which many lines of refuges from many directions made their ways toward Kahlberg. These refugee trains were easy prey for the low-flying Russian aircraft which constantly bombarded us. Tightly pressed against the cart, we waited out the attacks and were happy that we came out of this unharmed. All around us horrible scenes played out. The brittle ice was fatal to many refugees. Many wagons broke through and sank. Dead horses, wrecked carts and household items were strewn around on the ice. After the dangers we had gone through we were happy when we reached Kahlberg and had solid ground under our feet again.[10]

Travelling along the isthmus of Frisches Haff, they finally reached Schiewenhorst, north-east of Danzig. They waited and waited, in the hope of finding a passage on a ship going west. Their flight had lasted more than five months, yet all the time they still hoped that they could return to Argemünde, even if that hope diminished a little as each day passed. But Christel saw that 'the Russian noose' was becoming tighter and tighter. They pressed on, now with only a hand cart. Finally they secured places on a barge and reached Hela on 16 April:

Of the three ships that lay there, only *Goya* was taking people on board. We boarded at noon. We realised that the ship was overcrowded and we couldn't find a place below deck. So there was nothing for us to do but stay on deck, where we sat on our belongings near a pile of luggage and waited for the ship's departure. People increasingly poured onto the deck. I saw how the injured were continuously taken into the interior of the ship, where they were close to each other. It was said that there were about 3,000 wounded on board; in total, there would have been around 6,000 people on the ship.[11]

Christel Balsam's estimate of the number of those on board is probably close. Exactly how many people there were on the *Goya* when she sailed is unknown, but German sources mention between 6,000 and 7,000.

When the second air strike was over and bomb explosions were silent, it suddenly seemed as if every barge, skiff or rowboat in Hela was filled with people, all with a single goal: reaching the *Goya*. As the largest ship visible she became the magnet for the refugees.

Goya was armed with anti-aircraft guns, but against submarine torpedoes there was no other protection than her supposed high speed. (Kurt Gerdau)

Christel and the others got out to the ship next to the accommodation ladder. There were also companionways but all the entrances to the ship were inadequate to cope with the crush of desperate people trying to board. The harbour boiled with boats, while cranes hoisted the most seriously injured onto the deck. It became widely known that the *Goya* and the other ships would depart that day after dark. Sailing during the daytime was an invitation to be attacked and that all that could be hoped for was bad weather: clouds, fog, anything that would keep pilots away and that might hinder a successful submarine attack.

At half past three in the afternoon, in the midst of boarding and with the harbour still full of boats ferrying people out to the ships, the next attack came. This time there were twenty-two aircraft and they bombed not only the vessels but also the tens of thousands of people who stood on the docks and piers. Heinrich Rothlübbers saw how the discipline that had been more or less maintained now disappeared in a matter of seconds:

Fully loaded boats lying around us like a swarm were hit and sank in seconds. Women, children and soldiers hit by shrapnel screamed desperately for help. Those who were still alive tried with tenacious efforts to get on board. Soldiers from the widest range of regiments ruthlessly found their way up to the ship and the strongest of them even climbed up the anchor chain and the ropes that hung down from the upper deck ... And amidst all this chaos the Soviet hunter shelled the people ...[12]

The attack did not damage the ship significantly, but understandably it caused a huge panic on the quayside, making everyone doubly desperate to get on board. No soldiers or crewmen could, or dared to, stop the flood of people. They had long ceased counting, but the crew's conservative estimate after the third bomb attack was that there were far more than 6,000 people on the *Goya*. At five in the afternoon, the officers announced that they simply could not take any more. Every nook of the ship, every corridor, every little cargo space was full. And, of course, there was not enough rescue equipment for more than a fraction of those on board. Captain Plünnecke was deeply unhappy that his vessel was so overladen. He could only hope that everything would go well and, as they were about to weigh anchor, said, 'Now *Goya*'s fate lies in God's hands.'

Captain Otto Plünnecke had been wounded during an air attack. It was therefore deemed necessary that he be assisted by two other captains. Plünnecke, however, regarded this as an intrusion on his domain. (Kurt Gerdau)

At six o'clock the time of departure approached. Erich Sesse stood at the railing, talking with a sergeant, who grumbled that if something should happen they would end up in the cold water. It was not what Sasse wanted to hear and he lashed out against the sergeant and told him to shut up:

> It is the last trip and it will take me home. I had journeyed from Danzig to Riga in 1944; from the beginning of November 1944 I had gone from Windau in a double-bottomed ferry during a lightning operation at the end of the battle for the island of Saaremaa and landed on the southern tip of the Sworbe peninsula. In late November 1944, I barely escaped the advancing Russians on a landing barge. In February 1945 from Libau to Gotenhafen. All this I had happily gone through, so I would even make it through this journey![13]

When the anchor was finally raised, there arose, as with all the other ship departures, a terrible noise from the quayside and harbour boats. All those left behind were shouting at being left behind, some furiously shouting curses. Those on the *Goya* heard someone on one of the boats scream, perhaps a premonition of what was to come, 'Go to hell!'

THE CONVOY

Conforming with the usual practice, the *Goya* travelled in convoy with several other ships. Convoy number GO 712 was led by the steamer *Mercator* and the patrol boat *1604*. The *Goya* followed with the freighter *Kronenfels* and the water tanker *Ägir*, along with minesweepers *M-256* and *M-328*. Escort leader Kapitänleutnant Friedrich Keding chose the deep waterway, Fairway 58, which brought the convoy over the wrecks of both the *Wilhelm Gustloff* and the *Steuben*. Leaving Hela, the two escorts went first; *Kronenfels* lay on the landward side, *Goya* to the open sea, and slightly aft, with *Ägir* between them.

Anyone who had to descend to the lower cargo holds was met by a numbing stench. Thousands of people were crammed into these confined spaces and as there were no toilets down here, there was only ballast sand to use. Even though it was a cold, wet night, those who were able to make their way up to deck did so, Christel Balsam and her relatives among them. They had chosen a location on the ship far away from the holds where panic could easily break out if anything happened, although they tried to keep such thoughts away:

> When it got dark we prepared as best we could for the cold April night by covering our heads and shoulders, trying in this way to sleep.[14]

It grew colder but eventually they managed to drop off.

Erich Sasse stood for a long time on deck, but the rain finally forced him to try to find a place to sleep below deck. He lay down with some of his fellow soldiers behind the main stairway that led down below deck:

> Comrades Günter G. Landsberg-Warte and Joseph B. from Bonn-Beul went down to the engine room. It was hot in there, so I dissuaded them from remaining, and I even said that if she crashes nobody would be able to get out … We did not have lifebelts, because there were not sufficient belts on board for everybody and we had allowed the refugees to take them. It was very crowded and so we lay on the deck along with the other soldiers, and fell asleep quickly.[15]

The weakest link in the convoy set the pace. The *Kronenfels* could go no faster than 11 knots, so that was the convoy's maximum speed. This angered Plünnecke and the other officers on the *Goya*: her speed was her strength, and *Kronenfels* was depriving her of her advantage. Other factors too hinted at the difficulties the convoy faced. The Baltic remained relatively unchanging: the wind was gentle with visibility of 1 to 2 miles. The experienced civilian crew knew that the calm weather on a night like this was dangerous: those who had been on board when she was a submarine training target were well acquainted with the ideal conditions for a submarine attack.

'GUARD SUBMARINE' *L-3*

Vladimir Konovalov, Third Degree Captain and master of *L-3*, must have also felt the conditions were ideal to attack enemy ships. He knew his submarine well. She had been awarded the title of 'Guard Submarine',

Small vessels brought refugees to the harbours where the big ships were loading.

an honour that went only to the submarines of the Russian fleet that had distinguished themselves. It had been awarded when Konovalov was first mate on board. In October 1944, he had been promoted. Unlike Marinesco, he had a good reputation with his superiors as one of the most successful submarine commanders. On 31 January, the day after the *Wilhelm Gustloff*'s sinking, he had almost managed to crown his career when he sighted the *Cap Arcona*. She was one of the largest ships in the German fleet, and was heading towards Copenhagen with more than 8,000 people on board. Off Gotenhafen she was sighted by *L-3*. Konovalov launched three torpedoes: they all missed, which was a tremendous disappointment. But as he cruised off Hela in the middle of April, he knew that many ships were gathered there and sooner or later they would come out into the Baltic. He also hoped that the *Cap Arcona* would return: he would not miss again.

Nevertheless, *L-3* was not in top condition. After many long tours, the submarine was worn and her batteries were so weakened that when submerged she could only travel at 4 knots. Consequently, the master preferred to sail on the surface, although this risked easy detection. As darkness settled over the sea, and the crew started looking around. Konovalov, like any other submarine captain, knew it was at night time that the ships went westward. However, they quickly dived when the shadow of a warship approached.

Aboard the *L-3* were copies of captured German charts. The sea lanes were marked and therefore Konovalov knew that Fairway 58 was the route most vessels chose. He sailed towards the fairway and waited. In the distance, he saw light signals: someone was incautiously using a Morse lamp. Konovalov's hydrosonic equipment was no longer working, so he could not listen for enemy ships' propellers: he thanked a lucky star that the enemy had revealed itself by these signals. *L-3* now had to make a 90-degree turn at top speed but succeeded in coming up on the convoy's starboard side. Like a cat in the dark, they waited for the convoy's advanced vessels to pass and the real treasures to appear.

At ten o'clock in the evening, the convoy suspected that an enemy submarine was in the vicinity. *M-328* dropped depth charges but it was far from certain if a submarine was really so close. An hour and a half later the *Kronenfels* reported that she had mechanical damage, through her Morse signal operator. Korvettenkapitän Hahn, exploded in a fit of rage when he saw how carelessly the light signals were used. But the *Kronenfels* had no choice but to use lights – she lacked a radio. Even so, the *Goya's* officers felt that the signaller used his lights far too much to convey the information.

The damaged machinery reduced the convoy's speed significantly. It was now going no faster than 5 knots, so further increasing the risk of attack. Several on board the *Goya* thought that the vessels had actually stopped.

Kapitänleutnant Keding noted in his war diary that he considered letting *M-256* take the *Kronenfels* in tow, but this would cost them precious time:

23:42 Message from *M-256* by UK [radio]: 'Repairing machine on Kronenfels. Condition favourable. Towing is not required.'

UK station at the *M-328* in the chart house. I myself have used it, now and then, for my orders to come through quickly and without transmission errors. Immediately after satisfactory communication from the *M-256* I leave the UK station to the telegraph clerk and go to the end of the port bridge.[16]

Keding felt that the speed of 5 knots was acceptable and as the *Kronenfels* was apparently on her way to resolving the engine problems she would soon be able to reach her normal speed. And Keding had received no communications about submarines from his base, so he considered that there was no immediate danger.

ONLY A SMALL CARGO SHIP

Konovalov had followed the progress of the escort through the submarine's periscope. It was a godsend when the ships slowed their pace, but at the same time he was disappointed to find the largest vessel in the convoy was an ordinary cargo ship. But the target was almost impossible to miss, even though she was so very much smaller than the *Cap Arcona*. At 2345, *L-3* manoeuvred herself into position. The atmosphere was tense: everyone was waiting for the command 'Fire!' Eventually it came and four torpedoes were sent towards the freighter. To his chagrin, Konovalov saw that only two struck. But they proved to be enough: the ship quickly began to list and sink.

Just before this, Keding on *M-328* had his binoculars trained on the vessels astern of him, monitoring their progress. Suddenly he saw two huge columns of water rise up the *Goya*'s side, the water briefly obscuring the bridge. He understood what had happened and that he must track the submarine immediately.

Joseph Poiger was crewman on *M-328*. He was off duty and preparing coffee for those comrades who would follow him. He believed the time was just before midnight when he felt the ship shaken:

… by two huge explosions at two to three second intervals. I threw the jug or bowl and its contents into the nearest corner and threw myself to the stern to my 10.5cm anti-aircraft piece … Our ship left the scene of the accident and followed our hydrosonic scanners, which showed a distance of 1,200 meters [to the submarine]. Immediately the submarine alarm went

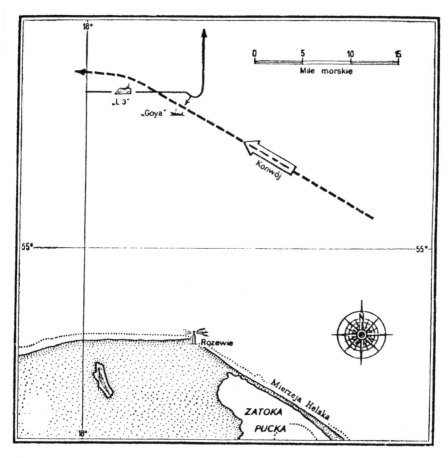

The *Goya*'s track on the evening of 16 April. The ship was close to the North Pomeranian coast, north-west of the Hela peninsula (Mierzeja Helska on this Polish map).

The *Goya* was hit by two torpedoes, one of them hitting her amidships in the engine room. As a result, she broke in two and disappeared in about seven minutes. (Kurt Gerdau)

off. We followed the sound on the scanners and threw two depth charges with the intention of sinking the submarine. This took about twenty minutes. With the greatest speed we went back to the accident and reached it after about 30–35 minutes, then about 0:40. Of the ship, nothing was left.[17]

Yet no other ship, bar one, stopped. The *Kronenfels* sailed on with *M-256* as if nothing had happened. Only the little *Ägir* stopped. Confusion and multiple mixed messages cost precious time.

The torpedoes struck the starboard side with a devastating effect. The first torpedo hit the bow and the second entered the engine room. All power was immediately knocked out and the lights extinguished. To Christel Balsam and her family this didn't mean much at first because they were on deck:

I was awakened by a detonation. It was toward midnight. Before I really understood what happened the vessel rolled to the side and there was panic. Cries and screams for relatives cut through the night. Everyone tried to get up on the side of the ship that rose. Then came a second detonation and the ship immediately began to sink.[18]

TOTAL PANIC

That which everyone feared, but nobody wanted to imagine, happened in seconds. And then panic spread everywhere. Erich Sasse woke and understood, though he was dazed, that he must get up and out as quickly as possible:

Suddenly two dreadful bangs tore me from sleep. My brain flashed: 'mines or torpedoes, get out!' In front of me planks had been torn up and my damaged hands are bleeding from splinters. Gun smoke, rioting and screams seep up from the lower holds. Drowsy, I stumble to the stairs up to the deck and notice how the ship lists to the port side …[19]

Behind him Sasse heard the sound of water and the cries of people trying to escape. The few exits were quickly blocked by the crush of bodies trying to reach the deck. But few in the lower cargo holds had any chance of survival: the lowermost deck had filled with water in moments. All the engine room staff not killed by the second torpedo were drowned.

Boatswain Heinrich Rothlübbers heard screams from the holds as the weight of people on a wooden stairway caused it to give way. He heard gunshots and assumed that soldiers were pushing their way to the front. Rothlübbers tried to think clearly: if he became caught up in the panic-stricken mass he would not reach the deck in time. Unfortunately, he was in one of the holds and the stairway was gone:

> My feet already splashed in water when I tried to reach the exit. Through the door high above me I saw a pale night sky. Hundreds of people crowded under the hatch opening, they wanted out, they screamed desperately for help when they did not succeed. The water rose constantly, approaching the deck with ever-greater force as the heel of the ship increased. Just a few more seconds, then everything would be over. A howling chorus, they waited helpless in the water of death, trapped in a trap. Would I be one of those who would die? No – I did not want to! Then a liberating thought came to me. The stair handrail, an iron pipe, was still in the same place. It was not easy to get through the crush of people and I had not a second more to lose. In the end, I managed to reach the railing. A jump – and I climbed up to the hatch opening. I had never been a good gymnast, but in this moment of greatest distress, I had received supernatural powers ... Now, I reached up to the edge and could then grab the hatch rim. A strenuous heave of the arms – and I was standing on the upper deck. I had just time to put on a lifebelt before a wave came over the deck and pulled me overboard and into the Baltic Sea.[20]

The water around the *Goya* was already bubbling with people. There had been no time to lower lifeboats: they had not even been swung out on their davits. Floats, which had been stowed with the idea that they would detach themselves in the event of a disaster, now drifted away but would later become of great importance. The water was about 4°C: only those who quickly made it onto a raft or were picked up by another ship had a chance of survival. To make matters worse, both soldiers and refugees were already weak. Hardly anyone had rested, and many had endured terrible suffering to reach Hela. And the many who had never been to sea before were probably in the most acute state of shock: finding themselves in an alien environment may have given them an added sense of hopelessness.

Up on deck, Erich Sasse, although almost without knowing where he was, noticed that the lights had gone out almost immediately. He became stuck in a throng of people but suddenly was thrown out like a projectile. He later assumed that compressed air being expelled from the ship's interior had more or less spat him out. The ship was going down quickly: the water suddenly reached his chest:

A panicked young girl was clinging closely to me and screamed 'Soldier, save me!' Mechanically I pushed her away and told her that she should hold on to a piece of wood; if she would hung on to me, we would both be lost. The ship went down underneath us like a stone while the bulkheads were crushed and the boilers exploded. People screamed desperately for help and pieces of luggage were thrown up from the bottom. I was afraid that the suction from the ship's destruction would drag me into the depths, but luckily this did not happen. I think it was because *Goya* was hit amidships at the height of the engine room by the two torpedoes. Since it was a freighter the open decks were flooded simultaneously and therefore there was no suction … No kind of emotions of horror took hold of me, it was just an indomitable will to live that filled me.[21]

The minesweeper *M-328* attacked the submarine with depth charges. The crew did not know if they had been successful but by the time they returned to the site of the *Goya*, most of those on board were already dead. (Kurt Gerdau)

Sasse rejected despair. He thought of all the horrors he had gone through at the front and now his body was so pumped with adrenaline that he could not feel the coldness of the water. But when he threw himself in, he felt his whole life went past as in a movie.

TALES FROM THE SEA

This same feeling of seeing one's life flash by was later recalled by Christel Balsam, who tried to climb up against the railing in an instinctive hope to get as far away from water as possible:

> A big wave hit us and swept away everything to the depths. All this lasted only a few minutes. As I cannot swim, it immediately became clear to me, 'Now I will die!' And like in a movie I saw in my mind my immediate family again. While this feeling lasted, I was pushed up to the surface again and got hold of a rope that belonged to a life raft. This wonder is inexplicable. All previous thoughts were forgotten. Right away I had received new courage to survive. On the raft there were already three soldiers.[22]

The soldiers pulled her up and when, after a few seconds, she calmed down, she looked around. To her surprise, Christel saw that were fires on the water. Oil had ignited and amid these pools of fire were hundreds of people screaming for help.

One of the commanders on the *Goya*, Kapitänleutnant Siegmund, had been in his cabin when the ship was hit. He ran to the bridge, where he saw neither Captain Plünnecke nor the other escort leader Korvettenkapitän Hahn, nor anyone else; the bridge was deserted:

> I tried to communicate with the engine room. In vain. The panic among the refugees and soldiers could not be suppressed, despite reassuring shouts, nor by showing them rafts and lifeboats. Barely in my right mind, I rush out onto the deck, looking at the sea raging towards me over the bow, sucked with the maelstrom down under the water, pushed up by an air-wave, head hits violently against a hard object, trying to hold on to a box, swimming in a field of screaming shipwrecked.[23]

Sergeant Willy Lietz's life was saved by a more unusual piece of flotsam. He was afraid of the cold, black water and for a long time he clutched the railing on the sinking ship. He was convinced that he would perish with the *Goya*. He didn't jump into the water but was eventually washed off the ship by a wave:

> Suddenly I was swimming in the frigid waters between corpses and the extra toilet [which had been] set up on the aft deck which went overboard with me. It was my salvation. I could actually cling to the wooden privy when the suction of the ship pulled me down two or three metres under the water and then catapulted me up again. I was almost hit by the cannon platform and ammunition boxes that slid down from the rear deck and struck the water beside me and sank immediately.[24]

He had swallowed water and diesel oil that had floated up from a fuel tank, which turned his stomach. Eventually he swapped his life-saving privy for a two-man raft that drifted past. Later, a grey-haired man in his sixties floated by in the water: Lietz assumed he was a refugee, one of the lucky ones who had a life jacket. The man held a bag in front of him and shouted to Lietz: 'So help me, then!' Lietz bent over the edge of the raft and asked the man to give him his hand, but he would not let go of the bag:

> When I once again shouted to him, 'Let the bag go, why don't you?' I got the answer, 'I cannot, it's all my money …!'
> I could not understand it. But I really could not help the poor fellow, I sat in the raft again, which had no floor but only cork ribs so I sat knee-deep in water. I saw the man being driven further out to the sea. Despite the seriousness of the situation I had to laugh at a man who would rather drown than be parted from his money.[25]

SAVED FROM THE SEA

Most of the survivors had been lucky enough to get up on to the *Goya*'s deck quickly or were already there. When the bow ripped apart and the holds quickly filled, this was the ship's death knell. After a few minutes the *Goya* broke in two and in seven minutes she had disappeared.

Hardly any of the wounded survived. The bedridden were doomed from the moment the first torpedo struck. Within a minute the holds were transformed into giant steel coffins. As the attack took place at night, most people were asleep and it took too long for them to understand what had happened. Thus the sinking was similar to that suffered by the *Wilhelm Gustloff* and the *Steuben*. The *Goya* sank, like the other two ships, in the same area of Fairway 58. Their hulls came to lie in a chain of death stretching in a north-westerly direction towards Denmark: a macabre line comprised of nearly 20,000 dead.

When Heinrich Rothlübbers threw himself into the water, he believed that his heart would stop: it was colder than he could have imagined:

> The April night was damp and cold, the sea was moving in a slight swell. With powerful strokes, I tried to get away from the vicinity of the ship so as not to be dragged down into the depths of the suction.[26]

Kapitänleutnant Keding, on *M-328*, noted in his war diary that he tried to depth charge the submarine as much as he could, and thereby protect the *Kronenfels*. Just after midnight he ordered the *Ägir* to sail closer to the *Goya*, but he did not know that the ship was already on the Baltic seabed. At 01.20, he noted that *M-328* was returning to the *Goya*, that the *Kronenfels* had repaired its damage and was now sailing at 7 knots, heading west. Keding then ordered *M-256* to continue escorting the *Kronenfels* while he would assist the *Ägir* in the rescue. But when *M-328* finally reached where the *Goya* should have been there was only a jumble of flotsam and desperate people.

The log on board *M-256* noted the *Goya*'s position, that she had sunk at midnight and was resting at a depth of 78m. The crew of the minesweeper now began to assist with the rescue of those in the water.

Joseph Poiger, on *M-328*, also had trouble grasping that the *Goya* had disappeared within, he estimated, five minutes. He saw people and wreckage everywhere:

> We were met by screaming, swearing, praying, moaning, cries for help, curses on starboard, port side, forward, aft, across our ship. The water tanker Ägir had already long been in the process of rescuing. The people who swam around in the water could not understand why we were not using all

efforts in saving people. But we had to sound constantly for the submarine so that our ship had to continually move so that we did not show a broadside to the submarine, or we, too, would get a torpedo hit.[27]

At one o'clock in the morning Keding received a message from Pillau that at 23.03 they had detected a Russian submarine. It was an hour too late. Keding replied that he was aware of submarines in the vicinity and that there was probably a submarine there still. If the base were to send rescue ships, 'only fast ships' would be of use. But with every minute that passed the chances lessened that they would find survivors. It was not as bitterly cold as when the *Wilhelm Gustloff* had sunk but the water was the same temperature and the Baltic had no mercy on those who were, after all, simply floating in life jackets. A life jacket often merely transformed death by drowning to death by hypothermia.

A ruthless struggle for places on the rafts ensued. In the dark, with no rescue vessels visible, a place on a raft was the only chance of survival, whatever the cost to others. Erich Sasse knew that he had to think only of himself:

Captain Keding was in command of *M-328*. He had assumed there was no danger from submarines as his base had not informed him of the presence of the Russian submarine *L-3*. (Kurt Gerdau)

In the darkness you could see only shadowy heads of the people who swam. Unfortunately we had to keep those even more unfortunate people around us away from our primitive raft, otherwise we would inevitably have been dragged down by the people who wanted help, swam and fought for their lives. It was a vile game of survival.[28]

'ONLY THE QUESTION OF YOUR OWN LIFE'

Several years earlier a few lines were written in a letter that corresponded almost exactly with what was now playing out:

Then there was a wild fight in the water between people to have some leave the raft so that someone could be saved. When I think about the whole thing I cannot understand how I could be saved but my cold-bloodedness to push away the others so that we could keep above the water helped a lot. It is terrible but at such a moment it is only a question of your own life.[29]

The author was Carl Olof Jansson and he wrote these lines on board the rescue ship *Carpathia* after surviving the sinking of the *Titanic*. The letter was written on 17 April 1912, thirty-three years less two days before *Goya*'s sinking.

However, on Erich Sasse's raft, he and his comrades in misery took pity on a girl and helped her on board. At the same time, they knew that one extra person might mean they all would drown. He shuddered at the sound of the girl when she climbed onto the raft, her breathing was a sort of gurgling. He thought of how a bottle was emptied and the sound that emerged when the water ran out. She was completely exhausted, but her weight made the raft sink deeper and now they sat literally in the water. Sasse's thoughts wandered, imagining that under them, somewhere in the depths, a victory was being celebrated in a submarine and a vodka bottle was being passed around. He thought about the madness of a war that he could not understand and about all the things he had participated in over the past few years, all the battles he had come through alive.

But reality constantly intruded. As the cold crept into the marrow of their bones, they tried massaging each other to maintain body heat. Sasse was thankful that he at least had a uniform – and several layers – which to

Survivors from the *Goya*. The type of life jacket worn by the man in the foreground was also used on the *Wilhelm Gustloff*. When worn by children the results were often fatal – the weight of a child was insufficient to prevent the life jacket turning upside down. (Heinz Schön)

some degree protected him. They were the reason he survived. Since the outbreak of the war, he had endured both cold and heat: he had frozen and sweated and felt lucky that those years had hardened him to endure the situation he now faced. Rescue finally came at the last moment:

> When we were rescued after nearly three and a half hours we had almost reached the end. For us it was a matter of indifference. When the rescuers came forward with brief light signals, we thought at first that it was the Russians, because we had almost accepted that it was over. We saw a dark shadow rowing towards us and then heard to our delight the German word 'Ranpaddlen!' ['Row on!'] They called out over the water with a megaphone. From a rubber raft that drifted around, a young woman jumped into the water and tried to swim to the rescue ship that was heading towards us. For some reason she drifted past the ship and was drawn into the propeller. A shrill cry proclaimed the ultimate. When the ship reversed, we were struck by fear that they would leave us castaways. But our time had not come.[30]

They were taken up into *M-256* by strong-armed sailors, but by then they were almost unconscious. Quickly stripped off, they were shepherded into cabins and laid, naked, in pairs next to each other, so that their body heat would return. Half an hour later, after being fed soup, Sasse started to revive.

He witnessed how the unconscious were rescued. They were put on blankets on deck and a doctor gave them injections, and detected their breathing by holding a mirror in front of their mouths while sailors pumped their chests. Sasse watched helplessly – hardly anyone could be saved: he thought it was because they had diesel oil in their lungs:

> Tragically this was also the fate of a pair of young siblings, who had tried to save themselves in one of the rubber boats stacked on the deck. When rescued the little blonde boy, who I think was between six and eight years old, was gripping his little sister, between two and three years old, by tufts of her hair. But she was hanging outside the raft and had drowned.[31]

Helmut Wolf belonged to the crew of *M-328* and participated in pulling both the living and the dead from the sea. Two girls were recovered who turned out to be twins:

One died shortly after she was rescued and was among the other dead [laid] on the aft deck. Now the surviving sister asked me to retrieve the ring from her dead sister to have that memento. It was not a pleasant task to search for it among the frozen corpses, but I found the ring and her sister was then very grateful for that.[32]

A FLOATING CEMETERY

The steamer *Mercator* had about 5,500 refugees on board who, realising what had happened to the *Goya*, began to panic. Captain Bohlen did what he could to calm them. He was ordered by Keding to sail for Copenhagen as soon as possible but to constantly change course to evade any possible submarine attack.

When the refugees boarded the ships in Hela, many families were parted (as was common in the evacuation). Some ended up on the *Mercator*, others on the *Ägir* and still others on the *Goya*. Anna Treter and her 5-year-old daughter were on the *Mercator*; her other daughter and her son were on the *Goya*. She could only listen helplessly to what others told her: that the *Goya* had been torpedoed, broken in two and disappeared in minutes.

On *M-328* everything was being done to save the shipwrecked. The crew pulled people from the water and they played searchlights across the sea to look for more, even though they knew that time was running out and they were still in danger from the Russian submarine. The ship moved slowly towards the mass of castaways to see where help was most needed: not an easy task when it was needed everywhere. The crew shouted at the top of their lungs to the swimmers to try to make their way towards the minesweeper. Joseph Poiger, like many of the crew, was working to try and save as many as he could:

Together, two men on the rubbing strake on our ship, both port and starboard at the stern, with one hand on the railing, with the other hand hauled up the castaways who swam in the sea. No sooner had we gotten yet another man up onto the deck, several others shouted, 'Help, help, I'm swimming, pull me up.' Some died in front of our eyes, close to our hands. This night between 16th and 17th April 1945 we crewmembers of *M-328* will never ever forget in our lives. Such a night was incredible. We saved those we could and put our own lives at risk. As cries for help became fewer, the sea claimed her victims. Whoever we could not pull up went under in front of us.[33]

Stoker Gotthardt Konitzer had the same experience. Earlier in the evening he had been out on the deck to get a little fresh air and when he went back down to the boiler room. He had taken off his life jacket to make it easier to work. Then came the submarine alarm. He grabbed the life jacket, rushed up on deck to his station, and then he heard the screams and cries for help in the distance. 'The Fat', as he called the *Goya*, was already gone, but the wreckage of the ship could be seen everywhere. Like Poiger, Konitzer more or less hung off the ship's side to pull up people:

Although the night was so cold, sweat ran down our bodies in litres. It was just our hands that continually became stiffer. Other crew members came and helped to pull up the survivors. Because the clothes on the castaways became increasingly heavy and their bodies stiffened; the longer they had been in the water, it became increasingly difficult for us to take them on board.[34]

Christel Balsam tried to understand what happened. It was dark but in April the night still gave off a dim glow and she could discern the outlines of people, of wreckage, but what she sensed above all else were the screams that cut through the air. The man who had helped her up, Wilhelm Malcharek, was as wet as Christel. They decided to exchange the flotation bag on which they had originally saved themselves for a raft that floated by. Christel managed to board the raft but Malcharek could not get up: he was near the end. She grabbed his belt and suddenly a rush of adrenaline gave her strength she could not have imagined, and she simply pulled Malcharek up on the raft. It was only then they discovered that there were two others already on it:

After a while the disaster scene was lit up by searchlights and you could hear the engine noise. We were convinced that we would be rescued. But then there was silence and the searchlights went out. They had not seen us! Disappointment came over us but despite this hopeless situation we clung tightly to the hope of daylight. Yes, when the day broke they would search further and would surely find us. Because of the weight of the four people on board, the raft was pushed under water and we sat in cold water up to our stomachs.[35]

When the dim light of dawn came they saw rafts and some lifeboats drifting but they were too far away for their cries to be heard. They had been staring for so long at the horizon that they thought they saw land, but it was only a mirage. They picked up flotsam they hoped could be used as a bailer, but it was no use: the raft remained half full of water. They were freezing and Malcharek tried, as the former teacher he was, to keep the cold away by letting his thoughts wander elsewhere. He talked about his memories of the war. He spoke about the time in the Crimea when his driver got lost. They found a cottage and a terrified woman let them in. Malcharek spoke several languages, one of which was Russian, and he began to entertain the woman, who after a few moments gave them both food and drink. The woman's mother was also there and she was a palm reader. She took Malcharek's and told him that he did not have a father but a living sister. She also told him that he would come in contact with water, lots of water, he would end up in a major accident, but he would survive. It was rubbish, he thought then; now when he told of the fortune teller, he had second thoughts about the prediction.

It was broad daylight, but still no ship had appeared. They began to doubt that they would ever be rescued and started to despair. It was true that they were not far from land, but it was land now under Russian control:

We lost courage and we began to have suicidal thoughts. In our distress we had not noticed at all that our legs had already gone numb through the cold of the water. For one of the soldiers any rescue would come too late. He died. Certainly the physical and mental sufferings had been too much for him. It was a painful moment. But then came the long-awaited rescue. Several ships appeared on the horizon and came towards us.[36]

They were overjoyed, but in the next second filled with worry: what would they do if the ships did not see them? They waved scarves and hats, and, finally, they saw one of the ships steering towards them. They had no strength left and had to be pulled aboard the minesweeper. Although exhausted, they changed clothes and took warming drinks. Finally, they could rest. Christel, almost unconscious already, fell asleep:

> It was only when I woke up that I became fully aware of the tragedy of this disaster. I was alone and 14 years old. Stepmother, brother and aunt were gone, my future uncertain. In this difficult time I received help and compassion from everyone on board.[37]

It was a minesweeping division that searched the area for survivors. Hans Constabel was one of the crew and he had helped to sweep the fairways on the North Pomeranian coast where cruisers and destroyers sailed. From the shore they saw searchlights and flashes of explosions. Suddenly they received orders to suspend their work, form up the boats and sail to a given position at top speed. At first hardly anyone knew what it was about, but then Constabel heard the name '*Goya*'.

As they approached the wreck site the vessels arranged themselves in formation so as not to miss anything. It was the morning of 17 April:

> We could see the wreckage and headed up towards it. When we finally came around Sergeant Michard shouted loudly 'Life jackets! Yellow life jackets!' Now, we could all see them. Bodies were found in them and they rocked back and forth by movement of the waves. Were they all dead already? We went close to them. The ladder was hung down the side of the ship. All participated. One was pulled up. Could barely hold the lifeless body. Eventually he lay on the deck. Staff Physician Körper undressed the victim's torso. Investigated for some time. Shook finally the head. We could all see it. 'Nothing to do – dead,' said our doctor. Everywhere the dead drifted![38]

They could not keep corpses on the vessel. Any papers found that could possibly provide identification were kept and the bodies returned to the sea. They did not think they would find anyone alive. But then someone shouted that he sighted a rubber raft and the vessel moved closer. There were people inside:

> One of them seemed to raise his hand slightly. It will turn out they are still alive. Cautiously we go up close to it. Now the rubber raft is beside us. Schonvogel throws over a rope. But the castaways are not in a position to move – they cannot take the rope.

Finally they managed it! Together they succeeded in pulling them up on our boat. One of them slips off, slips out of the hands of their saviours! Utters a terrible sound and disappears in the water![39]

The minesweepers were then ordered to go to Hela, and so again survivors were taken back to a place from which they thought they had escaped. However, from Hela they travelled in a new convoy and finally reached Copenhagen safely.

Anna Treter, on the *Mercator*, also reached Copenhagen. In a letter written thirty-seven years later she wrote:

All the rest of us left on the morning of 17th April and a few days later came to Denmark and a refugee camp. Since then I have not heard of my two children [who were on *Goya*]. I wrote at the time to the search service in Hamburg, but unfortunately I have not heard anything.[40]

LITTLE LOSSES

Between 6,000 and 7,000 people had perished, but again the Führer's headquarters regarded this latest sinking as an acceptable loss. From one of the last protocols issued before the Reich finally collapsed, it is possible to understand the reasoning:

The loss of a few thousand people in the steamer *Goya*'s sinking causes the Supreme Commander of the Navy to point out the extraordinary personnel losses as a percentage of only 0.49% of the previous transport in the eastern area. While an individual vessel's destruction is strongly felt as a painful loss, it is easily forgotten that, during the same period, a large number of ships with many wounded and refugees aboard safely reached the ports to which they were destined.[41]

News of the sinking was downplayed in the newspapers and on the radio, but that did not prevent knowledge of the *Goya* disaster travelling along the grapevine.

Vladimir Konovalov returned to base in triumph. As a hero with no record of alcohol problems or brothel visits, his superiors did not hesitate

Admiral of the Fleet Karl Dönitz was the leader of Germany after Hitler's suicide in the short period before the complete surrender.

to allow him to join the small band of who had received the highest military honour – 'Hero of the Soviet Union'. His sons would later also become submarine commanders.

Despite the loss of the *Goya,* the evacuation accelerated at an ever faster pace. Rear Admiral Konrad Engelhardt had several large passenger ships at his disposal, not only the *Cap Arcona* and *Deutschland* but also the *Robert Ley, Der Deutsche* and several others. His problem was a lack of fuel. The *Cap Arcona* in particular, although capacious, was extremely fuel-hungry and when in early 1945 shortages had become acute, the Atlantic giants were laid up and smaller ships shuttled between Hela and the western ports. The *Cap Arcona* and *Deutschland* were sent to Neustadt Bay, off Lübeck, where they anchored.

These vessels, which had previously been used to evacuate civilians and wounded soldiers, were to take on another role: floating concentration camps. Whether the pro-Nazi Grand Admiral Dönitz could have prevented this is debatable, but when he became leader of the Reich after Hitler's suicide on 30 April 1945, he did nothing to halt it. People were being rescued from the eastern parts of the Reich while at the same time extermination was still being maintained at industrial levels. One hand must have known perfectly well what the other hand was doing.

The wreck of the *Goya* on the seabed today. (Jonas Dahm)

8

DESTROYING THE EVIDENCE

Neuengamme is now part of larger Hamburg, a short journey on a local train from the central station. Here, until the early part of 1945, was one of the largest concentration camps in the German Reich, with a number of satellite camps scattered around the city. As the Allied troops approached Hamburg, the camp commandant, Max Pauly, fearing retribution, was determined to evacuate all the camps and destroy all the evidence of their existence. A large body of Nazis prepared themselves to undertake this eradication and 'destroy the evidence' became its guiding principle. Not only were the camps to be destroyed, but also all documents and the more tangible evidence of the existence of the camps – prisoners – were to be taken as far away from the hostile armies as possible. SS leader Heinrich Himmler had already declared *'Kein Häftling soll lebend in die Hände des Feindes fallen'* (No prisoner shall fall into enemy hands alive). In one way or another, all prisoners had to be liquidated.

At his trial at the Curiohaus in Hamburg in summer 1946, Pauly was questioned about what ultimately would have been the fate of the prisoners:

[Questioner] You said yesterday that Bassewitz [Count Georg-Henning von Bassewitz, senior SS officer] said that prisoners in Neuengamme were to be liquidated when the Allies approached.

[Pauly] Particularly the dangerous political elements that were in the Neuengamme.

– Might the actions in Fuhlsbüttel [a notorious camp in Hamburg] be something to do with this?

– I cannot say, but it is possible since the destruction of the political prisoners was already planned.

– Were you responsible for the execution of those who were executed on 21st or 22nd April?

– There was an order from Count Bassewitz.

– A special order for its people?

– For the <u>Fuhlsbüttel</u> actions there was a special order.

– Could this special order be the basis for an execution?

– It's possible.

– Did you have the opportunity to control it?

– No.

– You had to carry out such an order?

– Yes. Maybe I should say that I had previously given my word to Obergruppenführer Pohl on a separate instruction.

– What was the instruction?

– The Obergruppenführer had at the time told camp leaders that we need to think through how to kill the prisoners quickly with gas or other agents as the Allies approached.

– What was the word of honour? To remain silent?

– To remain silent.[1]

The first concentration camps had been built as early as February 1933, initially as temporary camps. This changed in 1934 when the camps came under the control of Heinrich Himmler and his SS, after which a more uniform system was developed. Some camps were transformed into extermination camps, although this happened relatively late in their history. They were planned to attract as little attention as possible. Extermination camps, in particular, were strategically sited so that the industrial killing was not located too close to civilian communities.

The extermination camp at Auschwitz had fallen to the advancing Soviet troops on 27 January 1945 before the SS had been able to destroy the evidence of its existence. The Nazis did not want this to happen again.

Himmler issued an instruction for the destruction of a camp, which was called 'Position A', but it is not clear exactly what he meant. The principle was that a camp would quickly be transformed so that the conquering enemy could not prove that they had found an industrial killing site. The plans for Dachau are illustrative: prisoners were to dig up the mass graves; bones were to be ground to make compost, ashes from the crematorium sieved to remove any fragments and then the crematorium used to burn the camp documents. The prisoners who participated in the work were to be killed, and the gas chambers and any other incriminating structures were to be blown up. As it happened, the SS had no time to implement this 'cleaning job' fully. In other places, such as Buchenwald, the prisoners rebelled and the plans came to naught. In other camps, prisoners managed to conceal documents before the SS could destroy them.

In the final weeks of Neuengamme and its satellite camps there were about 50,000 prisoners. They were not only Jews but political opponents, homosexuals, Jehovah's Witnesses, gypsies and a host of others. As well as men and women there were even child prisoners. No humanity was shown to them: in the autumn of 1944 tuberculosis experiments were conducted in Neugengamme's infirmary on twenty Jewish children, all aged between 5 and 12. To conceal what had happened from the Allies, on the night between 20 and 21 April 1945, just before Neuengamme was evacuated, the children were transferred to Bullenhuser Damm, an empty school building in Hamburg. Some were injected with morphine, others were simply lynched, their own body weight suffocating them. Two camp doctors and a few prisoners who knew too much shared their fate.

The Hamburg-South America Line's *Cap Arcona* was the flagship of the company, the queen of the south Atlantic. Sailing on her was the most comfortable way to travel from Europe to South America and many first-class passengers thought it the most elegant way.

THE WHITE BUSES

When the evacuation of the camps began, several people in Scandinavia organised the rescue of Norwegians and Danes in Neuengamme and other concentration camps. The operation was known as 'White Buses' after the colour of the transport used. Count Folke Bernadotte, deputy chairman of the Swedish Red Cross and nephew of the Swedish king Gustav V, a humanitarian with a strong Christian faith, came to be seen as the figurehead of this enterprise, although it was not his initiative.

The possibility of saving Scandinavians came about through the extraordinary contact between three people: Heinrich Himmler, massage therapist Felix Kersten and a Jewish Latvian businessman, Gillel Storch, who had come to Stockholm as a refugee.

Count Folke Bernadotte has personified the White Buses and the salvation of thousands of camp prisoners. He was perhaps too quick to claim the success of the operation for himself, something for which he would be criticised after the war.

Kersten, born in Estonia and holding, among others, Finnish citizenship, had become Himmler's masseur and as such he managed to temporarily relieve Himmler from the aches he suffered, so much so that Himmler felt he could not survive without this treatment. Kersten, in turn, was in touch with Storch in Stockholm. This triangle brought about the attempts to save all Scandinavians and as many Jews as they could from the camps.

Himmler may have declared that no prisoner would reach the Allies alive, but as the war drew to a close he allowed some Jews to purchase their evacuation to Switzerland. Indeed, corruption was rife throughout the concentration-camp system. The Norwegian physician Henry Meyer, a prisoner in Neuengamme, learned that everything could be bought in the camp:

> We started by sleeping on the floor, but soon beds, cabinets, sinks, mirrors and more were 'bought'. Due to a lack of tobacco among the Germans, most were paid with cigarettes … Corruption prevailed in the German camps – even life could be bought … Everything could be bought in Germany – it was just that prices were too often too high.[2]

Himmler may have had another motive for agreeing to the rescue of the Scandinavians – he may have thought that this would put him in a better light with the Allies. This was certainly one of the reasons Bernadotte believed the initiative was possible.

On 10 February 1945 a telegram from the Swedish State Department to the Embassy in Berlin announced that Bernadotte would come to the German capital to 'inspect the Red Cross expedition' but his main purpose was to obtain permission from the German authorities to evacuate Danish and Norwegian prisoners. Not only were the Swedes planning to evacuate prisoners, they were also looking for Swedish women who had married Germans, had been widowed and now had neither a home nor relatives in Germany.

At this time, it was not yet certain whether Himmler was willing to meet Bernadotte so the Swedish Embassy asked Walter Schellenberg, the Nazi head of foreign intelligence and advisor to Himmler, to use his influence. A meeting was arranged and Bernadotte flew to Berlin on 16 February.

Three days later they met and, Bernadotte later wrote, Himmler's side was surprisingly accommodating. Two weeks after the encounter, the Swedish Foreign Office relayed to their ambassador in London, Johan Beck-Fries, that Bernadotte's conversation with Himmler had been a triumph, that the prisoners would be gathered in a dedicated area in Neuengamme, and that a column of (white) buses would pick up those prisoners in the camp immediately threatened by the advancing Allies. The Germans had stated that they did not have the means to transport the prisoners, therefore it was best if it was organised from Sweden.

It was under cover of the greatest secrecy that this evacuation began. A circular issued on 28 February by the State Information Board to Swedish newspapers gave details of the operation but on the understanding that not a word should appear in print. The Information Board promised that a communiqué would come later: for the moment it was too delicate a subject.

The Scandinavian prisoners were moved to a separate part of Neuengamme, which was monitored by the Swedish Red Cross. For these prisoners, it was as if they stepped out through the gates of hell and out into the daylight. One of the Danes, Ernst Nielsen, described the feeling in a 1999 interview:

> The conditions were simply amazing, almost as if we had entered Paradise. On site there were no more orders and there was no conscripted labour anymore and no one beat us anymore. We were able to rest and sleep all the time, as much as we wanted.[3]

Curiously, the SS tried to keep some of the Scandinavian prisoners away from the part of the Neuengamme reserved for Danes and Norwegians. A former member of the Danish parliament, Axel Larsen, was one of them. He had been in the Sachsenhausen concentration camp and in March 1945 was taken along with several other Danes to Neuengamme. He was taken aside and put in a solitary cell in a bunker, where the SS had intended to execute him. An underground organisation that had formed in the camp suspected that Larsen was concealed somewhere. Another prisoner, an Austrian, had access to lists of names and succeeded in climbing, unseen, up on the roof of the bunker and made contact with Larsen through an air vent. He gave Larsen food and cigarettes and was able to tell the underground organisation that Larsen was indeed there and was about to be executed. Bernadotte was informed immediately and, as the SS and camp management held him in high esteem, was given immediate access to the bunker. Larsen was moved to join his compatriots.

On 20 April, all the mustered Scandinavian prisoners left Neuengamme – a column of more than 4,000 people. The Red Cross subsequently saved an additional 10,000 prisoners, but many of those who were not lucky enough to benefit from this special evacuation were later transported to ships in Neustadt Bay.

Most of the documents testifying to what had happened at the camps and who was responsible were destroyed. There had been detailed plans for providing new identities, money, clothes and everything else that was needed for the camp officials to disappear discreetly. Barracks, gallows and torture instruments were burned. The only evidence still to be disposed of were the remaining prisoners. They were sent from Neuengamme, partly by train, and partly on foot in the direction of Lübeck. The final major movement was of around 10,000 people, but transportation was spasmodic and at times, uncharacteristically, completely unplanned.

Prisoners were transported in livestock carriages, without food or water. Because the German rail network had been bombed continuously throughout the war, it was not possible to travel directly the relatively short distance between Hamburg and Lübeck. Indeed, it was not unheard of for a train to arrive in the evening at the same place it had departed from in the morning. In fact, it seemed as if the leadership of the SS themselves were not sure where these people were to go.

DEATH MARCHES

It was during this time that many of the notorious death marches took place, where prisoners were forced to walk briskly very long distances. Those unable to keep up were shot on the spot by the guards. Yet many prisoners managed to reach Lübeck and board the ships anchored there.

Several of these death marches began at Neuengamme's satellite camps and from there the prisoners walked north. Belgian Raymond van Pee was one of those forced to move from the camp at Bremen Schützenhof via Bremenvörde to Neuengamme:

> At midday came another order, we had to line up in rows of five and five and each group consisted of a hundred men. It was whispered that the camp would be evacuated ... After one kilometre we saw the first dead lying in the grass on the left and right side of the road ... Tuesday, 10th April, 1945. Five o'clock in the morning the doors [of the barracks] were torn open. After an hour's line-up for the roll call the first hundred prisoners leave the stone factory. We had nothing to eat. They promised us that we would get something at lunchtime.[4]

At the end of the sixth day, he and the other prisoners were so tired that they could not even fall asleep. They had seen their comrades – anyone with no strength left or who refused to continue – shot:

> Everyone felt guilty for our dead comrades. Would we have dragged them with us until we ourselves collapsed along with them? Or had we given up too early? For everyone, it was on our conscience.[5]

They reached the railway station in Bremervörde, where they were given about 150g of bread. After seven days, they reached Neuengamme but no one knew what to expect. It was on 13 April and shortly thereafter that everybody was taken further north towards Lübeck.

From there they were put on board ships such as the *Cap Arcona*. There remains the unanswered question – why did the SS chose a former passenger ship as a floating concentration camp? Was the ultimate purpose to tow it out to deeper water where it could be sunk and in doing so eliminate the 'evidence'? To place such a large number of people on ships that had no fuel and hardly any food or drink strongly suggests that this was indeed the SS's intention, but no documentary evidence has been found to prove it.

Nor is there a means of knowing exactly who was responsible. After the war, attempts were made by the Allies but those they captured blamed others or even each other. Only a few culprits were identified – but they included Karl Kaufmann, Gauleiter of Shipping, the man who selected the vessels that would be turned into floating concentration camps.

HAMBURG-SOUTH AMERICA LINE'S PRIDE

Kaufmann understood that a ship as large as the *Cap Arcona* would be able to accommodate a significant number of people: she was a vessel that had already transported about 8,000 refugees to Copenhagen. The problem was that she was still under the command of Konrad Engelhardt and his refugee transport organisation. Kaufmann also had to contend with the shipping company. For a long time, the Hamburg-South America Line had tried to protect their vessels, especially the flagship *Cap Arcona*, which they hoped would be back in civilian work as soon as hostilities were over.

The last journey the *Cap Arcona* had undertaken, however, had been fraught with problems. Mechanical damage meant that it was doubtful if she could leave Copenhagen. The other huge problem was the lack of fuel.

After the war, the British military authorities tried to discover why prisoners were taken to Neustadt Bay, Lübeck, and not Hamburg, which was much closer. One of the higher SS leaders, Georg-Henning Graf von Bassewitz-Behr, told them that the political and military leadership in Hamburg did not want thousands of concentration camp prisoners in the city at the very time that they were about to surrender uncon-ditionally. As no satellite camp was available, the SS leaders considered the ships at Neustadt were the best solution, albeit temporary. This also solved the problem of getting the prisoners away from the British troops.

For Konrad Engelhardt it was a shock when parts of the refugee fleet, under the order of Gauleiter Kaufmann, were taken from him. Kaufmann had rung Engelhardt on 15 April and told him that some ves-sels, including the *Cap Arcona*, would be requisitioned for 'special' tasks. Kaufmann informed him that the ship would take 8,000 prisoners from Neuengamme. Engelhardt angrily disagreed. 'It is absolutely out of the question!" he spluttered, but Kaufmann was immovable. Engelhardt explained that the ship was subordinate to the Navy, and that he was directly subordinate to Admiral Dönitz. Kaufmann said that this was no longer the case: he had given Engelhardt an order, he must abide by it. And, Kaufmann added, Engelhardt must inform the *Cap Arcona*'s officers.

Grand Admiral Dönitz had both the power to keep the *Cap Arcona* at the disposal of the refugee transport organisation or to deploy her for some other purpose, so Kaufmann must have had Dönitz's blessing for the order. Equally, Engelhardt was unable to countermand the order, which confirms that he understood that Dönitz explicitly or implicitly consented to a large passenger ship being turned into a concentration camp. Not only that, everyone was aware that the *Cap Arcona* was berthed because she consumed too much fuel. In late April 1945, there was hardly enough fuel for the smaller ships that shuttled between Hela and the western ports and so the *Cap Arcona* had been excluded as a refugee transporter. Her maintenance, including that of her life-saving equipment, had been seriously neglected: as she lay at anchor she could not be regarded as seaworthy. Thus was the *Cap Arcona*'s fate sealed.

Kaufmann suspected that the officers and crew would oppose this new role. However, he may have underestimated the *Cap Arcona*'s captain, Heinrich Bertram, a sailor of the old school whose ship was his kingdom.

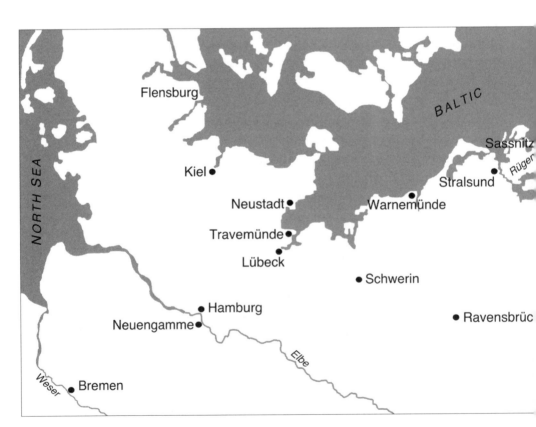

On 15 April, Captain Bertram travelled to Hamburg to try to find out from his shipping company, Hamburg-South America Line, what was planned for the *Cap Arcona*. They knew as little as Bertram, so he asked at the War Marine Division in Hamburg, who knew nothing either. He was still in Hamburg when a telegram reached the bridge of the *Cap Arcona*. First Officer William Hegener could not believe his eyes. No one could: he had to read the words several times:

> *Cap Arcona* will be cleared promptly for receiving a few thousand refugees from the concentration camps.[6]

Hegener immediately travelled to Neustadt in one of the ship's launches to get hold of Bertram and he eventually succeeded. Bertram insisted that it was absolutely not possible and he refused to entertain this absurd idea. He did not care that it was an order from Kaufmann: he was subordinate to Engelhardt and the vessel was subject to the Navy and the refugee organisation. Bertram returned to Hamburg and at the National Inspector of Shipping, which was Kaufmann's department, he learned that this was indeed the order. Although he protested, he was told that the 'shipments' were already under way and he and his crew must initiate preparations immediately for the prisoners who would soon reach Lübeck.

EVACUATION BY SEA

Prisoners were also evacuated from camps in other parts of the German Reich, including a satellite of the large Stutthof camp on Danzig Bay. They were taken on board two ships, *Elbing* and *Zephyr*, in a chaotic embarkation. During an air raid, about 100 prisoners managed to escape. The rest were packed tightly into the ships' holds, accompanied by both army and SS soldiers.

Elbing and *Zephyr* left Gotenhafen on 14 March for a westward journey of six days. Each prisoner was given one cup of water for the entire voyage, but very little food of any kind. About 100 of the 719 prisoners died, and their bodies thrown overboard. By April most of the survivors had been taken to Neuengamme, with the rest going directly to Lübeck. This was happening at the same moment that the refugee transport operation was in full swing and many refugees came in contact with the prisoners: their shocking appearance would haunt their memories for the rest of their lives. In retrospect it may seem surprising that the SS put so many resources into transporting prisoners when there was so little time and so few vessels to evacuate German civilians and soldiers, but the priority appears to have been to obey the edict to 'destroy the evidence'.

On 28 April more than 3,000 prisoners from the main Stutthof camp were embarked on four barges, including *Vaterland*, towed by the tug *Bussard*, and *Wolfgang*, towed by the *Adler*, which were then towed to the West. Each barge had four holds, each 8 by 5m. On the bottom, rotten straw had been strewn. Those prisoners without the strength to stand simply fell on top of their fellow passengers. The barges had no protection from the weather, but when the convoy reached Sassnitz the weather forced the barges to seek a harbour for shelter.

Ingmar Fredriksson, a sailor from the Åland Islands, was one of those forced to undertake the voyage. He had been second officer on the Finnish ship *Mercator*. When Finland broke its alliance with Germany in 1944, its sailors automatically became enemies of the Germans and the *Mercator* had unfortunately been in Danzig at the time. The crew was arrested and Fredriksson was sent to Stutthof. He kept a diary in the greatest secrecy, well aware that he could be shot if it was detected. But even on the barge, he wrote down what he experienced:

> The barge was about a 400 ton-cargo barge and we were around 1,000 people in it. We who were Scandinavians had the best space and yet we were so crowded that only half of us could sit, the other half had to stand.
>
> We divided ourselves into watches – sitting guards and standing guards. The Jews who were with the same barge lay on top of each other.
>
> We were then towed further west in the company of three barges, our barge had the worst tug and was therefore slowest.
>
> The Jews in the next compartment howled and howled throughout the day and night. In this condition, without food and water we were dragged along the German coast.[7]

Fredriksson noted that when they reached Stralsund, the city was in chaos. A tugboat came out with supplies but these were totally inadequate. A little margarine was distributed:

… and a small can of liver pate divided between six men and one cup of water per man.[8]

He had saved some supplies and noted that the last day of April was Walpurgis Night, a festival in Northern and Central Europe. Fredriksson thought he should celebrate it, despite the circumstances in which he found himself:

… eating one raw potato that I had saved and a piece of liver pate with margarine on.[9]

In Warnemünde the crew went ashore to see if there was any food but they 'got a negative answer', and the slow journey towards Lübeck continued:

At that time a lot of us drank the sea water and now quite a number had already died and been thrown overboard.[10]

Several mishaps occurred and other ships brought more prisoners westwards but when the convoy finally arrived in Lübeck only 2,665 people remained of more than 5,000 who had been transported from Gotenhafen and Stutthof.

As early as 20 April, inmates started to arrive in Lübeck, where there were now more vessels that the SS had requisitioned for their prisoners. *Thielbek*, *Athen* and *Elmenhorst* were moored there, although lack of fuel would later prevent *Elmenhorst* departing.

Thielbek, a cargo ship belonging to the Hamburg company Knöhr & Burchard, had been taken into a shipyard for repairs. She was towed into the industrial port of Lübeck on the night of 19 April and that evening high-ranking SS officers came on board to meet Captain John Jacobsen. He was told that very soon his ship would take aboard 2,000 prisoners. He protested indignantly, but was told that if he refused to obey the SS he would be shot on the spot. Jacobsen knew they meant business and that he had no way of preventing the prisoners coming on board.

Thielbek, with an eighteen-man crew, had no facilities to act as a prisoner transporter. There was a kitchen and toilets for the crew but for several thousand people there was nothing. No one could understand how these people could get food or even address their most basic needs. But the order was clear and no one on *Thielbek* dared oppose it.

Athen, a ship belonging to the German Levant Line, was ordered to go to the same berth as *Thielbek* and also to take on board prisoners. Adjacent to the vessels was a silo where the Red Cross stored food parcels for the prisoners who were on their way from Neuengamme. On 19 April, under cover of darkness, SS guards plundered the silo and took a large portion of the parcels.

On Friday, 30 April, the day Adolf Hitler committed suicide, 2,300 prisoners arrived in Lübeck from Neuengamme on cattle trucks. They were starving, but only a few of the Red Cross parcels were still there, so most of the prisoners continued to starve. It was early in the morning and they were immediately herded on board *Thielbek*.

One of the prisoners, Willi Lenz, saw that Untersturmbannführer Max Kierstein from Neuengamme was in command of the prisoners in Lübeck. Lenz had already experienced the train journey where many of his comrades had died of malnutrition or disease. When they came out on the dock Lenz saw:

> … a febrile man, with an unspeakable effort crawled out of his wagon, broke down, curled up on the quayside and was shot with a gun from a metre away by Kierstein, who had sprung forward. An SS man rolled him down the edge of the dock with his feet. The prisoner fell six metres down into the water. A large balloon of blood spread out in the water. You could see how the zebra-striped jacket swelled up before the body twisted and sank under the water. Kierstein was laughing! And yet ten minutes later this beast shot another defenceless sick man.[11]

The Russians and Poles were treated the worst. It was as if the SS found pleasure in confining these prisoners in the storerooms that were far forward, where potatoes and other foods were normally kept. These compartments had no daylight, standing height or ventilation: they were plain and simple stores. Among the prisoners was Alexander Machnew from Ufa in the Soviet Union. He had come on one of the freight trains and then forced down into the forecastle of the *Athen*:

> At four o'clock in the morning there were voices from SS soldiers. Closer and closer came the jingle-jangle sound of the locks on the trailer doors,

guards took away the prisoners. Our gate was also opened. There came a harsh commandment: 'Everyone out!' … This morning it was very foggy. SS soldiers formed a double line with three metre intervals through which we must get through.

From the talk of the guards standing around, I realised that we were in the port of Lübeck.[12]

Machnew thought there could have been 2,000 people in the hold and the moment he stepped on board he had more than death to worry about:

The first three days we got nothing to eat, nothing to drink. On the fourth day we were first given a small piece of bread. At noon, they sent down a bowl of soup in the hold and the soup was of the nature that it gave no joy to eat, despite our hunger. During our time in captivity we had suffered more than enough hunger pangs, but here at the bottom of the vessel we also were tormented by thirst and lack of air. The SS guards did open the door at times, but closed it again. The lack of oxygen became even greater.[13]

OWN INITIATIVE

In the meantime, the Swedish Red Cross had received permission to leave Sweden for Lübeck with two chartered ships, the *Lillie-Matthiessen* and *Magdalena*. They carried food parcels intended to be distributed among the prisoners, but if it was possible they would bring the prisoners back to Sweden.

More than once, it was the individual initiatives of Red Cross workers that brought prisoners on board. Lübeck was regarded as a relatively safe port: in 1944 Red Cross president Swiss C.J. Burckhardt had persuaded the Allies not to bomb it because the Red Cross wanted to use the port as a transhipment location for food parcels destined for Allied prisoners of war.

Dr Hans Arnoldsson worked for the Swedish Red Cross and belonged to Count Bernadotte's staff. He had participated in the evacuation of the Scandinavian prisoners but heard about the evacuation of the remaining prisoners from Neuengamme:

From an anonymous letter I received on 29th April I learned about this evacuation. The letter stated that in the harbour there was a ship named Athen and which had prisoners on board, who lived under the most difficult conditions and almost completely lacked food. The writer now requested the Red Cross for help. I could establish that on board there were 250 French, Belgian, Dutch [prisoners], and the rest mainly Russians. The total number of prisoners was about 2,200. Our Swedish boats Lillie-Matthiessen and Magdalena were lying in the harbour, ready to sail to Sweden after unloading their cargoes of packages for POWs.[14]

Arnoldsson negotiated with the German authorities that these 250 prisoners could be brought back to Sweden. On 30 April, at ten o'clock in the morning, the prisoners were lined up on the dock. Arnoldsson noted that it was quiet: everyone was stern-faced. None of them knew that they would be taken to Sweden:

The banana boat *Lillie-Matthiessen* on her way to Stockholm. In 1945 she was chartered, together with the *Magdalena*, by the Swedish Red Cross to ferry food packages to prisoners in Germany. (Gunnar Hedman)

The cargo ship *Magdalena* moored in Stockholm. In Lübeck as many camp prisoners as possible were taken on board. The commanders of the German guards would have allowed the Red Cross to take every prisoner, but this was impossible for these small steamers and many were left on the quayside. (Gunnar Hedman)

> Their joy was very great when they were told of the correct circumstances. Prisoners were mostly in very bad condition, a portion terribly thin, so-called Muselmann [a slang term meaning suffering from a combination of starvation and exhaustion]. Many had the typical striped prison clothes and some lacked the most essential piece of clothing.[15]

One of those transferred to a Swedish ship was the Belgian Albert van Nerun. Someone called out to French, Belgian, Dutch and Luxembourger prisoners to come up on deck where women at typewriters took their names:

Our surprise was when they did not ask for our numbers but for our names, our date of birth and nationality, and they wrote down the data. We dared not speak to each other about it. Quite a long while later, we left the ship under surveillance. We had to wait on the quay. It started to get dark. Then came a white bus from the Danish [sic] Red Cross. No, no cheers, not yet, don't show any joy. We were still surrounded by the SS. We entered [the bus] and went to another quay. There was a small vessel under the Swedish flag, *Magdalena*. Without the SS we went aboard. It was 30th April 1945. During the night we were taken to Trelleborg, Sweden. Rescued![16]

The Germans, however, still had the problem of removing all the camp prisoners left in Lübeck before the British arrived. An SS Hauptsturmführer was worried about facing Arnoldsson regarding the prisoners' condition: there were several cases of typhus and fears of contagion. The commandant had no orders, so was unsure what to do:

> He made a proposal that we should take over all the prisoners and take them to Sweden, which I unfortunately could not accept, as our resources would not have sufficed for such a number of people ... Then we loaded our 250 prisoners and I parted with a sickening feeling of powerlessness from the SS commander.[17]

Another group of prisoners who were seriously ill was transferred to the *Magdalena* but the ship could not accommodate more. The *Magdalena* departed as the other prisoners waited to be transported out to the *Cap Arcona*. Dr Arnoldsson had learned of the vessels in Neustadt Bay and he realised that this information must be passed on to the British:

> Then on 2nd May, in the afternoon, the British took the city. I understood that *Athen* had left the port. She joined the other evacuation vessels in Neustadt, which was still in German hands. There were now in port and at anchor four ships, all with Neuengamme prisoners on board. On the morning of 3rd May, I told the English authorities about the prison ships. Battles were then raging in the district of Neustadt and bombing activity was intense. The ships found themselves directly in the danger zone. The

British promised to investigate the matter and in the afternoon I was visited by two senior officers, who wanted to know all the details I knew concerning ships and their cargo and they promised to take action.[18]

The state of the accommodation for the prisoners on the ships was terrible, as Captain Walter von Lewinski would conclude. He had been sent as an expert from the Reich's Commission for the Maritime, and hence was subject to Kaufmann's orders. He later came to be on board the *Cap Arcona* on 3 May. He inspected the *Elmenhorst* and *Thielbek*:

According to the captains there were about 2,000 people on each ship, about twice as many as the ships could take on a short trip. Both ships were merely cargo ships, which were definitely not suitable for the accommodation of people and at best could be used as ferries. The prisoners were tightly packed in the holds and on deck. On Thielbek's aft deck and on shore, I saw a few corpses.[19]

When Heinrich Bertram of the *Cap Arcona* returned to Neustadt from Hamburg, he was determined to deny the boarding of prisoners as long as he could. He had his entire crew behind him (even though it was now much reduced). He knew it could be dangerous to oppose the SS, but at the same time, he could not take responsibility for so many people on a ship where there was insufficient life-saving equipment, supplies, water, toilets, and even the most basic requirements for a functioning vessel. On both 20 and 21 April, *Athen* came alongside the *Cap Arcona* with the request that prisoners be brought on board, but Bertram and his officers stubbornly refused to allow it. Without their agreement, it was not possible; the ship's high sides prevented any attempt. *Athen* was forced to return to Lübeck with the same number of prisoners on board.

The SS knew that the end of the war was fast approaching. They increasingly passed the monitoring of the prisoners to other guards and put into operation their pre-arranged plans to change identities, dress as civilians and disappear.

On 24 April, *Athen* once again returned to the *Cap Arcona* and was again denied permission to transfer prisoners. So once more *Athen* returned to Lübeck. For the officers on the *Cap Arcona*, it was just a matter of stalling until British troops took Lübeck and Neustadt.

This plan unravelled on 26 April. Bertram had again been to Hamburg but, having failed to achieve anything, returned in the morning. In Neustadt, a launch waited to bring him out to the *Cap Arcona*. He then became aware of an approaching SS officer. This was SS Sturmbannführer Gehring, accompanied by two SS soldiers:

> He showed me a written order in which it was stated that I would be shot on the spot if I continued to refuse to board prisoners. I understood that it was now clear that my death would not prevent the prisoners coming on board.[20]

Second Officer Thore Dommenget had signed on in Copenhagen after having served on the *Monte Rosa*, another of the Hamburg America Line ships, under Heinrich Bertram:

Heinrich Bertram, captain of the *Cap Arcona*. He was a 'sailor of the first rank' according to his second officer, Thore Dommenget. Knowing the limited capacity, provisions and life-saving equipment on the ship, Bertram delayed boarding the camp prisoners as long as he could but when, on the Neustadt quayside, the SS threatened to shoot him he had to capitulate. (Heinz Schön)

He was a sailor of the first rank. He was also a man who during the terrible Nazi era had moral courage. ... He was a man who was not afraid, he was not frightened by the Nazis ... Bertram had done everything possible to avoid this situation for the camp prisoners [that they came on board], he had tried the Navy, the shipping company of course, but it did not succeed. Then occurred the following ... [in Neustadt]: There came an SS officer with two men who approached me and asked:

'How do we get out to the *Cap Arcona*?'

'What do you want there?'

'We want to meet *Cap Arcona*'s captain!'

'But you do not need to go on board, he's right there!'

The [SS officers] explained that he'd be shot on the spot if he would continue to refuse [to accept the prisoners] ... He read through the order and said, 'Do you know, I have a wife and two children, and for that reason I will go with this insane order.[21]

Bertram explained his predicament to Dommenget: if he was shot prisoners would still come on board; his wife would be a widow and his children fatherless. There was no alternative.

9

THE MESSAGE WAS NOT PASSED ON

The *Cap Arcona* was the Hamburg South American Line's flagship, the South Atlantic's uncrowned queen and Hamburg's pride. Built in the Blohm & Voss shipyard in Hamburg, she was launched on 14 May 1927. By 19 November, she was ready to be handed over to the shipping company.

The journey from Hamburg to Rio de Janeiro took twelve days and another three days to reach Buenos Aires via Santos and Montevideo. Size, luxury and speed were the watchwords of the new ship. Like all other major passenger liners, *Cap Arcona* was a community in itself.

'Three times around the promenade deck was a kilometre,' the *Cap Arcona*'s Second Officer, Thore Dommenget, later recalled. She was 205m long, 25.7m wide and had a gross tonnage of 27,561grt. Driven by turbine engines with a maximum capacity of 28,000hp, she had a top speed of 21 knots. There was space for 1,315 passengers, a large number of whom were first class. The crew numbered 630, most of whom attended the needs of the first-class passengers, so that the long journey would be as comfortable as possible. Nothing was missing for the discerning passenger: the Cunard Line's catchphrase 'Going there is half the fun' applied equally to the Hamburg South American line.

Despite competition, especially from Italian and French ships that went to South America, the *Cap Arcona* remained the favourite among wealthy Argentinians. She became so popular and so prominently advertised that it led to the end of her smaller sister ship, the *Cap Polonio*, which was sold for scrap in June 1935.

In 1937 parts of the third-class accommodation were converted into refrigerated rooms: it was more profitable to transport meat from Argentina than third-class passengers. The following year, the *Cap Arcona*'s build cost had finally been paid off and the future looked very bright. On 8 August 1939, she began her ninety-second return trip to Germany, mooring according to schedule on 25 August at Überseebrücke in Hamburg. At the time no one imagined that this would be her final voyage across the Atlantic, but it was in fact to be the last ever commercial trip for any of the company's passenger ships.

Built to withstand the storms of the South Atlantic, the *Cap Arcona* sailed to South America via Madeira as a regular liner as well as a cruise ship.

The *Cap Arcona* in Buenos Aires.

The *Cap Arcona* leaving the landing stage in Hamburg.

The *Cap Arcona* (left) and her sister *Cap Polonia* in Hamburg harbour.

Above and opposite: The *Cap Arcona* quickly became a very popular ship among the rich and fastidious passengers – so much so that her sister ship, the *Cap Polonio,* became redundant and was scrapped. (Thore Dommenget)

After the outbreak of war, the *Cap Arcona* was included in the list of ships ordered to serve the German navy. She stayed in Hamburg for almost a year but on 29 November 1940, she relocated to Gotenhafen and became a barrack ship for 2,000 navy sailors and 300 *Marine Helferinnen*.

SINKING *TITANIC* IN THE BALTIC

One of the great but tragic ironies of maritime history was the sinking of the *Titanic* being replayed on the *Cap Arcona*. Staged scenes of panic on her decks were shortly afterwards to become a cruel reality. But, next to James Cameron's *Titanic* film project, the *Cap Arcona* was the largest piece of scenery ever used to depict *Titanic*. Yet director Herbert Selpin never saw his big movie completed and it was banned before it reached its intended audience.

Opposite and this page: The film
Titanic was intended to portray
the corruption of the British.
Unfortunately, this had a boomerang
effect. By spotlighting one person,
the director of the shipping company,
as a crook, it would not have been
difficult for audiences to see a parallel
with the leader of the German Reich.

Propaganda minister Joseph Goebbels had been impressed by *Der Untergang der Titanic (The Sinking of the* Titanic) by German author Pelz von Felinau (the same book Heinz Schön had been reading just before the *Wilhelm Gustloff* went down), a novel published in 1939. In it, Felinau gives *Titanic* a new hero: a German officer. The theme suited Goebbels perfectly: he wanted a movie that clearly depicted the corruption of British society, where money went before human life but where one person, a German, stood up and tried to stop the madness.

Money was no problem, but Goebbels needed someone who could handle the maritime environment, someone who could make a good seafaring film. There was one such director, Herbert Selpin, although he was not someone in whom Goebbels had great confidence. But there was no one with the same flair, so Goebbels agreed to give Selpin the commission. The script would, after all, be written by Walter Zerlett-Olfenius, a devoted Nazi.

For his own part, Selpin was no admirer of Goebbels and his sympathies for National Socialism were very low. However, it was an interesting commission. He needed a suitable stage for the exterior scenes and when the *Cap Arcona* was suggested, Selpin thought her perfect. She had long promenade decks: he could not imagine a more appropriate scene for his *Titanic*.

When Selpin arrived at Gotenhafen, very little had been done to prepare the ship for filming. The longer the recording dragged on, the worse his mood became. Many scenes had to be filmed at night, and frequently neighbouring warships 'accidentally' swept the film team with searchlights, which meant that recordings had to be redone. This and a host of other incidents increased both Selpin's rage and his alcohol intake. One day he went over the top and in a bar commented on the 'shit army' and the 'shit fleet'. Reported by so-called friends, Selpin was interrogated by the Gestapo. His filming was nearing the end, as was his patience, so he refused to recant. He was arrested on 31 July and found dead on 1 August. The Gestapo declared that 'he had hanged himself in his cell'. No further explanation was given.

Completing the film was passed to a more reliable director, Werner Klingler. However, before the film was released, it was shown privately to Joseph Goebbels. At the end he left in a rage. Even after his death, Selpin managed to take his revenge.

Titanic weaves the facts of the well-known ship disaster with a number of fictions. Before her encounter with the iceberg, a host of stock speculation takes place: the vessel has cost too much to build, putting her owners in financial trouble. The stock price is falling, something has to be done. 'Sir' Bruce Ismay (who was in reality the company's chief executive although not knighted) orders the ship to sail at top speed to New York; as owners of the world's fastest ship, the stock price will go up and the company will be saved.

The few honourable people on board are the German third-class passengers and the German third officer, Petersen. He protests loudly against the increase in speed as the ship has received warnings of icebergs. But nobody listens to him, the ship collides with an iceberg and sinks. The wealthy passengers bribe their way into the lifeboats, as does Ismay. He has a seat next to Petersen, who tolerates him only so that Ismay can be held responsible. At the resulting enquiry, Ismay is absolved, which demonstrates the rotten state of British morality and the corruption of the British system.

It was not the film Goebbels wanted. In 1943, the civilian population was suffering from the Allies' ceaseless bombings, and the German people were beginning to understand that real disaster was approaching and one person was responsible: Adolf Hitler. Selpin had also laid the blame for a disaster on a single person. The parallel was too close. In a country under constant aerial attack, the panic scenes were too close to home and Selpin had failed to make all the British villains. Some, such as the telegrapher, were even depicted showing great heroism.

The film could not be shown in Nazi Germany. It was labelled as 'Valuable to the State' – but banned at home. The premiere took place in Paris on 10 November 1943, and it was first shown in Stockholm on 28 January 1944. After the war, *Titanic* was again banned, but this time in the Allied territories for its anti-British content. It was, however, a great success in the 1950s in Eastern Europe, where it seemed to depict cold-blooded capitalism in the raw.

A SHIP IS MADE INTO A CAMP

It was with a heavy heart that Bertram and Dommenget went out to the *Cap Arcona* on 26 April after the meeting with SS Sturmbannführer Gehring. Bertram gathered his officers on the bridge and announced that it was no longer possible to oppose the SS. He spoke from the heart when he explained that as, far as they could, they had to treat all those who came on board with dignity, that they would try to get the prisoners to feel they were on a ship and no longer in a concentration camp. At the same time, he knew that there would be a large contingent of guards, including SS soldiers, and they probably had no intention of treating the prisoners any better than they had been treated before.

Bertram thought he might prevent bloodshed if once the prisoners were on board he could prevent the SS having the opportunity to execute the prisoners. He later told Dommenget that he really thought the prisoners might be taken to Sweden:

> In Hamburg, I was told that Count Bernadotte from Sweden even declared he was ready to take over the prisoners with the exception of the Germans. There would already be Swedish ships on their way and I would soon return to Neustadt.[1]

It was only a rumour, but one that was repeated so many times on the *Cap Arcona* that it came to be taken as the truth.

The first 2,500 prisoners were transferred under guard from the *Athen* to the *Cap Arcona* the same afternoon. For commanders and crewmen it was a shock – many had been led to believe that the German concentration camps were only for criminals and perverts, so the sight of these ordinary people, distressed and starving, was a brutal awakening.

Chief Steward Fritz Schwarz had been on the *Cap Arcona* for eighteen years. He had many memories from times of peace, he had experienced the war, and he had also participated in three refugee transports that *Cap Arcona* had carried out. What he saw when the prisoners came on board surpassed everything he had experienced:

> There were living dead who stumbled on board the *Cap Arcona*, dressed in rags or prison clothing, walking uncertainly along the gangway. Some supported others because many had no strength left. Only a few prisoners seemed to be German. You could hear Russian, Polish, Czech and French – and many other languages. There were old and young people. Or did they just look so old? … They streamed on board in hundreds.[2]

He noted that the prisoners had not been prepared for the glory of the ship that still remained, and he saw that they marvelled at the big mirrors. Schwarz wondered how many of them had ever been on board a ship before:

In the evening of the day when the first prisoners came aboard and I got a bit of peace, I went into one of these luxury cabins on the C Deck. I wanted to tell the people to spare the furniture. They stared at me when I entered the cabin. I did not heed the prohibition of speaking with the prisoners. My appeal was taken for granted and when they realised that I belonged to the civilian crew they began to speak. There were German concentration camp prisoners who were in the cabin and talked to me. I saw how their eyes glistened when I spoke to them, human to human, to me normal but to them it was clearly unreal. I was concerned when I left the cabin and I asked myself why these people were in concentration camps.[3]

Prisoners were shipped from both Lübeck and Neustadt and by 29 April there were about 7,500 people on board. A desperate attempt by Bertram to draw a halt when 5,000 detainees had been boarded did not succeed. He was brutally corrected by the SS and he found out that he was no longer the captain of his own ship. On the same day he returned to Hamburg to ensure he was relieved from responsibility of all future orders. He returned to Neustadt that same evening.

Initially, the SS had command of prisoners and ships. As before, the Russians and Poles were treated with particular cruelty and once again herded into the most confined areas in the bow, in front of the collision bulkhead. As on the *Athen*, where many had died of suffocation, there was not enough space to stand up and the oxygen supply was low. They were in what the crew called the banana room. However, and remarkably, after a doctor inspected these spaces, he succeeded in persuading the SS to have the prisoners moved to cabins on D deck.

As the SS slowly started to vanish, pressure relaxed and control was no longer as rigorous. Instead, older navy men were appointed as guards. Every day, however, one of the launches went to Neustadt with dead bodies for burial. The SS command tried to oppose this – it was surely enough to throw the dead overboard – but the officers stood firm and organised the funerals.

There were all kinds of prisoners in the concentration camps. One group that the Nazis regarded with particular disfavour were Jehovah's Witnesses because their religious convictions led to their refusal to undertake military service, which was tantamount to treason. Several thousand were taken to concentration camps. One of those who survived Neuengamme was Alfred Knegendorf. He had been forced onto the train transport to Lübeck, taken to board the *Thielbek* and afterwards he had been transferred to the *Athen*. On 27 April, he found himself on the *Cap Arcona*. He found out that even though he and some other Witnesses had a luxury cabin with a bath and shower (albeit without water) they had nothing to eat. He told his co-prisoners that they could possibly last for three days but no longer – unless the persistent rumour that the SS intended to blow up the ship proved correct:

> With a little rope that I caught I sounded the sea. It was 18 metres deep. Thus we had figured out: should the ship sink, water would come up to our window, and if she capsized the ship would rise about seven meters out of the water, as she was 25 metres wide.[4]

THE LIBERATORS ARE CLOSE

On 28 April, British troops crossed the Elbe at Lauenburg and established a bridgehead to Schleswig-Holstein. But fierce battles the next day halted the Allied advance. Despite this setback, the news reached the *Cap Arcona* that liberation was close. To the British units, it appeared that large numbers of German troops were concentrated in Schleswig-Holstein, which was partially correct. As the Allies had advanced, the entire German administration moved northwards, towards Flensburg and the border with Denmark. As well as the administration, what was left of the German army and naval leadership also headed north. The Allies assumed that there could be an opportunity – if an opportunity was given – for the German command to pull completely out of Germany and continue the fight in Norway.

Daily reconnaissance flights by the British reported that large numbers of ships were arriving in Lübeck and Neustadt. There was therefore good reason to suspect that what remained of German resistance would use these ships to get to Norway. It was a scenario that had to be avoided at all costs and therefore the Allies began to focus on bombing what was left of German ships. The British commanders reasoned that the ships in Neustadt Bay should be destroyed before they sailed.

Had the information that there were prisoners on board these ships not reached them?

Like all the prisoners, the Russian Alexander Machnew was aware that the end of the war was near. Even though it was strictly forbidden to listen to the Allied radio broadcasts, news somehow always managed to slip through and he understood that it was now only a question of days before liberation. But it also meant that the prisoners were neglected more than ever. The food that previously had been rationed now ceased to be distributed altogether; the fresh water brought out to the ship on one of the launches also stopped:

> In the middle of the ship at the entrance to our deck there was a pile that was growing and growing of the dead bodies of our comrades, a lot of naked starved bodies. No one was surprised by this and none of us were exempt from filling this place.[5]

Bertram had repeated conflicts with the officer who commanded the SS on board, Thümmel. There were not more than thirty SS guards on the ship, and they did not dare go down to the lower decks for fear of catching the diseases that were rife. This gave the prisoners the opportunity to organise themselves, and plot an insurrection. In fact, plans had been developing since boarding, but when the food and water stopped, the situation sharpened. It is clear that Captain Bertram knew about the prisoners' organisation: on the afternoon of 1 May he told its leader, Erwin Geschonneck, that Hitler was dead. The news ran around the ship, giving renewed hope.

It was decided that the advancing British troops must be contacted and told who was on the vessels. During the night of 29 and 30 April, some of the imprisoned Russian officers decided that the time had come to try to get to Neustadt. Eleven men who felt they were in good enough condition to swim, were chosen for the operation. They managed to get into the water, but they had totally misjudged their strength in relation to the distance between the ship and the land. They had apparently swum in the direction of Travemünde, a stretch of more than 5km.

A guard boat found three bodies and another one man still alive who was almost completely frozen. He was taken in a more or less unconscious state back to the *Cap Arcona*, where he was immediately shot. The others had simply disappeared. This did not diminish the thought of an uprising but the prisoners did not know how to go about it. They also feared that German submarines could be around the ships and might attack should there be an uprising. The German prisoner Rudi Goguel later described the feeling:

We were feverishly excited. Can you imagine how a person worries when he reads after ten years at the last signpost: freedom or death? We felt a part of the incredible responsibility that rested upon us if we did not do anything – or if what we did went wrong.[6]

Between prisoners and crew there arose some kind of mutual respect; they knew that the crew had nothing to do with the SS and they also noticed that they were treated in a different way by them. As the days went by and the Allies advanced, more and more SS men left the ships. Those who were left to guard the prisoners were often a kind of home guard, part of the decaying army of older men. An unsuccessful attempt to scrape together soldier material for the shrinking army was witnessed by Goguel. Many had been without food for a long time, and he saw the scene as almost farce-like:

On 28th April, SS-Oberscharführer Wiehagen of Neuengamme appeared on board to muster the German prisoners into a security unit for the SS. However, the appearance of the human skeletons seemed to convince him that there were no longer any fighters for the dying German Reich. In any event, he left with his task unfulfilled.[7]

On 1 May, as the British Army's 11th Tank Division neared, the Lübeck police commander ordered the *Thielbek*, already laden with prisoners, to depart. Because of her damaged rudder, she had to be towed to the River Trave, past Travemünde and out in the bay. With great difficulty, the *Thielbek* was manoeuvred towards the *Cap Arcona*.

FREIGHT

There were about 2,800 prisoners on board the *Thielbek*, in conditions that were even more vile than on the *Cap Arcona*. The *Thielbek* was a cargo vessel, her few cabins were only for the crew: she was not a ship suitable for carrying people. As early as 20 April, Third Mate Theodor Schotmann entered the disturbing note in his diary that they were taking on board prisoners from camps. As the *Thielbek* was still in the repair yard, nobody could understand who could have conceived this madness. On 25 April, he wrote that the prisoners had started to come aboard in large numbers but everything was much worse than he ever imagined. On 26 April, the situation became tense:

> Today, the prisoners at Thielbek have had a hot meal for the first time:
> Per man one quarter litre of cabbage soup.
> Like wolves they devoured it.
> If and when there is food again, nobody knows.
> The situation on board is becoming increasingly catastrophic.
> Above all, it stinks from the sanitary parts, literally up to the sky.
> For the concentration camp prisoners there is no water on board, neither to drink nor to wash.
> Nor are there toilets for them. But down in the cargo spaces, they know how to help themselves. From the hold room floor someone has lifted the planks so that you can look down into the flooring. It has been done on every deck. These openings they created serve as toilets. Down on the bottom, the excrement grows several centimetres day by day. It stinks terribly, the stench goes through all the holds.[8]

On 2 May, the convoy of barges from Stutthof and Gotenhafen reached Neustadt. Some of the starving prisoners saw scraps of food lying on the ground on the dockside. They managed to get up onto the dock before they were discovered, whereupon they were brutally thrown back into the barges again. All this played out in front of civilians, who merely thought they were looking at criminals: propaganda still had a firm grip even this late in the war.

ONE LAST CHANCE

The barges left Neustadt again, heading towards Lübeck, where on their way out they crossed paths with the *Thielbek* and *Athen*, and with the moored *Cap Arcona*. The convoy, however, went on to Travemünde. Here two prisoners managed to escape and they eventually reached the areas in Lübeck occupied by the British. These two told them about the prison transports, the barges and the ships, but the information did not reach high enough in the chain of command to prevent the tragedy that was to follow.

Lübeck before the outbreak of the Second World War. The town was to be heavily targetted by repeated air attacks. It was to here that the prisoners from Neuengamme were brought before being taken out into Neustadt Bay and the prison ships.

Other eyes were watching. A British spy was moving around the surroundings of Lübeck in late April 1945, recording the mass movement of people. He saw the prison transports but his only way of communicating with his superior was by postcards routed through Sweden. His reports were received far too late.

Just after the prison convoy left the harbour on 2 May for Neustadt Bay, British troops entered Lübeck. In the city there was a Swiss representative of the Red Cross, Paul de Blonay, who had important information. As he later stated:

In April 1945 I was at the harbour of Lübeck seeing about some shipments of Red Cross Parcels and I noticed a ship SS *Thielbeck* at the place where I was accustomed to unload Red Cross petrol supplies. Whilst I was walking past this ship, a box of matches dropped beside me. I could not find who had thrown it. This box contained a letter ... telling me about the state of some deportees – about 7,000 – in the three ships SS *Thielbeck*, SS *Athen* and SS *Cap Arcona*.[9]

De Blonay described the person he informed as a brigadier with the name of Roberts or Rogers. This could have been the British brigadier who captured Lübeck, Major General 'Pip' Roberts of the 11th Armoured division; Brigadier Churcher, of the 159th Infantry Division or Brigadier Harvey of the 29th Armoured Division. The officer passed the message on, but it is not known to whom. Major N.O. Till, who investigated the disaster at Neustadt Bay, reported:

The intelligence officer with 83rd Group RAF has admitted on two occasions ... that a message was received on 2nd May 1945 that these ships were loaded with KZ [concentration camp] prisoners but that, although there was ample time to warn the pilots of the planes who attacked those ships on the following day, by some oversight the message was never passed on ...[10]

All the files in the National Archives at Kew relating to the incident were made public in 1972. However, within these files, certain papers that were at one time in Till's report, such as the statement of the RAF intelligence officer and 'Reports by RAF', are missing. It has not been possible to discover why the information passed by Dr Hans Arnoldsson to 'two senior [British] officers' appears never to have reached the Royal Air Force.

Out in the bay, there were more than 9,000 people on the ships. The *Cap Arcona* was not as congested as the *Thielbek*, but everywhere the number of deaths from fatigue, hunger and disease were about to rise steeply. During the week about 300 prisoners died. The little food there was came from the few Red Cross parcels that had not been stolen by the SS; when the Scandinavian prisoners from Neuengamme were evacuated to Sweden, the remainder of their parcels were transferred to the *Cap Arcona*.

An air attack on a target at sea photographed by one of the aircraft. During the attacks on the ships in Neustadt Bay the pilots had little chance to see, let alone realise, that the white sheets hanging out were to mark surrender. (© Imperial War Museum)

Meanwhile, the German troops became more dissolute, given the uncertainty of their own futures. Neustadt's civil authorities had decided that the city would surrender without a fight but there was a nervous wait for the British tanks to arrive. The city centre was blocked to any prisoners who might turn up: the authorities were very concerned to ensure that the invading troops should not think that the prisoners had anything to do with the town.

The morning of 3 May saw the *Cap Arcona*, *Thielbek*, *Athen* and *Deutschland* still anchored on the roadstead. The *Deutschland* lay almost empty with no prisoners on board: although she had played a major role in the evacuation of troops and civilians from East Prussia, she was in the process of being converted into a hospital ship. Because of the shortage of paint, only her funnels were white and on only one side of one funnel was there a red cross.

The *Cap Arcona*'s second officer, Thore Dommenget, along with the ship's boy, Franz Wolff, and a few crewmen, had gone to Neustadt for the funerals of dead prisoners. Once these were over, Dommenget returned to the *Cap Arcona* while Wolff stayed ashore to try to find some supplies. It was a relatively mild May day, cloudy but still quite clear. It was two o'clock in the afternoon when Captain Nobmann on the *Athen* was ordered to return to Neustadt to take on prisoners from the Stutthof camp. Nobmann remonstrated with SS Untersturmbannführer Kierstein that his ship was completely full and the argument carried on until almost half past three. It came to an abrupt halt. British fighter-bombers thundered over the bay in the direction of the little armada of ships and a few moments later bombs began to rain down.

POSITION OF SHIP AFTER ATTACK

TRESS CONCENTRATION
ND A CIRCULAR HOLE IN A FLAT
AKE OF WIDTH 4 TIMES DIA. OF HOLE.

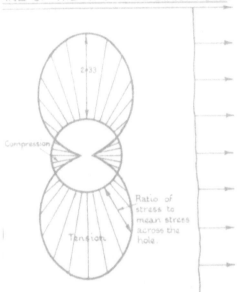

2·33

Compression

Tension

Ratio of stress to mean stress across the hole.

DAMAGE FROM 500LB M.C. B

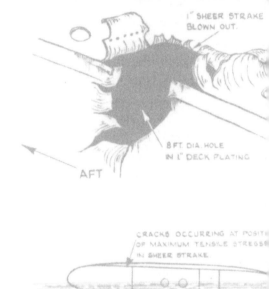

1" SHEER STRAKE BLOWN OUT.

8 FT. DIA. HOLE IN 1" DECK PLATING

AFT

CRACKS OCCURRING AT POSITION OF MAXIMUM TENSILE STRESSES IN SHEER STRAKE.

SEA-BED

CRACKS IN SHEER STRAKE DUE TO STRESS
CONCENTRATIONS AT THE CIRCUMFERENCE OF SIDESCUTTLES.

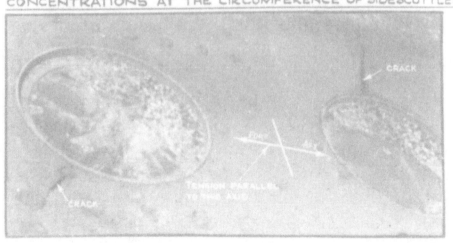

CRACK

TENSION PARALLEL TO THIS AXIS

CRACK

10

BRILLIANT ATTACKS

In what can only be described as brilliant attacks, 9 aircraft of 198 Squadron destroyed a 12,000-ton ship and a 1,500-ton cargo ship and 197 Squadron in Neustadt Bay destroyed a vessel of 15,000 tons. The 12,000 tonner, when left, is reported to have been burning from stem to stern. Two direct hits with 500 lb bombs are claimed on the 15,000 tonner on which a small fire was burning when 197 Squadron arrived. As a result of the attack, the ship on fire in 7 places and was later seen to be overturned.[1]

The Hawker Typhoon was developed as a replacement for the Hawker Hurricane and was introduced into service in 1941. It was a single-seater with a 2,200hp Napier Sabre engine. The early Typhoons were expected to reach 400mph at level flight, but then fuel consumption increased rapidly.

The Typhoon was relatively easy to fly, but was criticised for its slowness and a tendency to veer to starboard when taking off. However, its main defect was the engine cutting out at high speed. In fact, during the first nine months of operational use, more Typhoons were lost in accidents than in action. It was estimated that on average in every operation between July and September 1942, one plane crashed due to design or engine failure.

The plane was modified, made lighter, stronger and more stable. By incorporating extra fuel tanks into the wings, the range was increased from 1,110km to 1,754km. 'Tiffy', as it was nicknamed, flew at the battle of Normandy and, among other things, successfully destroyed 137 German tanks.

During continuous reconnaissance flights across northern Germany and the coastline of what was left of the Reich, pilots had spotted the large collection of ships at and around Lübeck, Neustadt and Kiel.

Typhoons armed with rockets about to take off. (© Imperial War Museum)

They had registered both merchant ships and warships, both of which were equipped with air defence and which could bite back effectively. They noted the uninterrupted gathering of ships:

> … but in mid-morning all aircraft carrying bombs or R.P. [rocket projectiles] were diverted to deal solely with the large concentrations of shipping making their way from Lübeck, Kiel and Schleswig in the general direction of Norway. The situation was somewhat similar to Cape Bon [on the coast of Tunisia, to which the remains of the German Afrika Corps had assembled], except that the enemy this time possessed the whole of his remaining fleet of war and merchant vessels, and none of H.M. Ships were present to seal off the area. Coastal Command, Ninth Air Force and 84 Group also took part in these attacks, and the full results will doubtless show that a very satisfactory join score was achieved. The group also participated in these attacks and the final result will undoubtedly show that a very satisfactory final goal was achieved. Certainly, the convoys which at the start were marshalled in an orderly way, were seen at the close of play to be wandering about the ocean in a very unseamanlike manner, and several fires from previous attacks were observed.[2]

At all costs the war had to be prevented from moving to Norway: Germany must be forced into an unconditional surrender. A major action was planned for 3 May to prevent any possibility of the ships travelling north. They had already noted that many ships had already gone in this direction, not only to Denmark and Sweden.

THE BRILLIANT ATTACKS

The first attack was led by the RAF's 198 Squadron from 84 Group (John Baldwin in command). The squadron and group were in the 2nd Tactical Air Force, headquartered in Süchteln, to the west of Dusseldorf. Nine Typhoon 1Bs, all equipped with rockets, had taken off from the Platlünne aerodrome at Nordhorn (north of Münster) at 14.00. At 15.30, five planes attacked the *Cap Arcona* and four attacked the *Thielbek*.

John Baldwin on a Hawker Typhoon. He later testified that the squadron he led had attacked a ship of '10,000/15,000 ton' but he had no knowledge that on board there were thousands of concentration camp prisoners. (© Imperial War Museum)

This was followed by a second wave from 263 Sqn of 84 Group, which took off from an aerodrome in Alhorn (west of Bremen) at 15.16. This squadron bombed the *Deutschland* and reported the burning *Cap Arcona*. Finally, a third wave from 197 Sqn, led by K.J. Harding, arrived (having taken off at 15.15 but travelled further than 263 Sqn's planes) and attacked the *Deutschland*. When he reached the bay he saw one ship burning fiercely and a second with a smaller fire raging on the bridge. He led his squadron for another attack, diving below the cloud base of 750m. He saw that the first pair of bombs had struck the *Thielbek* (all the others missed) and the ship had capsized.

The *Athen*, anchored in Neustadt, was also attacked and was the only ship to fire back at the aircraft. After several hits, Captain Nobmann raised a white flag and ordered the crew to immediately cease fire. Perhaps the flag was spotted: in any case the aircraft ceased their attack and more than 2,000 lives were saved.

On the *Cap Arcona*, the last thing that anyone had expected was an aerial attack. Second Mate Dommenget was as surprised as everyone else on board. He was in a makeshift mess room when the first bombs fell:

We had a mess on the deck in a room that used to be a playhouse for children. Then the first attack came. I would say that it was *Deutschland*. Then I went out to the bridge, where I should be, and Bertram said, 'We must quickly raise a bedsheet as a flag, and hoist it high!' It's clear what that means: we give up. This white flag I have also seen on the British photographs, the undamaged *Cap Arcona* and the white flag … But that was not the last thing we did [to prevent the attack] … the attack was later. I was in the lounge, a large room on *Arcona*, it crossed an entire deck. There the bombs hit and I have to say that in a few seconds, less than a minute, everything was on fire! I got up the stairs again to get up to the bridge … but I could not get through because of the smoke. What you must remember is this: the ship was built in 1927 and was in use until 1945. Fire-retardant material was not available at that time. So: it burned like tinder![3]

The older passenger ships such as the *Cap Arcona* were decorated with teak and mahogany panels, oak staircases, heavy drapes, large book-filled libraries, wooden decks and wooden lifeboats, all of which were combustible. If fire broke out, those stairways would funnel flames like blow torches, raising the heat to a level that would melt steel. Unless a fire was

Wooden panels, fabrics and other flammable material quickly transformed the *Cap Arcona* into a burning hell. The stairwell acted as an enormous funnel for the fire to rapidly spread through the ship. (Thore Dommenget)

extinguished quickly the vessel would soon be lost, even if fire-fighting equipment was there and working.

Thore Dommenget eventually managed to reach the bridge and sound the fire alarm, but it was not of great use when the fire was spreading rapidly and she was burning from the upper deck down. There was no water to put it out; there was no fuel to drive the water pumps; there was nothing anyone could do.

German and British sources do not agree on the timetable of events, but a British report summarised the attack from their point of view:

The first attack occurred at about 15.00 hours on 3rd May. The nearest 'bomb' fell about 50 metres away …

The second attack began around 15.20 and 4 or 6 aircraft were involved at first. The first hits were between the funnels on A deck level. They penetrated the superstructure and burst into the accommodation area causing fires. There was no hull damage at first, but numerous hits followed and all

Along the beaches of Neustadt Bay, the locals witnessed the air attacks on 3 May. When the wind was in the right direction they could hear the screams of the victims. They watched the burning of the ships throughout the afternoon. (© Imperial War Museum)

that was known was that fires developed which were never brought under control. The fire-fighting equipment was damaged and no seawater could be pumped on board. The whole superstructure was soon ablaze.[4]

Everyone in Neustadt, further up at Pelzerhaken, in Rettin, south of Haffkrug and on Timmendorfer Strand could see what was happening. The ships were a few hundred metres away, but they could hear and see everything that was happening. One witness was Fritz Hallenstedt:

We heard the detonations from the rockets and bombs and immediately rushed down to the beach. Here we saw *Cap Arcona, Thielbek*, which was nearby, and the big Hapag [Hamburg-South America Line] ship *Deutschland* were in flames… We saw all the desperate endeavours to get the boats in the water and so reach land. In these efforts, most of the boats slipped out of the davits and, crowded with people, fell straight into the water or were hanging with their bow or stern [still] in the davit. Terrible screams filled the air. We also saw hundreds of people jump overboard, throwing rafts, wooden beams and other stuff overboard. These crushed the swimmers who were already in the water and magnified the chaos.[5]

The 198 Squadron aircraft started the attack at about 750m and found that their rocket projectiles were very efficient: within a minute the fire on the largest ship was out of control. The pilots also saw that many had already begun to jump overboard.

Those on deck waved sheets and towels but to no effect. Later Dommenget met the pilots and asked them why they did not react to the white signals:

'Did you not see them?!'
'In an attack …? No, then it's impossible!!'[6]

Perhaps the pilots did not see or maybe saw too late the sheets and white cloths that were waved so desperately. Either way, no note was made in any surviving report. Once the attack started it could not be pulled back.

The attacks against the *Thielbek* and *Deutschland* were equally successful. The small crew on the *Deutschland* managed to save themselves but few on *Thielbek* had a chance. They were trapped in the deep holds, and when the rockets hit the ship, they ignited the straw and litter on the deck. Some rockets had probably penetrated the hull below the waterline. But no one was thinking about keeping the ship afloat: the preoccupation was with saving lives:

Thielbek had two cargo spaces, forward and aft which had iron ladders up. These were only thirty centimetres wide and it was therefore completely impossible for two thousand people to get up from the lower deck to the top. During the wild battle between people to come up, dreadful scenes unfolded. In fearful panic we fought and tried to fight our way up, but only a few managed. We had to make a road over the mountain of corpses … if one reached the edge of the hold, other prisoners hung on to him like grapes and pulled him back down to the hold again, and the ship already filled with water drawing its victims to the depths.[7]

Under a tarpaulin on the *Thielbek*, food was stored for all three vessels. When the list increased, several tons of it slid, which in turn increased this list, and the prisoners at the railing were caught by this food avalanche and crushed.

The *Cap Arcona*'s officers were on the bridge with Captain Walter von Lewinski. He had been sent by Gauleiter Kaufmann to report on the prisoner transport. He later told the British inquiry how quickly the ship turned into a ball of fire:

The first rocket hit amidships on the port side. The ship shook so vehemently that some of the lifeboats were thrown around each other. Almost at the same time as the rocket hit, the hunting pilots released all their bombs. There must have been fire bombs there. Captain Bertram and I ran under the deck. We wanted to investigate the damage to the ship. We did not get that far. The ship was shaking from the rocket attack. For several minutes only explosions were heard … Then you heard screams everywhere, without halt. The prisoners screamed in their fear of death.[8]

A CARPET OF FIRE

If Hell has ever been on Earth, it was probably on the burning ships in Neustadt Bay on 3 May 1945. The dry wood panels, textiles, paint and varnishes, mooring ropes and anything else that could burn burst into flames. Seconds after the first hits, the fire was out of control on the *Cap Arcona*. More than 200m of ship became a huge inferno.

As the flames took hold of the top deck, a carpet of fire spread over almost the entire ship. The heat made it almost impossible to get up to the main deck and smoke began to spread rapidly, all the way down to the depths of the ship. As the engines were not working, there was no power supply. There were smaller generators for the lighting, but there was no possibility of starting pumps and using the fire-extinguishing equipment. And importantly, the automatic bulkheads that might have halted the rapid spread of the fire could not be closed.

The prisoners, who had been banned from the open decks, were almost all down below. They could not understand why the ship had been attacked – they knew the Allies and their liberation were so close. But now smoke was the enemy and in their weakened state it killed many.

One of the prisoners, J. Schätzle, was in the former barber's saloon and he registered that there were several bombs in a few seconds:

While in conversation with a friend for many years, Longinius van Novara, fate reached us. Three small bombs crashed into our room and detonated.

An hour after the attack, the Atlantic steamer was in the grip of an uncontrollable fire. By the time this picture was taken by a British pilot the fire had spread to the lower decks, making it impossible for anyone to reach the boat deck. (© Imperial War Museum)

> Smoke and rubbish, chairs and tables, all swirled about each other. A second-long silence followed the wild inferno. The dust quickly settled. On the ship's side and the deck large holes gaped. A low wailing and cry for help was the first to break the calm.[9]

Prisoners who had been in cabins now threw themselves into corridors and passageways. The rockets spread the fire at a horrendously rapid rate and only a few stairwells remained intact through which the prisoners could escape.

Chief Purser Schwarz had been out on deck when the attacks began. He rushed down below to avoid being hit by splinters. After the first explosions, he thought he heard an uninterrupted series of detonations, believing that the pilots had carpet-bombed the ship. Schwarz had taken shelter in his cabin but he understood that the fire was everywhere:

To me it was obvious: if I do not want to burn, I have to get off the ship as quickly as possible. I could imagine what was happening now by the lifeboats.

As I ran through the forward stairwell to get on the deck, I saw a burning prisoner in front of me. Some of his comrades threw a blanket over him and tried to put out the fire on his clothes.

Through the thick smoke I managed to get up on the deck.[10]

He followed the many who were heading toward the bow. When he got there he looked out over the ship's side and saw people hanging on the anchor chains. He thought they looked like a bunch of grapes. No one dared to jump: seemingly they were afraid of drowning and the cold water. Meanwhile, more and more emerged from the ship's interior, and Schwarz saw several on fire as they came out. I've decided, he thought. Better to jump than be burned alive:

In the next moment I jumped over the rail. At the start I did not think about the height and, then, I realised that there was a considerable height, maybe twenty metres. I hit the water and – I guess because of the height – went deep down and came up again. And only then I felt the cold of the Baltic … When I noticed that one of the shipwrecked people attempted to get hold of me, I took off with a powerful swimming stroke. At about a hundred metres distance I turned around.

So, it was my ship, which had been my home for 18 years. The giant of 27,000 tons burned like a giant torch. I saw clearly the big shiny brass letters on the ship's side: *Cap Arcona*. And I saw how many prisoners were sitting on these letters. It's a scene I'll never forget.[11]

ROPES IN THE DAVITS

Second Mate Dommenget was on port side of the boat deck beside the foremost lifeboat. The wooden arches that formed the top of the high windows in one of the lounges reached this deck – they were so high that they went from the A deck to halfway up the height of the boat deck:

And then there was an explosion and these teak arches flew out … making it almost impossible to get to the other boats.[12]

The fire had literally exploded in the lounge, with a power so great that the teak arches flew off like projectiles and the flames shot out like glowing brands through each archway. Then the fire took hold of the davit ropes, with devastating results.

On 8 September 1934, the cruise ship *Morro Castle* caught fire off the American East Coast, a few hours away from New York. She was returning from Havana with 316 passengers and a crew of 230. Constructed according to older fire regulations, the *Morro Castle* had Manila ropes in the davits, not steel wire. When the ship caught fire, these ropes caught alight and only half of her twelve lifeboats could be lowered. One hundred and thirty-five people were lost.

Following this disaster, fire protection on ships was seriously reviewed. One recommendation was that Manila ropes would be replaced by steel wires. Unfortunately, this had not happened on the *Cap Arcona* (or, as we have seen, on the *Wilhelm Gustoff* before her). Dommenget had good reason to recall this during the seconds that followed:

When the fire took its grip of the salons, the woodwork burned at an incredible speed. The teak-framed fanlights in this picture were actually looking out onto the lower part of the boat deck. When these frames caught fire they acted like flamethrowers, preventing anyone moving on the boat deck. (Thore Dommenget)

… as often happen in shipping circles, the ropes had not been replaced, it meant that you had to change davits etc, etc. It did not happen … So we had ropes … You cannot lower a lifeboat if the ropes have burned up – and that was just what happened. The stern rope first, maybe there were a hundred people in the boat and crash! – they fell in the water, then the other rope burned and the boat fell down on top of them. The [lifeboats] were … our only opportunity to save people.[13]

One of the Polish prisoners, Tadeusz Kowzan, had instinctively climbed up as high as he could and he was struck by how quickly the fire spread beyond control:

The bombs had slammed into the middle of the ship and from there the thick flames fanned out. People crowded at the ship's sides. More and more gathered on the top deck and there was terrible congestion. Every person who fell down died when he was trampled on. And the fire spread more and more, it became hotter all the time, and the smoke became more suffocating. When they could not see rescue, some prisoners began to jump into the sea and swim.[14]

When boats could no longer be lowered, jumping into the water might seem the only option. But one could be killed by the impact of hitting the water, or falling onto floating debris. There were few life jackets (the SS had removed most of them – perhaps another indication of their intentions). In summer, a trained swimmer might have been able to reach land but now it was too far and too cold.

On C deck prisoners managed to reach one of the smoking rooms, where they took everything made of wood they could find and threw it out of the portholes to be used as floats by those in the water. Further up, on A deck aft, a few hundred prisoners had gathered. The bridge could still be seen even though it was on fire. Smoke had engulfed the bow and it was only the aft decks that offered refuge. Heinrich Mehringer was one of those jammed here:

Like a storm wave, an enormous sea of fire rushed out of the structures on our deck. The many refugees at the railing were so tightly packed by those who pressed against them that no one had a chance to lift a leg and climb over the rail. The fire ate through the woodwork of the deckhouse so quickly that many of the unfortunate were engulfed by the fire before they realised it.

I myself was burning on my back and head, but in the excitement, I did not feel the heat but cold. Then I saw, at the moment of greatest danger and at the last moment, an iron pipe above me that served as a holder for sun umbrellas. With a stretched arm, I reached it and with superhuman powers I pulled myself up with one outstretched arm. Then I came to stand on the heads of the many assembled people … maybe ten people were lucky enough to do the same as me, then the fire had taken command of the conglomeration. We now ran for our lives on our comrades' heads, like on a street.[15]

They reached the railing and climbed over it onto a lower-lying deck, probably the aft docking deck, where a crewman tried to give first aid to some of the injured prisoners. Mehringer looked up at the deck he and the others had just left. The fire was engulfing it: they could only look helplessly. He knew from earlier days how a crematorium smelled, but this stench went beyond anything he knew. What he saw was painfully stuck in his mind:

On the deck above us, all our comrades burned. After a while, the fire had no nutrition anymore. A silence of death lay upon us. As soon as we could, we tried to look up and we were offered a terrible image: more than two hundred, charred people burnt beyond recognition fused into a lump from which a horrible stench streamed.[16]

Alfred Knegendorf had, like everyone else, been completely surprised by the attack. He and his co-prisoners were in their cabin when they first heard the rocket attacks, then the fusillade from the aircrafts' guns:

A moment later we ran to the door. When we got into the corridor it was filled with prisoners and smoke. A huge panic had broken out. Only slowly and with difficulty could we move forward. It was at the last minute that we managed to get on to the deck. Had we stayed for a few minutes in the smoke-filled corridor under deck we would have suffocated … Meanwhile the whole ship, from stem to stern, had become a single sea of flames and smoke, the heat became increasingly unbearable and the screams of the condemned on this ship must certainly have been heard on land. So loud, so awful, so fearful was it.[17]

WATER OR FIRE

Hundreds of people threw themselves off the ship. If they were lucky they landed uninjured in the water, if not they fell onto wreckage – or were hit by objects thrown out of the ship. One SS soldier had jumped with his lifebelt on and had probably died when he hit the water. The body lay with its arms stretched out. It made a good float – one prisoner climbed up and sat like a dwarf on top of the corpse.

Captain Bertram told Dommenget that it was over, the ship was no longer salvageable:

> 'Try to save yourself!' Then I went into my cabin, where the floor was already bent upward [by the heat], it was high up in the ship. There hung my life jacket on a Norwegian uniform jacket I received, a rather thick thing … Then I had a gun in a belt although it wasn't allowed. Then I went to the forecastle, which is in the bow … There was a so-called banana hatch: under the hatchway there were about three hundred people … they only had an iron ladder that was welded on the wall that they could come up on – but only one by one. Here on the bow was the safest place, but from earlier experience I know that it's impossible to say to a panicking human mass 'One by one!' I could only watch. Some came up – the strong![18]

Along the side of the ship, there was an emergency gangway. Some were hanging by the side of the bow, and Dommenget knew that it would be possible to climb down there. He was heading down the ship's side when two prisoners grabbed his shoulders. He was strong and had a firm grip on the gangway's rope railing, but with two men hanging onto him he could no longer move:

> I had both hands on the rope and underneath me there was a knot. I said 'Guys, now you jump!' And they did too. Probably they died shortly afterwards – they were undressed. One cannot say to five thousand concentration camp prisoners that they should get dressed – they hardly had anything anyhow.[19]

On deck the risk was being burned alive; 20m below the risk was freezing to death. And to jump from a height of 15 to 20m with a lifebelt could result in a very quick death. The force of hitting the water could break a neck: it was actually safer to jump without a lifebelt. With so much debris in the water, it is easy to understand why many hesitated to jump from the *Cap Arcona*'s boat deck. But as the fire came closer and the heat increased, hesitation diminished:

> I swam in the water and I saw how *Thielbek* went under. You know if you take a jar of peas and press it under the water and the jar splits, then the peas come out and the jar is left down there, that's the ship. On *Thielbek* only a handful of people could save themselves.[20]

When the *Thielbek* quickly went down, perhaps more than 1,000 people quickly came up and the thought of peas in a jar whirled through Dommenget's head, but thanks to an inflatable lifebelt, he was saved. He swam away, turned around and saw how the third mate went out through a ventilator even though 'he was quite fat, but the fat saved him!'

Second Officer Thore Dommenget in 2001.

The water was ice cold and despite his uniform it penetrated Dommenget's skin like a thousand needles. He swam to one of the ship's floats and climbed up onto it:

> Twelve people could save themselves. At twelve it was full, but they became thirteen, eighteen, and then it sank. Now, I had a lifebelt and then someone called 'Comrade, can I get hold of you?' But it did not work. Then I picked up my gun, but of course I did not use it, but said, 'Let go, otherwise I will use it!' He released me and I got off the float and saw Neustadt Bay and saw that Kaufmann's yacht lay close. I swam there … the yacht had no fuel, no mast …[21]

Dommenget's gun was wet and had not been fired since the First World War, but it still terrified a Russian prisoner who had made his way to the same yacht. Dommenget placed his gun and belt in the boat, which pacified the Russian. They were less than 100m from the burning ship. The second mate looked at the *Cap Arcona*, which was now burning from front to end 'like a single torch'. Through the portholes flames licked as the fire penetrated deck after deck.

All sides of human nature were on display that afternoon. Despite his clothes, by the time Dommenget finally managed to climb onto the yacht he was completely frozen. Some camp prisoners who were already on board started to massage his body so that he slowly recovered his body heat. In the distance he saw an old man in a rowing boat. It was a bizarre sight: the old man had rowed out to see what was going on and had it not been for the burning ships and all the people, the idyll would have been perfect:

> I begged him to help me and he took me ashore. I walked from Pelzerhaken in the direction of the pilot's house … and I said I must definitely call … and a German navy officer answered and said that 'the English are already here'. Then an English officer answered, I think, and I told him 'Thousands of people are out in the bay dying, you must do something for them to get them to shore!' Then I went to Augustus Platz … I saw a jeep and two soldiers … and I stood there wondering what happens now? It was almost comical and I was just staring at the soldier … and he turned around and said, 'You're a prisoner now, hands up!' He came up to me … and I said 'I am a merchant naval officer, I'm civilian.' And then he said, 'That's OK, my brother's in the merchant navy, too, have a cigarette!'[22]

But the war was not quite over. A German minesweeper sailed out of Neustadt. Using megaphones, the crew called for 'German soldiers'. Alexander Machnew could only look on with bitterness and rage at how every prisoner who tried to hold on to the ship's railing was mercilessly pushed back in the water again. If that did not discourage them, the crew opened fire:

> They shot the comrades floating in the water. Those who were shot in the rapid fire disappeared into the water without a sound.[23]

He could never forget how two prisoners fought desperately in the water over a plank:

> Both wanted it, but for two it was too small. One won only by pushing the head of the other under the water. Should this winner be alive today, he may sometimes think that he can thank someone else for his life.[24]

Captain Bertram had gone forward as the fire swept the bridge and the deck. He reached the anchor chain and climbed down. He would later be rescued from the water. Unbeknown to him, his 13-year-old daughter was watching the burning ship from the shore.

THE CAPSIZE

Later in the afternoon, the fire had eaten through the *Cap Arcona*'s decks and, in combination with the hits in her sides, the Atlantic mammoth began to slowly lose stability:

> The fire was raging for three hours, after which an explosion occurred (which may have been caused by evaporation due to the heat of a small amount of fuel oil in the tank) and the vessel turned over to port and capsized.[25]

Erwin Geschonneck, the German political prisoner who had led the prisoners' resistance organisation, had jumped into the water and had avoided being shot by the minesweeper 'rescue vessel'. He actually swam back to the *Cap Arcona*. After what felt like hours (but was probably just one) he managed to climb the anchor chain, through the hawse pipe and up into the ship:

Up there sat some desperate people. Suddenly the horizon rose and the ship dropped. Some of us could hold onto the railing, everyone else was thrown into the water and pulled under the ship. For several hours we sat on *Cap Arcona*'s side and waited until the Englishmen, who in the meantime had taken the bay, sent out boats and brought us to land.[26]

The water is only 18m deep in this part of the Bay and the *Cap Arcona* lay like a beached whale, an island of smoking, distorted steel that slowly began to cool.

Alfred Knegendorf had stayed on the ship with another prisoner who did not dare jump because he could not swim. Alfred heard a powerful detonation somewhere inside the vessel and then noticed how the *Cap Arcona* started leaning to port. He realised that the ship was about to capsize:

With all my strength I clung to the railing. Then I waited until the ship sank more and more. Then I slid down and sat on *Cap Arcona*'s keel. The ship's body was very hot, but here was the best chance to survive. I was also one of the few men who did not get wet. With a piece of rope I tried to save some who were in the water. In that way I pulled up twenty men out of the water.[27]

The *Deutschland* photographed from the air. The ship has capsized but parts of her are still burning. A plume of smoke rises from the interior. (© Imperial War Museum)

When areas of the hull had cooled down enough, survivors climbed back onto the remains of the Atlantic giant. These areas were very limited: the majority of the ship was still aglow. (Stadt Neustadt in Holstein)

He sat there all afternoon and waited until the evening when he was rescued. He landed as a free man in a liberated Neustadt.

The *Deutschland* was also sticking up out of the water but the smaller *Thielbek* had sunk. Perhaps fifty people survived from this ship: about 2,000 people were drowned in a few minutes, an hour after British troops took Neustadt, which surrendered without resistance. When the British realised what had taken place, they launched a rescue effort. However, there was still much confusion in the town: German soldiers were still there and among them were SS soldiers who did not hesitate to kill prisoners wherever they found them.

MASSACRE ON THE BEACHES

Before the British took Neustadt, and before the attacks, the barges with the prisoners from Stutthof had been towed out of Lübeck, towards the *Cap Arcona* and the other ships. This time, Captain Bertram refused to accept a single extra person. The *Thielbek* and *Athen* were also at bursting point: on the *Thielbek* the prisoners were literally standing on top of each other. Two barges were untethered from the moorings on the ships; the tugs towing the other two barges simply released them and departed. The Åland seaman Ingmar Fredriksson noted in his diary that those on the barges had been left to their fate:

> Our guards held a conference and a rumour told us that Himmler had ordered that everyone should be drowned and that no one should fall into the hands of the English alive. When a nearby vessel was blown into the air so that the wreckage was whirling around us, our guards left in a hurry and left us alone out there.
>
> We were not slow to throw away the moorings and cut the anchor chains. The wind lay on land and we set ourselves up with blankets like sails to sail our strange craft to land.[28]

The dead floated ashore long after the aerial attacks. To their number were added prisoners who had survived transport on the barges from Stutthof but were then executed by German soldiers on the beaches. (© Imperial War Museum)

Rumours about people in striped prison uniforms landing spread rapidly through Neustadt. SS soldiers were despatched and a number of merciless executions took place on the beaches north of the city. Fredriksson had managed to get ashore when he saw the soldiers approach:

> Soon some marines came to the place and commanded us to stay on the strip of beach. However, the landing continued all the time, and I was careful to wash and shave for the first time since I left Stutthof.
>
> While I was shaving my old guards had received a report about our landing and were now racing towards us. Those who were still aboard the barges were thrown into the sea and had to wade ashore, and those who were not quick enough were shot down.[29]

The barges were discovered by German soldiers and the SS. A survivor, Nathan Roloff, saw how a department of marines turned up with a commander, who Roloff later understood was a Lieutenant Ziemann. His first action was to kick a saucepan from a fire in which one of the female prisoners was warming water for her child:

> Then he gave schnapps to them [the soldiers]. The marines began to shoot the prisoners, who with great effort had managed to come ashore. Although several hours had passed, hundreds of prisoners remained on the barge. To speed up the landing, the marines went on the deck of the barge. In the presence of the German navy officers, the marines began to beat the prisoners, mainly women and children, who were on deck with their guns and to kick them overboard.[30]

Surviving prisoners described how drunken soldiers shot wildly. Some of the prisoners were chased like animals. The number shot on the beach has never been established.

Ziemann was subsequently tried for these murders, but there was deemed to be insufficient evidence to prove his guilt. Other reports claimed that boys in the Hitler Youth had also shot prisoners.

On the other barges, the course of events was different. These prisoners were transferred to the *Athen*, which remained in Neustadt. Where the ship might go after the attack in the bay was uncertain. The SS and the soldiers gathered all the prisoners they could find and force-marched them into

Neustadt. They had been without food for almost a week. On the way into the city about 170 who could not keep up with the pace were shot.

The Germans continued to search for the escaped, but the chase was halted by the air attacks. And then, between four and half past four, just over two hours after the attacks, British units reached Neustadt and began to occupy the city. Fate once again played a tragi-comic role when survivors from the ships began to appear in the city as the British tanks rolled in: the troops thought they were about to find another concentration camp.

The Åland sailor Ingmar Fredriksson had survived Stutthof, the barges and the shooting on the beach and had even survived the British air attacks unscathed:

> We took the opportunity to crawl into a nearby house and we looked from there to see what would take place.
>
> A while later when the English were in the city we went and reported to them.
>
> The English opened the military warehouse and distributed food to us and we Scandinavians were lodged in the former marine facilities. Sadly, in the morning the streets were lined with corpses – people who had eaten too much and died after a long hunger.[31]

The Red Cross arranged for the Scandinavians to be sent to Flensburg, then on to Sweden, where they were quarantined. However, typhus broke out and several died in a hospital in Helsingborg on the south coast. They were buried in the nearby Pålsjö Cemetery.

The British in Neustadt were confused. They could not understand why concentration camp prisoners were appearing all over the city. Eventually it became clear, and the city's hospital was emptied to make room for the prisoners from barges and survivors from the vessels. But, as Fredriksson had seen elsewhere, when the skeletal prisoners were fed their digestive tracts could not always cope with the sudden nutritional supply.

The British collected all the survivors who could be found along the beaches, and took the small excursion boat *Neustadt* out to the *Cap Arcona*. Here they found the survivors who had taken refuge on the upturned ship's starboard side: the sea had quenched the fires and parts of the side were now cool enough to stand on. It was still quite hot, but the forward part of the vessel was still largely intact. The survivors were not aware that Neustadt was now under British control.

Exactly how many actually died on the *Cap Arcona* and *Thielbek* will never be known but more than 8,000 people lost their lives, not counting those who died of fatigue, hunger, thirst or disease related to their treatment by the Nazis. Prisoners from twenty-four different nations had been aboard the ships, and for most their captivity did not end in freedom but in an inferno. In all, about 450 people survived. Of these only about fifty had been on *Thielbek*. It was a cruel irony: what appeared to be the objective of the Nazis – the death of all the prisoners – was almost completely achieved by British pilots.

The local population of Neustadt was forced to bury the bodies found along the shore and those recovered from the sea. At first, British soldiers believed there must have been a concentration camp in Neustadt. (© Imperial War Museum)

There was a widespread belief around the Neustadt Bay that the prisoners on the ships were criminals and at first there was little willingness to help the prisoners. When the truth emerged about the ships, it came as a shock to many. (© Imperial War Museum)

PEACE

A few days later, on 5 May, the war in Europe was over and all of liberated Europe celebrated. The pilots who had attacked Neustadt were no exception:

> Hangover day today with aspirin before breakfast. Nobody felt like flying, especially after last night's celebration, so the day drifted in silence.[32]

When Dommenget was in Neustadt, he ran into Franz Wolff, the *Cap Arcona*'s ship's boy. Wolff had been in the city during the attack and then had tried to organise a rescue ship. He had since been hired by the British. As they were chatting, Dommenget suddenly heard a soldier behind him:

> Suddenly I heard a voice behind me, 'Who's this chap?' And then Franz Wolff, who didn't speak any English, said: 'Zweite Officer Cap Arcona.' [Second Officer of the Cap Arcona] 'Do you know something about sailing?' 'Yes, Sir, maybe a bit.' 'This afternoon three o'clock we will have a race around the wrecks. Will you be here?' 'Yes, Sir.' That was the first regatta around the two ships![33]

The British pilots came to look at the effects of the rockets and bombs. They showed great interest in the impact.

Later a formal survey, led by the British Bombing Survey Unit, was undertaken of the sunken ships in northern Germany and Denmark. The intention seems to have been to find out what impact the rockets had, to study the impact of the explosions, to understand how effective the weapons were and to see how they could be used tactically in the future. They also wanted to know the effect of mines, other types of bombs and the impact of the cannon.

Opposite and overleaf: The damage assessments later undertaken on the ships sunk off the north German coast catalogued the devastating effects of the fires. The preoccupation was with the effectiveness of the projectiles: the victims were not mentioned. (National Archives)

DEUTSCHLAND

DAMAGE FROM R.P. 60 LB H.E. & 500 LB M.C. BOMB FUZED ·025 SEC.T.D

SERVICE	BUILDING DATE	CONSTR.	LENGTH	BREADTH	DEEP DRAUGHT	SPEED	G.R.T.	DEAD WEIGHT	DEEP DISPL'MT
PASSENGER LINER	1923	RIVETED	646'	72·1'	32·8'	19	21,046	12,806	25,000

CODE	
★	500 LB M.C. BOMB
✸	R.P. 60 LB H.E.
X	20 mm H.E.I.
·	20 mm A.P.

P = PORT
S = STARBOARD

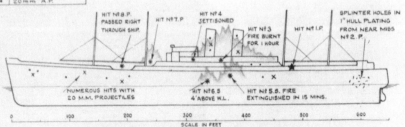

HIT Nº 8.P. PASSED RIGHT THROUGH SHIP.

HIT Nº 7.P.

HIT Nº 4 JETTISONED

HIT Nº 3 FIRE BURNT FOR 1 HOUR

HIT Nº I.P.

SPLINTER HOLES IN 1" HULL PLATING FROM NEAR MISS Nº 2.P.

NUMEROUS HITS WITH 20 M.M. PROJECTILES

HIT Nº 6.5 4' ABOVE W.L.

HIT Nº 5.5. FIRE EXTINGUISHED IN 15 MINS.

SCALE IN FEET

POSITION OF SHIP AFTER ATTACK

STRESS CONCENTRATION
ROUND A CIRCULAR HOLE IN A FLAT STRAKE OF WIDTH 4 TIMES DIA. OF HOLE.

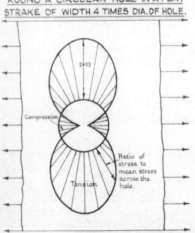

2·33

Compression

Tension

Ratio of stress to mean stress across the hole.

DAMAGE FROM 500LB M.C. BOMB

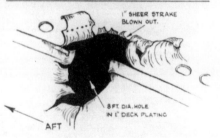

1" SHEER STRAKE BLOWN OUT.

8 FT. DIA. HOLE IN 1" DECK PLATING

AFT

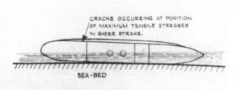

CRACKS OCCURRING AT POSITION OF MAXIMUM TENSILE STRESSES IN SHEER STRAKE.

SEA-BED

CRACKS IN SHEER STRAKE DUE TO STRESS
CONCENTRATIONS AT THE CIRCUMFERENCE OF SIDESCUTTLES.

CRACK

TENSION PARALLEL TO THIS AXIS

CRACK

"CAP·ARCONA"

DAMAGE FROM R.P. 60LB H.E.

SERVICE	BUILDING DATE	CONSTR.	LENGTH	BREADTH	DEEP DRAUGHT	SPEED	G.R.T.	DEAD WEIGHT	DEEP DISPLT
PASSENGER LINER	1927	RIVETED	644'	84·6	28·6	19	27,561	11,319	27,000

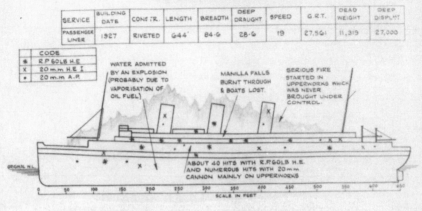

CODE
*	R.P. 60LB H.E.
X	20 m.m. H.E.I
·	20 m.m. A.P.

WATER ADMITTED BY AN EXPLOSION (PROBABLY DUE TO VAPORISATION OF OIL FUEL)

MANILLA FALLS BURNT THROUGH & BOATS LOST.

SERIOUS FIRE STARTED IN UPPERWORKS WHICH WAS NEVER BROUGHT UNDER CONTROL.

ABOUT 40 HITS WITH R.P. 60LB H.E. AND NUMEROUS HITS WITH 20 m.m CANNON MAINLY ON UPPERWORKS

ORIGINAL W.L.

0 50 100 150 200 250 300 350 400 450 500 550 600
SCALE IN FEET

POSITION OF SHIP IN NEUSTADT BAY

VIEW SHOWING DISTORTION OF BRIDGE DUE TO INTENSE HEAT

EXIT HOLE OF R.P. 60LB H.E. WHICH FAILED TO DETONATE

CLOSE UP SHOWING EXTENSIVE DISTORTION OF UPPERWORKS DUE TO FIRE

A delegation travelled for a month and looked at a total of fifty-two vessels, among which the *Cap Arcona* and *Deutschland* attracted great interest. It was found that the rockets used against the *Cap Arcona* could be more efficient and the fire resulting from the rockets:

> ... one could easily get under control ... but due to the chaotic conditions on the last [ship], this resulted in the ship being burned out and finally capsizing (probably due to an explosion in the fuel tanks).[34]

They were relatively pleased with the rockets, although it was found that they were not primarily a weapon to destroy ships.

A somewhat more personal assessment of the conditions in Germany was set out in a British war diary in May 1945:

> After an interval of some one hundred and thirty years, German territory was again overrun by invading armies. For the first time a United Germany was overrun and never before in history had a country been so devastated prior to land fighting on its territory. In attempting to fight to the 'last ditch', Germany became so chaotic the civil administration was brought to a standstill. It is doubtful whether at any time in the Middle Ages were there so many homeless and aimless wanderers on the roads.[35]

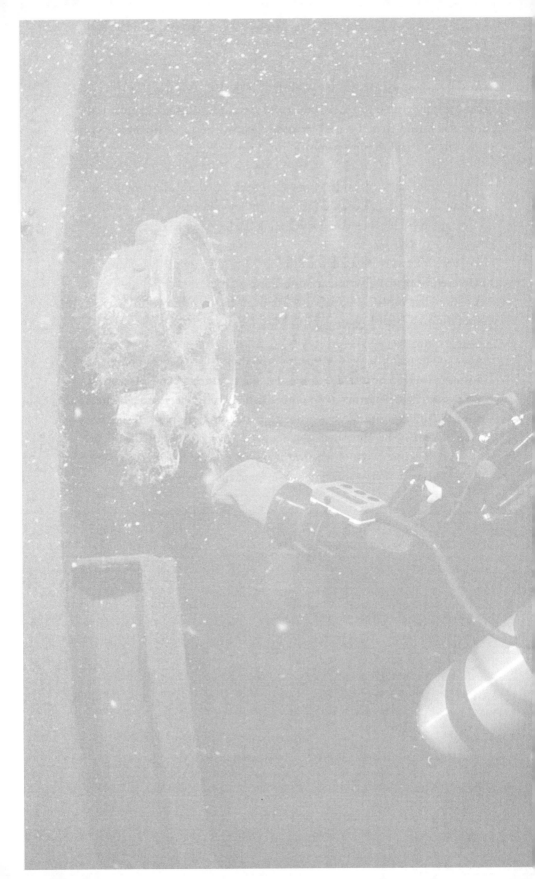

11

AFTERWAR

By the time peace in Europe was sealed in the early days of May 1945 history's biggest evacuation by sea had been completed. Konrad Engelhardt realised that not everyone had been saved but Unternehmen Rettung had succeeded in bringing 2 million people from East Prussia to the West. Four ship disasters had ended the lives of more than 25,000 people, but they were quickly forgotten when the news spread around the world of the genocide, of the 6 million deaths in the holocaust camps. In the new Germany, there was little interest in looking back at what had happened on these ships; its focus was on building up a new nation. Many of the survivors from the *Wilhelm Gustloff* and the other ships chose not to speak about their experiences – for them too it was more important to look forward than back. But over the intervening years, attitudes have changed. A desire to preserve the memory of what happened has grown stronger and the story of the *Wilhelm Gustloff* in particular has become much better known.

Today, the wrecks of the *Wilhelm Gustloff*, *Steuben* and *Goya* lie in a row along the north coast of Poland and a mass of stories have been spun about the *Wilhelm Gustloff* in particular. She lies at a depth accessible to an advanced amateur diver, even though diving is banned on her. That the ship is a mass grave, with thousands of bodies still inside, has not deterred them.

A sunken ship always has the power to create myths and legends and the *Wilhelm Gustloff* is no exception. For her, the most persistent is that of the Amber Room but no evidence for it being on the ship has ever been found.

But the *Wilhelm Gustloff*, *Steuben*, *Goya* and *Cap Arcona* are not myth creators in the same way as the *Titanic*. That ship, the largest in the world, sank in peacetime, between the two big news centres of London and New York, at a time when there was a dearth of interesting news, with a number of rich and well-known people on board, on the ship's maiden voyage.

These were 'assets' that none of the Baltic ships had. They were either refugee boats or floating concentration camps destroyed during an avalanche of news in the winter of 1944 and the spring 1945. The comments from the Führer's headquarters after each disaster are clear enough: it was tragic that these ships had sunk, but one must count on a certain 'acceptable loss'.

In today's Germany, certain organisations and individuals have tried to increase interest in these events for the worst of motives. The Rechtsradikalen, the Radical Right, has used them to focus on the Russian atrocities, at the same time ignoring the most inhuman conditions in which concentration camp prisoners were kept and transported.

The use of the *Wilhelm Gustloff* by Nazi apologists was the theme of Günter Grass's novel *Im Krebsgang* (*Crabwalk*), published in 2002. It fictionalises elements of the story of the *Wilhelm Gustloff*'s sinking but it is based on factual accounts. The book received considerable attention in Germany: for example the magazine *Der Spiegel* had on its cover of 4 February 2002 'Die deutsche Titanic' (The German Titanic).

A film about *Gustloff* was released in 1959, *Nacht fiel über Gotenhafen* (*Night Fell over Gotenhafen*) and more recently a TV movie *Die Gustloff* (2008) was made. One can expect more. There is certainly a market for ship disaster media, given the success in Germany of James Cameron's *Titanic* and the huge *Titanic* exhibition in Hamburg.

The killing of concentration camp victims by Allied bombing is a heart-rending tragedy. Between 8,000 and 10,000 camp prisoners met a horrifying death in the Baltic, in the gunsights of British planes and almost within sight of British troops. Only hours later they would have been freed. What happened in Neustadt Bay is an inconvenient truth in the British narrative about the Second World War. Too many questions remain about the passing of vital messages but unless missing papers emerge they will not be answered.

The wrecks of the *Cap Arcona*, *Thielbek* and *Deutschland* were left in Neustadt Bay for several years. The *Thielbek* was raised during January and February 1950. The remains of only 200 people were found. It can only be assumed that the current washed the others away through the loading hatch.

The *Thielbek* was later put back into service under the name *Reinbek*. There were plans to raise and restore the *Cap Arcona* and *Deutschland* but they were too far gone. The *Cap Arcona* was set on fire once again and finally broken up in 1949.

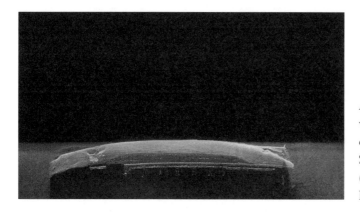

A digital visualization of the sunken Steuben. (Magnus Petersson)

Around Neustadt Bay bodies floated ashore. Thousands of people have been buried around the bay. Eighteen different cemeteries, 'memory groves' and memorials shelter almost 3,500 victims. The rest were either washed out to sea or buried by local residents in unknown places. In the first months after the disaster bodies were washed ashore almost each day on the beaches, but by and by they became fewer and fewer.

Victims have continued to be washed ashore or uncovered on the sand beaches through the years. As the victims were scantily buried in the first days, they were later formally reburied. And, each year a ceremony is held in Neustadt in memory of the disaster. Now, there is probably no one alive who witnessed the tragedy in Neustadt Bay on 3 May 1945.

But as early as 7 May 1945 the British survivors and the local population organised a memorial service in Neustadt, with a procession paid for by the town. They gathered on the beach between Neustadt and Pelzerhaken where today there is one of the largest memorials to the tragedy.

The greater the distance in the time from the events, the greater the interest in war losses in the Baltic. That the disasters of the Baltic finally have increased attention is the result of dedicated individuals and their hope that these histories may not be forgotten. The best example is the Cap Arcona Museum in Neustadt in Holstein, where supportive research is undertaken. It is a small museum with an archive dedicated to the tragedy, open to the general public. The museum shows selected objects from the *Cap Arcona* but it is first and foremost an educational museum where the focus is placed on discussing the events that led up to the bombings on 3 May.

Den Opfern
des Untergangs
der
„Wilhelm-Gustloff"

EPILOGUE

The story is not yet at an end. Expeditions return to the *Wilhelm Gustloff* and new questions emerge. Nobody, however, will ever know how many died, nor will the question of responsibility ever be resolved, but the victims will have died in vain if we do not recognise the horror of the events and what led up to them.

But are we capable of that?

During the convention at Ostseebad Damp in January 1995 to commemorate the loss of the *Wilhelm Gustloff* I sat next to a survivor, Eva Dorn. On her other side was a man who was very anxious to show her his collection of photographs from the Second World War. He was clearly a supporter of Admiral Dönitz, as many of the pictures were of him: Dönitz, the man who in the chain of responsibility for the tragedies in the Baltic must sit very near the top.

Eva looked at him and then turned to me and said, 'Some people never learn.'

The audience at the memorial meeting in Ostseebad Damp in January 1995. The majority of people in this photograph were survivors of the *Wilhelm Gustloff* sinking.

Left: Horst Woit (left) and Heinz Schön on the boat prior to the wreath-laying ceremony on the Baltic at Ostseebad Damp in January 1995.

Below: Robert Hering, captain of *T-36*, and Wilhelm Gustloff's Second Officer Paul Vollrath, photographed in Ostseebad Damp in January 1995. (Heinz Schön)

NOTES

INTRODUCTION

1 Interview Thore Dommenget.

1 THE BEGINNING

1 Sennerteg, p. 23.
2 Fredmann, p. 76.
3 Fredmann, p. 77.
4 Buttar, p. 90.
5 Buttar, pp. 90–91.
6 Schön: Ostsee '45, p. 12.
7 Malmberg: Flykten från
   Hangö, Hufvudstadsbladet
   3 December 1991.
   (Newspaper article)
8 Wetterholm 1994, pp. 96–97.
9 Ekman 1983, pp. 282–283.
10 Ekman Hufvudstadsbladet,
   23 September 1984.
11 Ekman Hufvudstadsbladet,
   23 September 1984.
12 Ekman, Hufvudstadsbladet,
   23 September 1984.
13 Ekman, Hufvudstadsbladet,
   23 September 1984.
14 Schön 1995, p. 36.
15 Sennerteg, p. 117.
16 Ekman 1983, p. 243.
17 Schön 1998, p. 97.
18 Schön 1998, p. 100.

2 KRAFT DURCH FREUDE

1 Schön 1987, p. 10.
2 Schön 1987, p. 14.
3 Paust, p. 114.
4 Kahl, p. 34.

3 THE WORKERS' DREAM SHIP

1 Schön 1998, p. 19.
2 Schön 1987, p. 71.
3 Schön 1985, pp. 112–113.

4 THE BEGINNING OF THE END

1 Schön 1998, p. 56.
2 Schön 1992, pp. 69–70.
3 Schön 1992, p. 70.
4 Schön 1998, p. 98.
5 Bekker, p. 170.
6 Interview Horst Woit.
7 Interview Horst Woit.
8 Typed story Milda Bendrich.
9 Interview Margit Schilder-Brook.
10 Interview Margit Schilder-Brook.
11 Interview Margit Schilder-Brook.
12 Schön 1998, pp. 72–74.
13 Interview Eva Dorn-Rotschild.
14 Interview Eva Dorn-Rotschild.
15 Lange, Rudi, p. 6.
16 Schön 1985, p. 85.
17 Fechner, p. 145.

18 Schön 1985, p. 233.
19 Schön 1985, p. 233.
20 Interview Heli Beneicke.
21 Interview Heli Beneicke.
22 Interview Rudolf Geiss.
23 Interview Eva Dorn-Rotschild.
24 Schön 1985, p. 239.
25 Lange, Rudi 1990, p. 8.
26 Schön 1998, p. 91.
27 Typed story Milda Bendrich.
28 Interview Margit Schilder-Brook.
29 Schön 1998, p. 96.
30 Schön 1992, p. 144.
31 Interview Heli Beneicke.
32 Interview Eva Dorn-Rotschild.
33 Interview Eva Dorn-Rotschild.

5 THE SEA OF DEATH

1 Schön 1998, p. 101.
2 Schön 1998, p. 100.
3 Interview Eva Dorn-Rotschild.
4 Schön 1985, p. 442.
5 Schön 1998, p. 107.
6 Schön 1998, p. 107.
7 Fechner, p. 147.
8 Schön 1998, p. 102.
9 A. Bock from Svensk Sjöfarts Tidning, No. 16, 1958.
10 Typed story Milda Bendrich.
11 Interview Margit Schilder-Brook.
12 Interview Heli Beneicke.
13 Interview Heli Beneicke.
14 Lange, Rudi 1990, p. 11.
15 From letter to Mrs. Ilse Kunandt.
16 Interview Eva Dorn-Rotschild.
17 Schön 1998, pp. 128–129.
18 Flottentorpedoboot T 36, p. 11.
19 Typed story by Horst Woit.
20 Typed story by Horst Woit.
21 Interview Margit Schilder-Brook.
22 Interview Margit Schilder-Brook.
23 Schön 1998, p. 111.
24 Interview Eva Dorn-Rotschild.
25 Interview Heinz Schön.
26 Typed story Milda Bendrich.
27 A. Bock from Svensk Sjöfarts Tidning, No. 16, 1958.
28 Interview Heli Beneicke.
29 Interview Heli Beneicke.
30 Interview Eva Dorn-Rotschild.
31 Flottentorpedoboot T 36, p. 11.
32 Typed story by Horst Woit.
33 Lange, Rudi 1990, p. 12.
34 Lange, Rudi 1990, p. 13.
35 Lange, Rudi 1990, p. 13.
36 Lange, Rudi 1990, p. 14.
37 A. Bock from Svensk Sjöfarts Tidning, No. 16, 1958.
38 Fechner, p. 151.
39 Interview Eva Dorn-Rotschild.
40 Interview Margit Schilder-Brook.
41 Interview Eva Dorn-Rotschild.
42 Interview Eva Dorn-Rotschild.
43 Flottentorpedoboot T 36, p. 11.
44 Flottentorpedoboot T 36, p. 11.
45 Interview Eva Dorn-Rotschild.
46 Interview Eva Dorn-Rotschild.
47 A. Bock from Svensk Sjöfarts Tidning, No. 16, 1958.
48 Fechner, p. 151.
49 Schön 1998, pp. 131–132.
50 Interview Margit Schilder-Brook.
51 Interview Margit Schilder-Brook.
52 Interview Margit Schilder-Brook.
53 Interview Margit Schilder-Brook.
54 Flottentorpedoboot T 36, pp. 12–13.
55 Flottentorpedoboot T 36, p. 13.
56 Interview Eva Dorn-Rotschild.

57 A. Bock from Svensk Sjöfarts Tidning, No. 16, 1958.
58 Flottentorpedoboot T 36, p. 13.
59 Interview Heli Beneicke.
60 Schön 1998, p. 144.
61 Schön 1998, p. 147.
62 Schön 1998, p. 149.
63 Schön 1985, p. 402.
64 Interview Eva Dorn-Rotschild.
65 Interview Eva Dorn-Rotschild.
66 Typed story Milda Bendrich.
67 Schön 1992, p. 243.

6 THE BEAUTIFUL WHITE *STEUBEN*

1 Brustat-Naval, p. 49.
2 Vita vackra 'Steuben' Norddeutscher Lloyd Stockholm.
3 5 Vårkryssningar till Medelhavet, p. 1.
4 Schön 1995, p. 169.
5 Schön 1995, p. 269.
6 Schön 1992, pp. 270–271.
7 Schön 1992, pp. 270–271.
8 Schön 1992, pp. 281–282.
9 Brustat-Naval, p. 50.
10 Brustat-Naval, pp. 50–51.
11 Schön 1992, p. 305.
12 Brustat-Naval, p. 51.
13 Brustat-Naval, p. 52.
14 Schön 1992, pp. 306–307.
15 Schön 1992, p. 307.
16 Schön 1992, p. 309.
17 Schön 1992, p. 315.
18 Schön 1992, p. 381.
19 Schön 1992, p. 415.

7 THE MOTOR SHIP *GOYA*

1 Hahn, p. 16.
2 Typed story by Charlotte Dölling.
3 Typed story by Charlotte Dölling.
4 Typed story by Charlotte Dölling.
5 Typed story by Charlotte Dölling.
6 Typed story by Charlotte Dölling.
7 Typed story by Anna Treter.
8 Typed story by Erich Sasse.
9 Schön 1992, p. 435.
10 Typed story by Christel Balsam.
11 Typed story by Christel Balsam.
12 Schön 1992, p. 440.
13 Typed story by Erich Sasse.
14 Typed story by Christel Balsam.
15 Typed story by Erich Sasse.
16 Gerdau 1985, p. 169.
17 Typed story by Joseph Poiger.
18 Typed story by Christel Balsam.
19 Typed story by Erich Sasse.
20 Schön 1992, p. 467.
21 Typed story by Erich Sasse.
22 Typed story by Christel Balsam.
23 Schön 1992, p. 464.
24 Schön 1992, p. 477.
25 Schön 1992, p. 477.
26 Schön 1992, p. 474.
27 Typed story by Joseph Poiger.
28 Typed story by Erich Sasse.
29 Wetterholm 2000, p. 15.
30 Typed story by Erich Sasse.
31 Typed story by Erich Sasse.
32 Letter from Helmut Wolf to Kurt Gerdau.
33 Typed story by Josef Poiger.
34 Schön 1992, p. 480.
35 Typed story by Christel Balsam.
36 Typed story by Christel Balsam.
37 Typed story by Christel Balsam.
38 Constabel, p. 32.
39 Constabel, p. 32.
40 Letter from Anna Treter to Kurt Gerdau.
41 Schön 1992, p. 485.

8 DESTROYING THE EVIDENCE

1 Goguel, p. 29.
2 Aftenposten 28 November 1945.
3 Hertz-Eichenrode, Part I, p. 170.
4 Hertz-Eichenrode, Part I, pp. 170–172.
5 Hertz-Eichenrode, Part I, p. 174.
6 Schön 1992, p. 518.
7 Diary by Ingmar Fredriksson.
8 Diary by Ingmar Fredriksson.
9 Diary by Ingmar Fredriksson.
10 Diary by Ingmar Fredriksson.
11 Goguel, p. 26.
12 Schön 1992, p. 534.
13 Schön 1992, p. 534.
14 Arnoldsson, p. 157.
15 Arnoldsson, p. 158.
16 Hertz-Eichenrode, Part I, p. 264.
17 Arnoldsson, pp. 158–159.
18 Arnoldsson, pp. 160–161.
19 Hertz-Eichenrode, Part I, p. 258.
20 Interview Thore Dommenget.
21 Interview Thore Dommenget.

9 THE MESSAGE WAS NOT PASSED ON

1 Hertz-Eichenrode, Part I, p. 247.
2 Schön 1992, p. 520.
3 Schön 1992, p. 521.
4 Schön 1992, p. 531.
5 Schön 1992, p. 536.
6 Goguel, pp. 46–47.
7 Goguel, pp. 30–31.
8 Schön 1992, pp. 547–548.
9 WO 309/873, Deposition of Paul de Blonay, exhibit no.42, 119.
10 Hertz-Eichenrode, Part I, p. 276.

10 BRILLIANT ATTACKS

1 War Diary AIR 24/1498.
2 War Diary AIR 24/1498.
3 Interview Thore Dommenget.
4 A Survey of Damaged Shipping, AIR 15/474, p. 21.
5 Hertz-Eichenrode, Part I, p. 268.
6 Interview Thore Dommenget.
7 Goguel, p. 57.
8 Schön 1989, p. 218.
9 Goguel, p. 58.
10 Schön 1989, p. 221.
11 Schön 1989, pp. 221–222.
12 Interview Thore Dommenget.
13 Interview Thore Dommenget.
14 Goguel, p. 60.
15 Goguel, pp. 62–63.
16 Goguel, p. 63.
17 Schön 1992, p. 532.
18 Interview Thore Dommenget.
19 Interview Thore Dommenget.
20 Interview Thore Dommenget.
21 Interview Thore Dommenget.
22 Interview Thore Dommenget.
23 Goguel, p. 66.
24 Hertz-Eichenrode, Part I, p. 270.
25 War Diary AIR 15/474.
26 Goguel, pp. 78–79.
27 Schön 1992, p. 534.
28 Diary by Ingmar Fredriksson.
29 Diary by Ingmar Fredriksson.
30 Goguel, p. 73.
31 Diary by Ingmar Fredriksson.
32 War Diary AIR 27/1169.
33 Interview Thore Dommenget.
34 War Diary AIR 15/474.
35 War Diary AIR 25/698.

BIBLIOGRAPHY

PRINTED SOURCES

Adolf Bock – marinmålare, professor. Catalogue to the exhibition about Adolf Bock, Helsinki 1990.

Arnoldsson, Hans, *Natt och dimma.* Bonniers, Stockholm 1945.

Bekker Cajus, *Flucht übers Meer. Ostsee deutsches Schicksal 1945.* Bechtermünz Verlag, Augsburg 1999.

Bengtsson, Roger och von Zweigbergk, Jürgen, *Den torpederade gotlandsbåten Hansa. Människor, minnen, mysterier.* Förlags AB Wiken 1992.

Bernadotte, Folke, *Slutet. Mina humanitära förhandlingar i Tyskland våren 1945 och deras politiska följder.* Norstedts, Stockholm 1945.

Bock, Adolf, 'När 5.000 människor gick till botten i Östersjön i januari 1945'. *Svensk Sjöfarts Tidning* Nr 16, 1958.

Brustat-Naval, Fritz, *Unternehmen Rettung.* Koehlers Verlagsgesellschaft mbH, Herford 1985.

Buttar, Prit, *Battleground Prussia: The Assault on Germany's Eastern Front 1944–45* [Kindle Edition]. Osprey Publishing, Oxford 2012.

Constabel, Hans, *Hol nieder Flagge! Ereignisse um ein Standgericht Mai 1945.* Convent Verlag, Hamburg 2001.

Daenhardt, Rainer och Schön, Heinz, *Do céu ao inferno. Do Funchal ao Báltico: o maior desastre naval História.* Publicações Quipu, Lisbon 2000.

'Die deutsche Titanic' *Der Spiegel* Nr 6, 4 February 2002.

Eichenrode-Hertz, Katharina: *Ein KZ wird geräumt. Häftlinge zwischen Vernichtung und Befreiung. Die Auflösung des KZ Neuengamme und seiner Aussenlager durch die SS im Frühjahr 1945.* Catalogue of the touring exhibition Volume 1: Texte und Dokument. Volume 2: Karten. Edition Temmen, Bremen 2000.

Einhorn, Lena, *Handelsresande i liv. Om vilja och vankelmod i krigets skugga.* Prisma, Stockholm 1999.

Ekman, Per-Olof, *Havsvargar. Ubåtar och ubåtskrig i Östersjön.* Schildts förlag, Helsingfors 1983.

'När vi lotsade ut ryska ubåtar'. *Hufvudstadsbladet* 23 September 1984.

Sjöfront. Schildts Förlag, Helsingfors 1981.

Fechner, Eberhard och Jannet, *La Paloma Seemannsgeschichten.* Quadriga Verlag, Berlin 1996.

Fredmann, Ernst, *Sie kamen übers Meer. Die größte Rettungsaktion der Geschichte.* Staats und Wirtschaftliches Gesellschaft e.V., Köln 1971.

Furuhammar, Leif och Isaksson, Folke, *Politik och film.* Pan/Norstedts, Stockholm 1971.

Gerdau, Kurt, Goya *Rettung über See. Die grösste Schiffskatastrophe der Welt.* Koehler, Herford 1985.

– *Kampfboot 328. Von der Selbstverständlichkeit der Pflicht.* Koehler, Herford 1989.

Goguel, Rudi, *Cap Arcona. Report über den Untergang der Häftlingsflotte in der Lübecker Bucht am 3. Mai 1945.* Röderberg-Verlag GmbH, Frankfurt am Main, andra omarbetade uppöagan. Second edition, 1972.

Gunston, Bill, *The Illustrated Directory of Fighting Aircraft of World War II.* MBI Publishing Company, Osceola, Wisconsin 1998.

Hahn, Günther Ernst, Goya *Zielschiff + Transporter.* Published by the author, 1999.

Hansen, Hans-Walter, *Marinemaler Adolf Bock.* Leben und Werk. Koehlers Verlagsgesellschaft mbH, Hamburg 2001.

Kahl, Werner, *Den tyske arbetaren reser.* Berlin 1941.

Die Kinder vom Bullenhuser Damm. From the serial Hamburg Porträt. Museum für Hamburgische Geschichte, Hamburg no year.

Kludas, Arnold, *Die Cap-Schnelldampfer der Hamburg-Süd. Königinnen der Südatlantik.* Koehler Verlagsgesellschaft mbH, Hamburg 1996.

Die Geschichte der deutschen Passagierschiffahrt. Volume V. *Eine Ära geht zu Ende 1930 bis 1990.* Ernst Kabel Verlag, Hamburg 1990.

Lange, Rudi, *Rettung über See. Der Untergang der 'Wilhelm Gustloff' Auf den Spuren der Geschichte nach 43 Jahren.* Published by author Lange & Partner, Hamburg 1990.

Lange, Wilhelm, Cap Arcona. Das tragische Ende der KZ-Häftlings-Flotte am 3. Mai 1945. Neustadt in Holstein (Förlag), Tredje upplagan Neustadt 1992.

'Die Katastrophe der Häftlingsflotte in der Neustädter Bucht am 3. Mai 1945'. Article from *Jahrbuch für Heimatkunde* Oldenburg/Holstein, 1985.

Disaster at Neustadt Bay. Zusammenfassende Information zum Untergang der KZ-Häftlingsflotte in der Neustädter Bucht am 3. Mai 1945. Neustadt in Holstein (Förlag), Neustadt 2000.

– 'Der 2. Weltkrieg im Neustädter Raum. "Cap Arcona" – der Untergang der KZ-Häftlings-Flotte in der Neustädter Bucht am 3. Mai 1945'. In *Neustadt in Holstein 1244–1994. Aspekte zur Stadtgeschichte. Festschrift zur 750-Jahr-Feier.* Neustadt in Holstein (publisher), Neustadt 1994.

Malmberg, Thure, 'Ett sekel för skeppare'. *Hufvudstadsbladet* 31 January 1975.

'Flykten från Hangö ett blodbad till sjöss'. *Hufvudstadsbladet* 3 December 1991.

'Jag har försökt glömma ...' *Hufvudstadsbladet* 6 May 1995.

Meyer, Henry. 'Fanger og leger i Neuengamme.' *Aftenposten* 28 November 1945.

Mielke, Otto, *SOS Schicksale deutscher Schiffe. Nr. 23 MS. Wilhelm Gustloff Katastrophe bei Nacht.* Arthur Moewig Verlag, München 1953.

Müller, Wolfgang and Kramer, Reinhard, *Gesunken und Verschollen. Menschen- und Schiffsschicksale Ostsee 1945.* Keohlers Verlagsgesellschaft, Herford 1994.

Nesbit, Roy Conyers, *Failed to Return. Mysteries of the Air 1939–1945.* Patrick Stephens Ltd, Wellingborough 1988.

Norddeutscher Lloyd Bremen. *Vita vackra Steuben.* Advertising brochure for *General von Steuben*, Stockholm 1938.

Paust, Otto, *KdF Das große Urlauberschiff.* Wilhelm Limpert-Verlag, Dresden 1936.

Polmar, Norman and Noot, Jurrien, *Submarines of the Russian and Soviet Navies, 1718–1990.* Naval Institute Press, Annapolis, Maryland 1991.

Poralla, Peter, *Unvergänglicher Schmerz. Ein Protokoll der Geschichte Danzigs Schickslsjahr 1945.* Verlag Hogast GmbH, Freiburg 1987.

Reichenberg, Hans, 'När Östersjön var ofredens hav'. Articles in *Klubb Maritim Södra Kretsen* 1990:1-3, 1992:1-3 and 1992:1.

'Schlauchboot-Generalprobe'. *Der Adler*, Issue 20, Berlin 6 October 1942.

Schmidt, Rudolf and Kludas, Arnold, *Die deutschen Lazarettschiffe im Zweiten Weltkrieg.* Motorbuch Verlag, Stuttgart 1978.

Schwadtke, Karl-Heinz, *Deutschlands Handelsschiffe 1939–1945.* Stalling Verlag, Oldenburg 1974.

Schön, Heinz: *Die Cap Arcona Katastrophe Eine Dokumentation nach Augenzeugen-Berichten.* Motorbuch Verlag, Stuttgart 1989.

–*Die 'Gustloff'-Katastrophe. Bericht eines Überlebenden.* Motorbuch Verlag, Stuttgart 1985.

Hitlers Traumschiffe. Die „Kraft durch Freude" Flotte 1934–1939. Arndt-Verlag, Kiel 2000.

– *Die Cap Arcona Katastrophe. Eine Dokumentation nach Augenzeugen-Berichten.* Motorbuch Verlag, Stuttgart 1989.

Die KdF-Schiffe und ihr Schicksal. Motorbuch Verlag, Stuttgart 1987.

Die letzten Kriegstage. Ostseehäfen 1945. Motorbuch Verlag, Stuttgart 1995.

Ostsee '45. Menschen Schiffe Schicksale. Motorbuch Verlag, Stuttgart 1992.

– *SOS Wilhelm Gustloff. Die größte Schiffskatastrophe der Geschichte.* Motorbuch Verlag, Stuttgart 1998.

Der Untergang der 'Wilhelm Gustloff'. Tatsachenbericht eines Überlebenden. Karina-Goltze-Verlag, K.G., Göttingen 1952.

Schuhler, Odin, 'Ubåtar i västerled'. *Sveriges Flotta* 6–7, 1975

Sellwood, A.V., *The Damned Don't Drown. The Sinking of the Wilhelm Gustloff.* Allan Wingate Ltd, London 1973.

Sennerteg, Niclas, *Stalins hämnd. Röda Armén i Tyskland 1944–1945.* Historiska Media, Lund 2001.

Terry, Antony, 'Brewery clue to £20m booty.' *The Sunday Times* 24 August 1969.

Thorén, Ragnar, *Ryska ubåtskriget i Östersjön 1941–1945. Den svenske marinattachén i Helsingfors 1942 – 1945 Ragnar Thorén rapporterar.* Probus Förlag, Stockholm 1992.

Wetterholm, Claes-Göran, *Breven från Titanic. Meddelanden från Postmuseum nr. 47.* Postmuseum, Stockholm 2000.

– *Titanic.* Prisma, Tredje upplagan. Third edition, Stockholm 1999.

– *Vrak i svenska vatten.* Rabén Prisma, Stockholm 1994.

Watson, P., *The Nazi Titanic.* Da Capo Press, Boston 2016.

Advertising brochure for the *Steuben* [in Swedish] Norddeutscher Lloyd Stockholm 1939.

INTERNET

www.fleetairarmarchive.net/Aircraft/Typhoon

MANUSCRIPT SOURCES

Christel Balsam, handwritten account about her flight from Argemünde and journey with the *Goya* dated 16 December 1985. Access to the account was given to me by Kurt Gerdau.

Milda Bendrich, typed account of the journey with *Wilhelm Gustloff*. The account is dated 9 June 1981 and access to it was given to me by her daughter Inge Bendrich.

Flottentorpedoboot *T 36*. Memorial publication for the meeting of former crew members of the torpedo boat on 12–14 November 1993 at Hotel Palm, Linz, Rhein. No place, 1993.

Charlotte Dölling, account of the journey with the *Goya* 11–15 March 1945. Typed account, access given to me by Kurt Gerdau.

Ingmar Fredriksson, handwritten diary between August 1944 and May 1945. Access to diary given to me by Thure Malmberg.

Rudolf Geiss, letter to Ilse Kunandt about the sinking of the *Wilhelm Gustloff*.

Josef Poiger, typed account of what he saw from *M-328*. Access to the account was given to me by Kurt Gerdau.

Erich Sasse, typed account about the journey with the *Goya*. Access to the account was given to me by Kurt Gerdau.

Anna Treter, two letters to Kurt Gerdau about the flight from East Prussia and how her two children ended up on the *Goya*. The first letter is dated 26 October 1982, the second without date but probably in the later part of 1982. Access to the letters was given to me by Kurt Gerdau.

Horst Woit, typed account about the flight and the journey with the *Wilhelm Gustloff*. Access to the account was given to me by Horst Woit.

Helmut Wolf, letter to Kurt Gerdau about life aboard *M-328*, dated 24 October 1988. Access to the letter was given to me by Kurt Gerdau.

NATIONAL ARCHIVES, UK

AIR 15/474 Report book: *A Survey of Damaged Shipping in North Germany and Denmark.*

AIR 24/1448	LC 027728
AIR 24/1498	2011
AIR 24/1498	4139
AIR 24/1498	027721
AIR 24/1518	2023
AIR 25/698	2011
AIR 25/707	2023
AIR 25/710	027720
AIR 27/1109	5822
AIR 27/1137	033077
AIR 27/1138	
AIR 27/1157	033077
AIR 27/1169	LC 027728

AIR 27/1170   5820
AIR 27/1170   XC 027728
AIR 27/1548   5751
AIR 27/1(5)48   32(5)40
AIR 27/1770   033077
AIR 27/1848   340(7?)4
AIR 27/2103   033077
AIR 29/409
FO 1006/102
WO 171/4144
WO 171/4184

National Archives, Sweden: the Archive of the Red Cross, The Folke
    Benadotte Archive.

INTERVIEWS BY THE AUTHOR

Heli Beneicke, 1995
Margit Schilder-Brook, 2002
Thore Dommenget, 2001
Ingeborg/Eva Dorn-Rotschild, 2001
Rudolf Geiss, 2001
Kurt Gerdau, 2001
Heinz Schön, 1994, 1995 and 2001
Wilhelm Lange, 1995 and 2001

ACKNOWLEDGEMENTS

The creation of this book on the shipping disasters of the Baltic is the result of the assistance of many individuals. I am greatly indebted to Heinz Schön, himself a survivor of the *Wilhelm Gustloff* and the foremost chronicler of the ship's history. Wilhelm Lange, who has undertaken meticulous research about the tragedy in the Neustadt Bay and built a great archive on the event, helped immensely, as did Kurt Gerdau, who has written extensively about the refugees' flight on the Baltic and put his archive at my disposal. My thanks also go Käthe Schön, the wife of Heinz, and Doris Gerdau the wife of Kurt. Günther Ernst Hahn, the son of Felix Hahn, gave me considerable information on the *Goya*, for which I am most grateful.

The survivors I have met or have corresponded with have all given me their stories. Heinz Schön invited me not only to his home but also gave me the opportunity to partake in the last great meeting with survivors from the *Wilhelm Gustloff*, in Ostseebad Damp in January 1995. Eva Dorn-Rotschild and I sat together for three days for a very substantial interview in the house of her daughter Anne. My thanks also go to Thore Dommenget, Margit Schilder-Brook, Rudolf Geiss, Horst Woit and Heli Beneicke for interviews, as well as to Horst Woit, who put me in contact with Inge Bendrich in Australia, who put her mother's story at my disposal. The maritime historian Thure Malmberg has been a constant source of information about history of the Finnish war.

Many thanks to the artist Karl Magnus Petterson, who contributed the fascinating interpretation of the *Steuben*. My thanks also go to diver and photographer Jonas Dahm for his fascinating and beautiful wreck photos. These images are published through the company Deep Sea Productions.

Many thanks also go to the following individuals and institutions:

Björn Fontander
Frihetsmuseet Copenhagen
Gunnar Hedman
Imperial War Museum, London
Matthias Jansson
Bo Jerndell
Anne Krichner and family
Arnold Kludas
Ulla Neurath
Norsk Sjøfartsmuseum
National Archives, Kew
Public Archives, Stockholm
Thomas Rockwell
Röda Korset/Red Cross, Stockholm
Ina Schmidt
Birgit and Bernd Schwartz
The magazine *Båtologen*
Dorcas Wagenknecht

However, without the support and initiative of my friend and translator Eric Kentley there would never have been a book in English. He has pushed me through the whole work and has done an incredible miracle by transforming the Swedish into wonderful English. I must also mention his partner Diana Cashin, who was a constant source of support!

Claes-Göran Wetterholm
Stockholm and London, January 2020

All pictures the collection of the author, unless otherwise stated. Maps by Eric Kentley.

INDEX

The History Press

The destination for history
www.thehistorypress.co.uk